W9-BXH-302

Introduction to Databases

James J. Townsend

ST. PHILIP'S COLLEGE LIBRARY

Introduction to Databases

Copyright © 1992 by Que Corporation.

All rights reserved. Printed in the United States of America. No part of this book may be used or reproduced in any form or by any means, or stored in a database or retrieval system, without prior written permission of the publisher except in the case of brief quotations embodied in critical articles and reviews. Making copies of any part of this book for any purpose other than your own personal use is a violation of United States copyright laws. For information, address Que Corporation, 11711 N. College Ave., Carmel, IN 46032.

Library of Congress Catalog No.: 91-67629

ISBN: 0-88022-840-7

This book is sold *as is*, without warranty of any kind, either express or implied, respecting the contents of this book, including but not limited to implied warranties for the book's quality, performance, merchantability, or fitness for any particular purpose. Neither Que Corporation nor its dealers or distributors shall be liable to the purchaser or any other person or entity with respect to any liability, loss, or damage caused or alleged to be caused directly or indirectly by this book.

94 93   4 3

Interpretation of the printing code: the rightmost double-digit number is the year of the book's printing; the rightmost single-digit number, the number of the book's printing. For example, a printing code of 92-1 shows that the first printing of the book occurred in 1992.

Screens reproductions in this book were created by using Collage Plus from Inner Media, Inc., Hollis, NH.

Publisher: Lloyd J. Short

Acquisitions Manager: Rick Ranucci

Project Development Manager: Thomas H. Bennett

Managing Editor: Paul Boger

Book Designers: Scott Cook and Michele Laseau

Production Team: Brad Chinn, Jeanne Clark, Keith Davenport, Mark Enochs, Dennis Clay Hager, Carrie Keesling, Betty Kish, Bob LaRoche, Laurie Lee, Jay Lesandrini, Linda Quigley, Linda Seifert, Louise Shinault, Kevin Spear, Allan Wimmer, Phil Worthington, Christine Young

Dedication

For Marcella

Product Director

Timothy S. Stanley

Production Editor

Frances R. Huber

Editors

Sara Allaei
Lorna Gentry
Susan Pink, TechRight MS
Editorial Services
Susan M. Shaw
Diane L. Steele
Barbara Tilly
Colleen Totz

Acquisitions Editor

Tim Ryan

Technical Editor

Mark P. Marchi

*Composed in Cheltenham and
MCPdigital by Que Corporation*

About the Author

James J. Townsend is president of Information Strategies, a database consulting firm in Washington, DC. He designs custom database applications for business and government, including major U.S. government agencies and Fortune 100 companies. Before joining Information Strategies, he was a fellow at the Georgetown University Center for Strategic and International Studies. He may be contacted at Information Strategies at (202) 462-1290 or via CompuServe address 70304,2750.

Trademark Acknowledgments

Que Corporation has made every effort to supply trademark information about company names, products, and services mentioned in this book. Trademarks indicated below were derived from various sources. Que Corporation cannot attest to the accuracy of this information.

ALPHA Four is a registered trademark of ALPHA Software Corporation.

Apple, Mac, and Macintosh are registered trademarks of Apple Computers, Inc.

Ashton-Tate, dBASE, dBASE II, and dBASE IV are registered trademarks of Ashton-Tate Corporation.

Clipper and Nantucket are trademarks of Nantucket, Inc.

COMPAQ is a registered trademark of COMPAQ Computer Corporation.

DataEase is a registered trademark of DataEase International, Inc.

DataPerfect and DrawPerfect are registered trademarks of WordPerfect Corporation.

DECnet is a registered trademark of Digital Equipment Corporation.

FASTBACK is a registered trademark of Fifth Generation Systems, Inc.

File Express and Novell are trademarks of Novell, Inc.

FoxPro is a trademark of Fox Holdings, Inc.

IBM and OS/2 are registered trademarks of International Business Machines, Inc.

Lotus is a registered trademark of Lotus Development Corporation.

Microsoft, LAN Manager, and SQL Server are registered trademarks, and Windows is a trademark of Microsoft Corporation.

Norton Utilities is a registered trademark of Symantec Corporation.

ORACLE is a registered trademark of Oracle Corporation.

Paradox, Quattro Pro, and Reflex are registered trademarks of Borland International, Inc.

PC-File is a registered trademark of Buttonware, Inc., and is also a trademark of Jim Button.

PC Tools is a trademark of Central Point Software.

Professional File is a trademark of Software Publishing Corporation.

Q&A is a registered trademark of Symantec Corporation.

Quicksilver is a trademark of WordTech Systems, Inc.

R:BASE is a registered trademark of Microrim, Inc.

SpinRite is a trademark of Gibson Research Corporation.

UNIX is a registered trademark of AT&T.

Trademarks of other products mentioned in this book are held by the companies producing them.

Acknowledgments

Thanks to everyone at Que Corporation for taking a chance on a book not devoted to a specific software product. Special thanks to:

Tim Ryan, acquisitions editor, for returning my phone calls and pleading the cases for this book.

Tim Stanley, product development editor, for providing comments on early drafts of the manuscript.

Mark Marchi, technical editor, for providing a knowledgeable technical review.

Fran Huber, production editor, for indefatigable editing of the manuscript and for guiding me through my first editorial review at Que.

All the others at Que—editors Sara Allaei, Lorna Gentry, Susan Pink, Susan Shaw, Barbara Tilly, and Colleen Totz, and the production and business departments—for being on the team that made this book possible.

Thanks to the manufacturers who provided software, including Lotus Corporation, Ashton-Tate, Alpha Software, Borland, DataEase International, and Symantec.

I am grateful to all those who read drafts of the manuscript, including John Batdorf, Howard Berger, Christa Carpentiere, Joan Carpentiere, Joe Carpentiere, Tina Carpentiere, Steven Duffield, Martin Fox, Chris Guziak, Laurel Lamb, Bill McHenry, Shelby Smith, Phil Winkler, and many electronic interlocutors on CompuServe who provided a wish list of topics for this book.

Special thanks to Jeff Chapski of Information Strategies for patiently wading through the thickets of my prose, patiently matching figures and tables to the text, and sticking with the project from start to finish.

Finally, to the clients of Information Strategies, for providing the opportunity to put all these theories to the test, exposing me to more problems and challenges than I possibly could have come up with on my own.

—J.T.

Contents at a Glance

Table of Contents

3   Planning Your Database 53

4   Organizing Your Data 63

7   Using Views 155

8   Generating Reports 187

9   Honing Your Reporting Skills 231

10 Designing Menus 243

Introduction

No one can survive the next decade in business, government, or academia without using a computer. From elementary school through retirement, computers are indispensable tools of modern life. Sooner or later, nearly everyone will become a computer user, and most computer users will encounter a database.

Introduction to Databases is intended to be a survival manual. It describes fundamental relational database concepts and good design practices. It explains what database software guides assume that you already know: the principles of database design. *Introduction to Databases* illustrates the theory of databases with practical business examples. You can use this information to develop your own database application or to understand what to expect if someone else builds an application for you.

This book is not a substitute for the user manuals provided with database software or for software command reference books. It does not tell you which function key to press to cut a line or how to change a field from blue to red. From my experience as a database developer, databases seldom fail because the user misunderstands a command; instead, databases usually fail because the user does not understand the data and how it fits in with the policies and operations of a business.

This book encourages a hands-on approach and is oriented toward readers who do not have the time to read more scholarly books before plunging into their first database project. You can work through the examples offered here with your favorite database software. To maximize the value of the lessons presented, build an application while reading this book. Start with the examples in this book, and then apply the principles to your own application.

Who Should Read This Book?

Very few companies use even the least powerful computers to their fullest capacity. For a computer-literate person, this idle power is a resource waiting to be used to increase productivity.

Although computers are widely available, the computer revolution will not really be complete until the people who use computers can write programs for themselves. As many executives already have discovered, designing critical business applications is too important to be left to computer professionals. Fortunately, you no longer have to depend on professional computer programmers to write computer programs.

In recent years, database software has been simplified so that business users can create powerful and complex applications without writing a line of programming code. You no longer need to be a programmer to build and use a database. Many people in business, frustrated with the shortcomings of off-the-shelf software and the long lead times of their computer departments, have taken matters into their own hands. In the process, they have saved their employers untold millions of dollars.

Introduction to Databases is designed to meet the needs of the following people:

- Business people who are responsible for managing databases

- Business students, undergraduate and graduate, who will be working with databases

- Computer science and management information systems students who want a down-to-earth introduction to databases

- Purchasers of database software who are bewildered by the documentation that comes with the software

- Computer programmers and information center support staff who have had no formal training in database design

- Computer hobbyists who want to explore databases and database design

- Anyone who feels overwhelmed by vast amounts of data

Why Should You Read This Book?

There are many rewards for mastering databases. If you understand and manage your data, you are likely to prosper over the coming decades. By building your own databases, you can make your work simpler, more effective, and can add to your work a higher degree of consistency and organization than you could have achieved without a database.

This book can help you become an asset to your organization. Even if you do not build the database yourself, an understanding of databases will help you manage the computer professionals involved in database development.

Which Database Software Should I Use?

This book discusses database design concepts that are useful regardless of which database software you use. The book has a certain prejudice in favor of relational databases, especially for solving complex problems, but does not endorse any specific database product. *Introduction to Databases* uses several popular packages to illustrate database concepts in action.

Hardware and software come and go with amazing speed. Five years from now, the leading packages may be unrecognizable from the packages used today. Database software vendors only now are taking advantage of the graphical user interface revolution, led by the Apple Mac, Microsoft Windows, and UNIX X-Window. The coming years are sure to bring many new developments.

The topics discussed in this book are much less subject to change than the computer industry. The same analysis techniques apply today, with fancy graphical databases used on workstations, as applied a decade ago on mainframes, minicomputers, and PCs. Database theory is based on logic and mathematics, not on the latest marketing slogans.

If you do not see examples from your database among the screen shots for this book, do not panic. You can apply the principles you learn to any database software you choose. Reading about more than one package may help you understand database design better than working within the confines of your favorite program. You even may learn about features that you would like to see in the next release of your program.

You might want to read this book before you purchase new database software. Chapter 14, "Choosing Database Software," offers advice on evaluating your options.

ST. PHILIP'S COLLEGE LIBRARY

What Is Covered in This Book?

This book follows the stages of database development chronologically, starting with determining requirements for the application and working through all the stages of implementation. The first three chapters of the book are the most important because they lay the foundation for all the steps that follow.

Chapter 1, "Why Use a Database?" helps you decide when a database is the right choice for solving a problem. Chapter 1 compares the strengths and weaknesses of word processing programs, spreadsheets, and databases, and offers a checklist to determine whether a database is right for you.

Chapter 2, "Analyzing a Project," teaches you how to determine the requirements for your database application. It shows you how to conduct interviews with users and introduces all the database terminology that you will need to understand a database. You learn also how to draw database schemas to show how different parts of the database are interrelated.

Chapter 3, "Planning Your Database," applies the concepts you have already learned to large, complex projects. It discusses special management issues relating to large projects.

Chapter 4, "Organizing Your Data," explains how to arrive at a sound structure for your database through a process known as *normalization*. This chapter gives rules for minimizing redundant data entry to make your database faster and more reliable. Organizing your data is the precursor to building database elements.

Chapter 5, "Building Tables," explains how to create tables—the fundamental building blocks of every database. This chapter defines field types and methods for choosing the right field for your needs. It also includes conventions for naming tables and fields.

Chapter 6, "Building Forms," introduces aesthetics into the design process and shows you how to make pleasing data-entry forms to make your database easy (if not fun) to use. Sample good and bad forms illustrate the principles outlined in the chapter.

Chapter 7, "Using Views," deals with advanced forms design, especially forms that include data from more than one table. The approaches taken by different software packages are illustrated with screen shots and step-by-step instructions.

Chapter 8, "Generating Reports," explains the steps in report writing, from record selection to sorting, formatting, and printer control. It shows all types of reports, including listings, letters, labels, and summary reports.

Chapter 9, "Honing Your Reporting Skills," discusses processing procedures such as posting and archiving. It also covers importing and exporting files and ways to standardize your reports.

Chapter 10, "Designing Menus," illustrates how a good menu structure can make your database more accessible and secure. This chapter discusses style conventions for menus and alternative methods for grouping menu choices.

Chapter 11, "Testing Your Database," takes your database through its paces and attempts to identify flaws in the design. It shows you how to create a test plan and offers tips for successful testing.

Chapter 12, "Creating System Documentation," helps you prepare documentation for the people who will use and maintain your database. It includes rules for style and content and outlines of sample documentation.

Chapter 13, "Database Administration," describes the care and maintenance of a database when the database is operational. The chapter covers hardware and software considerations, including issues such as backups, software upgrades, and security.

Chapter 14, "Choosing Database Software," guides you through the process of choosing database software. It shows you how to express your needs in the right terms to narrow your software options and provides objective and subjective criteria to weigh when making your decision.

Chapter 15, "Client-Server Architecture," is an overview of the most exciting recent database technology development. It defines client-server terminology and analyzes the costs and benefits of this architecture.

The Glossary defines commonly used database terms. The Bibliography lists sources for additional information on databases, including books, magazines, and on-line information.

Conventions Used in This Book

Introduction to Databases uses several conventions of which you should be aware. They are listed here for your reference.

Direct quotations of words that appear on-screen are represented in a `special typeface`. Listings and queries appear in the same `special typeface`.

Information that you are to type is indicated by *italic type*. Words used for the first time and defined in the text also appear in *italic type* (for example, "a *database* is a collection of information you can search or otherwise manipulate").

File names appear in all uppercase letters (for example, CLIENTS). Names of database tables appear in initial capital letters (for example, Clients table). Field names appear in all uppercase letters (for example, NAME).

Special tips, notes, and warnings are placed in shaded boxes to distinguish them from the normal flow of text.

This icon tells you that the following list is a checklist.

Why Use a Database?

Unless each man produces more than he receives, increases his output, there will be less for him than all the others.

Bernard M. Baruch

In a world full of information, organizations and individuals who understand and manage their data are most likely to prosper. Computers have become indispensable tools for managing information, and a range of software packages are available to tackle different aspects of information storage and retrieval. Of all the computer software you can master, databases will have the most far-reaching impact on your work.

What is a database? In general terms, a *database* is a collection of information you can search or otherwise manipulate. A baseball card collection is an example of a noncomputerized database. A baseball card collection has a structure that makes it easy to look up relevant facts about your favorite players and even contains built-in graphics (the photo on the face of the card). This book discusses computerized databases and the techniques you can master to build your own database.

Database design can provide tremendous personal satisfaction. You perhaps can learn more about business and government through database design than through years of apprenticeship. I have had the opportunity to learn about different organizations and to meet new friends in my database work. Working with databases has introduced me to a number of unlikely heroes who work in large corporate or government bureaucracies and have saved their institutions millions of dollars by building their own databases.

Many of these computer explorers are self-taught. They have in common the initiative to accomplish their goals no matter what barriers arise. Access to powerful database software has made their accomplishments possible.

This book can set you on the road toward becoming a hero within your organization. Even if you do not build the database yourself, you will understand the automation projects around you better and will be able to ask probing questions of others involved in database development.

Untapped Power

Many companies do not use even their least powerful computers to the fullest capacity. Employees use powerful hardware for nothing more demanding than writing memos or printing invitations to the company picnic. For a computer-literate manager, this idle power is a resource waiting to be used to increase productivity.

How can a database help you? Databases are powerful tools for anyone who collects, sorts, distributes, or analyzes information. Databases enable an individual to store and track large sets of data—more information than one person possibly can remember—quickly and accurately.

Databases have a wide variety of uses. A representative list of applications follows, but you may think of more opportunities for database applications for your organization.

- **Accounting**
  Accounts payable
  Accounts receivable
  Account balances
  Fixed assets and depreciation
  Job costing
  Payroll, including deductions and taxes
  Invoicing
  Tax estimate control system
  Bank statement reconciliations

- **Banking and Finance**
  Collections management
  Scheduling for billable hours
  Portfolio valuation and control
  Loan management
  Safe deposit box rental tracking
  Securities transfer

- **Business and Office Administration**
  Church: parishioner information
  Medicine: patient history
  Law: client case details

Sales and service
Garage/repair shop activities
Utilities usage and billing
Purchasing
Equipment rental reservations
Shipping and receiving
Voter registration
Wholesale distribution system
Warranty information
Troubleshooting tips

- **Education**
Class scheduling
Faculty/administration data

- **Fleet Management**
Scheduling
Expense analysis
Service parts tracking
Delivery schedules and routing

- **Fund Raising**
Donor tracking
Planned giving
Nonprofit accounting
Contribution allocation

- **Insurance**
Claims tracking
Beneficiary details
Policy holder/beneficiary details
Worker's compensation

- **Legal Services**
Docket, deadline tracking
Case tracking
Billable hours tracking
Client, staff management

- **Maintenance Management**
Service call analysis
Replacement parts

- **Medical Services**
Billable time per ambulance unit
Response time per unit
Emergency room log

Patient histories
Automatic medical form completion
Accounts receivable
Electronic claims submission
Hospital statistical information on doctors, nurses and patients
Medicare/Medicaid log
Patient care and nursing schedule
Nursing home coordination
Medical case profile

- **Member Tracking**
  Political campaign management
  Conference planning
  Club/association tracking

- **Personnel/Administration**
  Detailed personnel history
  Human resource tracking
  Pension requirements/allocations
  Shift and vacation scheduling
  Payroll with corresponding deductions, taxes, and so on
  Match personnel to job requirements

- **Planning and Project Management**
  Daily/weekly/monthly/yearly scheduling
  Meeting, conference, seminar or convention planner
  Project task coordinating

- **Production and Inventory Control**
  Sales and inventory processing
  Bill of material generation
  Inventory and purchase ordering system
  Manufacturing production and analysis reporting
  Batch/job formulas, procedures and components
  Product testing statistical data
  Point of sale tracking

- **Real Estate**
  Automatic rent billing
  Management of leases, tenants, buildings, maintenance, and so on
  Mortgage tracking

- **Safety**
  Inspection scheduling
  Materials and government safety specifications for all products
  Emergency situation instructions

1

- **Sales**
  Client tracking
  Customer requirements
  Direct mail
  Order entry and tracking
  Salesperson assignments by territory or product
  Telemarketing

- **Travel and Recreation**
  Hotel and motel registration
  Tour reservations

- **Personal**
  Personal daily planner
  Computerized telephone book that generates address labels for holiday greeting cards and reminds you of anniversaries, birthdays, and so on
  Personal Budgeting and Tax Preparation

- **Others**
  Museum exhibition detail tracking
  Images for security

You need software to reach these goals. *Database management systems* (DBMS) are software packages used to implement database applications. You can choose from dozens of DBMS packages, including best-selling PC packages such as AskSam, Clipper, DataEase, dBASE, FoxPro, Paradox, Q&A, and R:BASE. See Chapter 14 for tips on selecting the best tool for the job.

The Benefits of Using a Database

Many jobs are too big for one person working alone. Researchers at the University of Arizona have compiled the most extensive unclassified database in the world on Soviet and East European computing. The analyses of all the researchers have been pooled into one database, which consolidates thousands of entries from dozens of scholars into one easily accessible resource. The database stores the notes entered by researchers in a consistent format. Databases, together with computer networks, make such collaboration possible regardless of the geographic location of users. Consequently, a researcher in Boston can share notes with colleagues in Washington, D.C., or Berkeley without having to arrange costly face-to-face meetings.

The use of databases enforces a consistent means of entering information, removing much of the inaccuracy of manual record-keeping. You can design a database so that a user can enter only a valid dollar amount for an invoice amount rather than an invalid entry of *dog* or *cat* (which can happen with paper ledger sheets). To catch errors quickly, the data-entry screen uses a predetermined format that validates information as it is added.

In many organizations, databases capture information spanning a longer period than the tenure of an individual. Consequently, databases represent the collective memory of an institution. Corporate databases can contain historical information on every activity in a company, from sales to personnel to manufacturing specifications. A database can track each customer order from shipping through billing and payment. As the period of time covered by a database grows, long-term trends in the data become visible. For example, tracking vehicle fleet repairs over several years reveals the operating cost and reliability of each year, make, and model vehicle in the fleet. Performing this analysis by manually tabulating maintenance orders would be difficult or impossible, but databases make such calculations commonplace.

Databases handle large volumes of data, data from varied sources, data that covers a long period of time, and many reports on the same data.

Building a database is like building a small working model of the reality you are trying to track. The database captures the most important elements that you want to monitor for feedback on the progress of the business.

A database systematically stores information for retrieval or analysis. When successful, a database becomes central to an operation and adds value to the work being performed. A wholesaler can track returns of defective goods to measure the reliability of its suppliers. A pizza delivery service can use a database to provide better customer service; the database can store the last order of a customer or special directions to an address.

A database also captures the personality and rules of an organization. The process of building a database helps refine your business practices by bringing them into the open, making them explicit and objective. What you track in your database reveals what you care about in your business. The database contains rules reflecting the real-life concerns of management. You can set up a database so that credit can be granted based only on established rules; you can give credit limits to customers based on past purchases and payment record.

1

Databases can last a long time. The life of a database has only two stages: development and maintenance (as database developer Larry Reutzel at Mobil Oil Corporation told me when he worked on a large project). Database applications rarely die unless the organization or function served by the database ceases to exist. Even if the computer hardware and programming language change, the data is converted, and the database continues.

If you are creating databases for your own use, you are in an excellent position to understand your requirements and to convert these business rules into a database. If you are creating databases for others, you can learn the proven techniques for converting the needs of users into finished systems.

Software Tools

Before you begin to build a database, make sure that building a database is the appropriate way to address your needs. Many of the purposes of a database can be fulfilled by other means, with or without a computer. In some cases, business problems are not amenable to automation, but can be improved by better management, training, or other changes.

Even when automation seems to be the answer, a database may not be the best tool. To find out, you must understand your needs and goals, the software options at your disposal, and the cost of each option. The most widely used types of software for business data management are word processing programs, spreadsheets, and databases.

Word Processing Software

A database is not a panacea, despite all its inherent charm and allure. A word processing program is sufficient to record text. You can use word processing software to keep simple lists, such as small mailing lists, or to record the results of manual procedures, such as counting products or customers. Many word processing programs also include limited mathematical functions and search capabilities.

Spreadsheets

Electronic spreadsheets perform more powerful mathematical calculations than word processing programs. Designed as computerized versions of ledger sheets, spreadsheets store data as rows and columns of numbers. You can use spreadsheets to calculate totals, averages, standard deviations, and other statistics that would take hours if performed by hand. Spreadsheets enable you to modify data easily and they instantly recalculate all derived values. You can use spreadsheets for "what-if" calculations based on several sets of business assumptions. You can forecast corporate revenues and profits for various assumptions of economic growth or build a model to decide whether to open a new location. Table 1.1 is an example of a simple spreadsheet.

Table 1.1. Budget Tracking—Sales Department

	1st Qtr	2nd Qtr	3rd Qtr	4th Qtr	TOTALS
Travel	$10,000	12,000	9,000	15,000	46,000
Meals	$ 5,000	4,000	7,000	10,000	26,000
Auto	$ 3,000	2,000	4,000	5,000	14,000
	$18,000	18,000	20,000	30,000	86,000

Although spreadsheets accommodate text and numbers, text functions are more limited than mathematical functions. Spreadsheets typically do not include word processing features such as spell checkers or word wrap. Some users write memos in Lotus 1-2-3, using long cells (data-entry fields in spreadsheets) for the body of the memo, but this practice is not recommended.

Because most spreadsheets are based on a two-dimensional model, they become unwieldy when you work with large numbers of rows and columns or when the number of data entries varies for each row or column. Imagine a spreadsheet wide enough to show transactions for every inventory item at your local department store. The useful size of a spreadsheet is limited. In most spreadsheets, you can enter only a limited number of records. In Quattro Pro, for instance, you can enter up to 8,191 records in one spreadsheet—a healthy number of records, more than you probably need to hold your Christmas card address list, but not big enough for many business applications.

Spreadsheets are limited in their reporting capabilities. A friend of mine uses a spreadsheet to track his earnings and expenses as a musician. He organizes his spreadsheet by taxable categories, with a monthly entry for each category. This setup simplifies his tax preparation, but the spreadsheet is useless for reporting the amount of money paid by each client for the year or comparing earnings to expenses for a particular performance. The spreadsheet does not capture the data in sufficient detail to perform these calculations.

Databases

Database programs meet different needs from word processing software or spreadsheets. Whereas the output of a word processing program is fixed, and the reports from a spreadsheet somewhat predictable, output from a database program is more flexible. You can use database software to generate many kinds of output, from letters and invoices to summary statistical reports. Moreover, database programs provide simple facilities for transferring their information (*exporting files*) to spreadsheets and word processing software for further manipulation.

Database software generally provides better capability for sharing data among several users than a word processing program or a spreadsheet. Multiuser databases contain special safeguards to ensure that data is updated properly, even when several people use the same file.

As table 1.2 indicates, spreadsheets and databases are more powerful than word processing for some functions, but also more expensive and difficult to learn. When you need to perform mathematical calculations, spreadsheets and databases offer the only real options.

Table 1.2. Features and Cost Comparison: Word Processing, Spreadsheets, Databases

	Word Processing	Spreadsheet	Database
Text Handling	Excellent	Poor	Fair to Poor
Mathematical Functions	Poor	Excellent	Excellent
Ease of Use	Excellent	Good	Good
Training Cost	Low	Moderate	Moderate-High
Software Cost	Low	Moderate	High
Volume of Data	Low	Moderate	Moderate-High
Multiuser Access	Low	Moderate	High
Report Flexibility	Low	Low-Moderate	High

A Database Checklist

Use the following checklist to decide whether a database will fulfill your needs:

❏ Are you using a high volume of information? Do you have more information than you can rely upon one person to remember?

❏ Do you need extensive reporting?

❏ Does your work follow predictable patterns?

❏ Do you need to monitor historical trends?

❏ Do you share information with co-workers?

❏ Does your information contain text and numbers?

❏ Do you have more information than a spreadsheet or word processing document can handle? How many spreadsheets or pages of text would you need to store your data?

❏ Does your information require extensive searching or sorting?

If you answer *no* to all these questions, you may continue reading this book for sheer enjoyment. If you answer *yes* to more than four questions, consider a database. If you answer *yes* to six or more questions, a database program is the information tool for you.

Custom Database Applications

Unfortunately, database software straight from the box doesn't address business needs in the same direct way as a word processing program. For your database to be useful, you must develop a database *application* to apply the database to the problem at hand. A database application consists of data tables, forms, reports, procedures, and menus designed to serve a particular business function. You can design an application for a dental office, for example, which you write with database software such as dBASE, and which automates billing, scheduling, and insurance claims.

Until recently, building a database application required substantial programming experience (and patience) to write, test, and debug programs hundreds or thousands of lines long. This situation is no longer true. A number of database management systems (DBMS) are available for building, with little or no programming, full-blown applications, and even more intuitive database interfaces are on the way. You now can develop

1

in hours or days on the PC an application that would have taken months to build in COBOL or BASIC. Easier-to-use database software places custom applications within the reach of more people than ever before. This trend toward simpler, more approachable database software is likely to continue.

With some database packages, you can accomplish tasks through simple menus or point-and-click visual representations of the database rather than through traditional programming. The stampede of users to the Mac and to Windows on the PC show that graphical interfaces appeal to users. (A *graphical user interface* is a design for the part of a program that interacts with the user and represents computer processes and entities as on-screen graphic images.) In addition to a more pleasing interface, DBMS have become less demanding on the programmer. The database management system automatically handles many difficult or tedious database chores. The developer often is insulated from the minute details of physical storage structure for the data. Query optimizers in database software help to find the fastest route to the desired result, even from a badly written query. Off-the-shelf applications are available for you to customize to your special requirements.

Even with easier-to-use database software, you still must understand your data. A large portion of this book is devoted to analyzing problems and designing databases to solve them. Fortunately, business skills and common sense play at least as large a role in successful database design as programming aptitude.

Databases resemble the organizations they serve. Unlike general purpose software such as word processing software, a database application becomes an intimate part of a business. Consequently, you cannot easily substitute one application for another. Although database management systems may be generic, a database application usually is tailored closely to a single use. A manufacturing and distribution database system is of little use to a dentist, even if both systems are written using the same database management system.

All the power of databases comes with a price. When a misbehaving word processing program destroys a memo or letter, the damage is immediately obvious and relatively easy to fix. Databases, however, can wreak more insidious havoc, gradually producing erroneous results undetected by users until the problem becomes very costly to reverse. Imagine the addresses in your billing address database being switched randomly from one customer to another, or the customers' billing amounts transposed. Before starting a database project, be sure that you understand the technical and not-so-technical skills needed to succeed.

What Skills Do You Need?

Above all, designing a database application requires *in-depth knowledge of the problem you are trying to solve*. A technically flawed application that addresses the proper business needs is better than a slickly executed but misconceived application. Without question, the most essential aspect of any application is its design.

Database design calls for *communication skills*. Determining requirements calls for extensive discussions with users to explain the implications of their decisions on the finished system. A database designer also needs *writing skills* to express requirements and to prepare user documentation.

The developer needs *analytical aptitude* to sift through requirements, to organize data, and to create application elements that best fulfill the needs of users. The designer must keep in mind the broad goals of the application, even while poring over the smallest details of a report or form.

Finally, the developer must have mastery of the particular DBMS used to build the application. The developer must understand the unique features, strengths, and limitations of the package so that the DBMS does not prevent the application from succeeding. For larger database projects, this phase of development is often passed on to a team of programmers who develop distinct software modules.

Why Build Your Own Database?

With so much software on the market, why go to the trouble and expense of creating your own database application? After all, packages are available for nearly every use imaginable, tracking everything from prenatal care to cemetery monuments.

One of the most compelling reasons to design your own database is that you have special needs, which off-the-shelf packages cannot fulfill. Perhaps your business delivers pizzas and dry cleaning at the same time. You need to track preferences for pepperoni and starch in shirts on the same customer record—not a likely feature on packaged software. You may prefer to have the software precisely fit the way you do business rather than contort your business to fit the assumptions of the software.

Commercial software applications may be too expensive for your budget. Complex packages can cost tens or hundreds of thousands of dollars, making them less than cost effective, especially if they don't suit your business exactly. A homegrown solution looks more appealing when it means saving on expenses.

You may want to build your own database application for the following reasons:

- You understand your data best
- No adequate off-the-shelf software exists
- You cannot wait for the corporate management information systems (MIS) department to develop a database
- The database is less expensive to develop yourself

A good reason to build your own database is the time needed for someone else to develop an application. Corporate management information systems (MIS) departments often are swamped with requests for new systems and burdened with the upkeep of existing applications. Even high priority projects must wait for programmers to become available. As table 1.3 shows, the backlog of applications runs from a minimum of six months to over one year, depending on the hardware platform (jargon for the type of computer).

Table 1.3. The Applications Backlog†

Platform	Months
Mainframe	14
Mini	9
PC	6

†Standard and Poor's *Industry Surveys: Computers and Office Equipment* (28 June 1990) C92.

If your project is at the bottom of a corporate waiting list, you may want to seize the initiative yourself. Frustrated managers often reallocate their budget for paper clips and long lunches to purchase PCs and software for new applications. They easily can get approval for hundreds or thousands of dollars worth of travel and entertainment, but must lobby long and hard to spend money on computer projects.

I offer you one final, little-known reason for creating your own database application: it is fun. There is no satisfaction quite like creating something from nothing, something that makes work easier and more productive. You can recognize database developers by the "parental glow" that comes from the pride of building applications.

Database design is as much an art as a science. This book reveals some of the secret tricks of the database trade and the step-by-step approach needed to achieve the best results. To start designing your database application, turn off the computer and sit down in a comfortable chair with paper and pencil.

A Sample Database Session

Before delving into the steps in database design, look at where you want to end up. The following section shows highlights from a database session. The application in use is the Business Lead Information Tracking System (BLITS), a contact management tool for sales professionals or business executives. BLITS tracks clients and related information, including companies, activities, scheduling and correspondence. It prints basic reports such as form letters, phone lists, mailing labels, follow-up schedules, and activity histories. BLITS includes all utilities necessary to maintain the database, access word processing software for correspondence, and search for clients by any desired criteria.

Typically, databases use menus to offer the user a list of actions (Chapter 10 discusses in detail the design and creation of menus). The first thing the user sees in the application is the application main menu. BLITS has four main menu options: Edit Data, Search, Run Reports, or Utilities. You choose the option by typing the letter or number of the choice.

After you select an action, other options appear on-screen for further information; for example, if you select Run Reports, another menu appears, asking you which report you want to run. If you then select Directories, another menu appears asking you which directory you want to run, and so on. You select these secondary menu options in the same way you select the primary options. If you choose 1: Edit Data, the options shown in figure 1.1 appear across the top of the screen.

From this menu, the user selects the file to edit. In this particular application, records can be added, modified, or deleted from the same form. You Edit Data in the CLIENTS file, for example, to perform one of the following tasks:

- Enter a new person into your database

- Retrieve a person's record and make an address change

- View the phone numbers for all people in New York

- Remove one or more people from the database

Databases use special screens for entering and viewing information. Figure 1.2 shows the data-entry form for CLIENTS as the form appears to

1

the user; figure 1.3 shows a sample client record. (Chapters 6 and 7 discuss techniques for creating forms and views.)

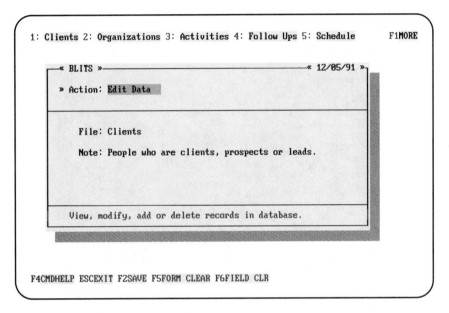

Fig. 1.1. *The BLITS Edit Data menu.*

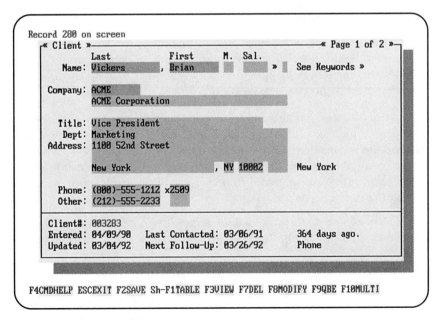

Fig. 1.2. *The CLIENTS data-entry form.*

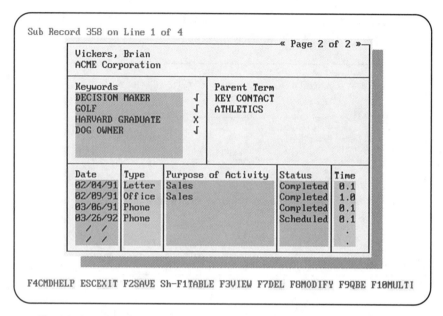

Fig. 1.3. *A sample client record.*

The first page of the CLIENTS data-entry form contains the name and address of the client or prospect (again see fig. 1.2). The second page displays all key words associated with the client and an activity history for the client (again see fig. 1.3).

Use reports to retrieve information from the database. You can send reports to the printer, to the screen, or to a disk file. Reports from BLITS include mailing labels, form letters, activity reports, and follow-up calendars. Figure 1.4 shows a sample report.

This brief discussion highlights some of the key elements of a finished database application. Of course, as in Hollywood, much more goes on behind the scenes than is apparent to the viewer. A database application is the result of quite a bit of planning and software craftsmanship. This book shows you how to create your own database application, overcoming all the obstacles in your path.

This book addresses the stages of database design in chronological order, from the first inkling that you need a database until it is signed, sealed, and delivered.

```
Phone Listing

October 15, 1991                                                    Page 1

Organization                          Name                  Phone

* Unlisted                            Abel, Robert          (301)-341-1000
                                      Dorsal, Rick          (201)-966-4246
                                      Lawful, Diana         (301)-341-1000

Aetna Insurance Company               Brixius, Nicholas     (301)-459-2323
                                      Miller, Mike          (203)-636-5016
                                      Tannenbaum, Carl      (301)-262-5111

Agricultural Marketing Service        Ace, Erick            (301)-653-7908
                                      Grason, Susan         (703)-528-8200

Alpha-Beta Corporation                Taylor, Randy         (213)-234-5666

American Computer Machines Enterprises De Almeida, Mark     (516)-781-0069

American Cyanamid                     Walsh, James          (201)-831-2000

American International Group          Larkin, Chris         (000)-486-5269

American Life Insurance Company       Riccioli, Richard     (302)-594-2233

American University                   Biles, George         (703)-425-0546
```

Fig. 1.4. *A sample report.*

Summary

Databases offer a powerful alternative to spreadsheets and word processing software for storing large volumes of data. New advances in software
technology make designing your own custom database application easier
than ever.

If you have run up against the limitations of word processing software
and spreadsheets for storing large volumes of data, learning about databases is the next step. Now is a good time to learn about databases,
because the current crop of DBMS is easier to use than ever before. Databases are not for everyone, but if you want to master your data universe,
they are definitely for you.

Analyzing a Project

The man who gets the most satisfactory results is not always the man with the most brilliant single mind, but rather the man that can best coordinate the brains and talent of his associates.

W. Alton Jones

The planning stage is the most crucial phase of a database project; it lays the foundation for all following stages. Poor planning is more often the cause of database failures than is flawed execution.

Planning saves time and money. Early in a project, the cost of major design overhauls is low; at later stages, changes become increasingly difficult and expensive. A problem costing $100 to correct in the design phase costs $1000 to fix when the system has become operational. Costs aside, planning saves hours of work. A sound database design makes maintaining your application simple even as business rules change. A flawed design, even if masterfully executed, yields a crippled, inadequate application.

Take the time to write down goals and requirements for the database, even if you will be the only user. This list will help you reach your goals faster. Luckily, having sole control of the process is easier than steering your database through a committee.

How Much is Enough?

If analysis is such a good thing, how do you know when to stop? The amount of time you devote to analysis is proportional to the scope of the application and the resources available to you. The level of organization in the existing process also affects the time required for analysis. Automating a well-defined, structured system takes less time than designing all the business rules necessary to build the database.

A good rule of thumb is that analysis takes from one-fourth to one-third the total project time. If the total project time is projected at two months, expect to spend the first two weeks doing analysis. Take whatever time you need to produce the documents discussed in this chapter.

Analysis can be highly formalized, with group sessions followed by elaborate documentation of requirements. Small projects, however, perhaps call for only informal analysis, such as a database schema scrawled on a cocktail napkin or casual discussions with users. If you plan to computerize your stamp collection, you probably don't need to gather a team of experts for a week-long requirements meeting (see fig. 2.1).

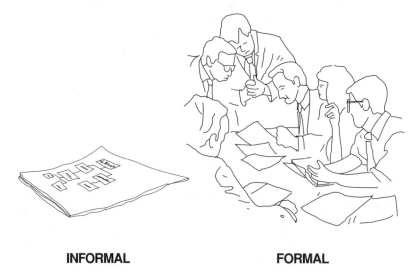

INFORMAL   **FORMAL**

Fig. 2.1. The formality spectrum.

Wherever your project falls on the formality spectrum, you need to understand all the steps in database analysis to make an informed decision about which steps you can skip. Beware of underestimating the importance of an application. Even small databases become quite important to their users. "Quick fix" provisional databases tend to last much longer than their builders anticipate. I once worked on a database that was set up to say *1989* in all the reports because it was intended to last only a year while the mainframe system was created. The next year, the company called me in to change the reports to say 1990, and by 1991, I had inserted variables that changed automatically for successive years of "temporary" operation. A small, PC-based, temporary application often forestalls the need for its planned mainframe successor—particularly after costs for the larger project are determined. Be as comprehensive as possible from the start in describing the system's intended lifespan so that you do not have to work in new elements at the last minute.

To achieve quick results, try to keep the number of project participants to a minimum. The more people involved in a project, the more time the project consumes. Meetings take longer and are more difficult to schedule, and shared responsibility may translate into lower accountability.

Although you can spend an unlimited amount of time on analysis, don't let analysis paralyze your project. In database design, as in most human endeavors, perfection is the enemy of excellence. After you have eliminated the worst uncertainties, declare a halt to analysis and continue with the project.

Approaches to Analysis

You can approach a database project in two ways: working forward from general goals to specifics (the *top-down approach*) or working backward from specifics to goals (the *bottom-up approach*). Working forward, you start with no assumptions and build from general to specific goals toward the fine details of the data forms and reports. You interview users, build the database structures, and finally create sample reports.

Working backward, you use the final product of the database, usually reports, to determine data storage requirements. Working backward from printed forms and reports to identify what you need to track in the database is one of the most useful analysis techniques. To begin, spread all the printed output from the manual system (or computerized system) on a table. Add sketches of new reports to be created from scratch. Virtually all the fields you will enter into the database are contained in the reports. Users will not have to enter some fields given on the paper form, such as totals and averages, which can be calculated from other fields.

This chapter gives examples of both approaches to determining database requirements. You may work forward and backward, even on the same project.

Levels of Analysis

To build a database, you must perform three distinct levels of analysis: *conceptual*, *logical*, and *physical*. Each level represents a stage between the business practice you are automating and the database application.

The broadest analysis takes place at the conceptual level and produces a conceptual model. A conceptual model helps describe the entities you are tracking, how they relate to one another, and the business rules that govern those entities. A conceptual model is not tied directly to computer applications, but is necessary for designing paper forms or systematic manual procedures. Banking, accounting, order entry, and other common business functions employed detailed conceptual models long before the computer age.

The next stage of analysis, at the logical level, produces the logical model. At this level of analysis, you translate the conceptual model into a database table structure using a particular data model. You define data elements and data integrity rules at the logical level. The logical model is not confined to any particular hardware, operating system, or database; it is the same whether the application is destined for a roomful of mainframes or a laptop PC. You can use the same logical model as the starting point for any database software.

The final level of analysis is the physical level. At this stage, the constraints of the computer (hardware and software) come into play. The physical analysis concerns such details as storage methods, disk drive access, and indexing. Every DBMS has its own strengths and weaknesses, so the design is compromised to work around the weaknesses and to take advantage of the strengths.

Changes made at any stage of the analysis affect all subsequent stages. For instance, identifying a new business entity within the conceptual model will change the logical and physical models of the database. Inevitably, mistakes made early in the process come back to haunt you.

Be sure to go through all three levels of analysis to create your database and to keep the levels separate in your mind. If you skip a stage and jump right into making compromises for your particular software and hardware, you may needlessly reduce your flexibility. The conceptual and logical designs are useful on their own and will be helpful if you later decide to move the application to new software.

Goals of Analysis

The objective of the analysis process is to determine the requirements for the application, so retreat to a windowless room with a PC and a large bag of chocolates and start creating. For an engaging primer on requirements, see Donald C. Gause and Gerald M. Weinberg, *Exploring Requirements: Quality Before Design* (New York: Dorset House Publishing, 1989). At the end of analysis, you should have the following information:

- A list of business goals

- A list of entities to track

- A database schema

- Sample report outputs

- Processing requirements

In a formal project, the preceding items are combined in a requirements document. The following table of contents is from a typical requirements list:

Introduction
Goals
System Overview
Data Entry Forms
    Lakes, rivers, streams
    Boats
    Lures and baits
    Tackle
    Fishing outings
    Fish caught
    Expense accounting
Reports
    Chronological log
    Fish by weight
    Fish by species
    Weather, seasonal analysis
    Lure effectiveness
    Boat performance
Procedures
    Backup database
    Export data to Fish and Wildlife Service
Operating Environment
    Equipment
    Operating system
    Printers

The most important aid to analysis is the assistance of people who are closest to the problem—the prospective users of the system. Guessing what users want in a database system is a poor substitute for asking them directly. Although user interviews take time, they are necessary. The time and effort spent meeting with users is rewarded later in the design process and in the finished application.

Throughout the development process, check to make sure that your perspective is consistent with the users' perspective. Continued contact with the users keeps the project on track and helps refine the nuances of the application. *Prototyping* is the most effective way to maintain contact with your users. In prototyping, programmers build a working system and place it in the users' hands as soon as possible. Prototypes help users learn more about the application and refine their requirements for it. Prototyping also prevents the database creator from straying too far from user expectations.

When polled for their requirements, users usually assume responsibility for the system and actively work to ensure its success. Given a system imposed from above, however, users may point to the system's inevitable flaws as excuses for not using it. Users involved in the design of a new system have a greater stake in its success. They are more receptive to training and have more patience with the application's "birthing pains."

Because analysis is so important, some companies hire facilitators to oversee requirements meetings. Facilitators are highly paid computer "midwives" who bridge the gap between the computer users and programmers. They conduct formal user interviews throughout the development process and present prototypes for user testing and evaluation.

When developing a database for your own use, you must face the awkward task of being your own prosecutor, defense attorney, and judge, but at least you do not have to worry about your user ignoring requests for information. When the time comes for your interview, sidle up to the mirror, look yourself in the eye, and answer the questions posed in your soliloquy as honestly as possible.

Rules for Conducting User Interviews

Regardless of the subject of your interview, adherence to the following guidelines will improve your chances of success. If these suggestions are too strict, modify them to suit your own interview techniques.

- *Have an agenda.* Holding a meeting without an agenda is like showing up for midterms without studying. Some people get by with it, but the payoff is better when you are prepared. An agenda focuses the discussion and gives you license to silence participants when they deviate from the plan. Assign a period of time for each part of the agenda so that obstructionists cannot filibuster the meeting by wasting too much time with preliminaries. Distribute the agenda in advance so that participants can do their homework.

- *Encourage "blue sky" thinking.* Ignore questions of feasibility. This is not the time to set application limits; you will have plenty of opportunities for setting limits as development proceeds. Use all the brainstorming tricks you know to catch a glimpse of the users' goals. You may be surprised at how many of their wishes you can fulfill.

- *Focus on the problem at hand.* Try to understand the business problem at hand and all the ways the application might help solve that problem. Stop discussion that leaps ahead to potential problems with the solution and thereby stifles creativity.

- *Don't foreclose your options too soon.* Examine the entire business problem before focusing on the specifics of your database project. The database may cover more areas than you anticipated. Boundaries established without the benefit of analysis may misdirect efforts toward automating unimportant aspects of a process. You may spend 90 percent of your resources to fix 10 percent of the problem. Worse yet, you may automate the least important part of the process.

- *Create a quiet, stress-free environment.* Making progress is difficult when participants are interrupted by phone calls or other demands. Encourage participants to arrange their schedules so they will not be diverted from the meeting. As shown in figure 2.2, you can use many props to create a good environment. Hot coffee, desserts, and any other appropriate creature comforts help participants feel relaxed and creative.

WHAT YOU WOULD LIKE TO USE   **WHAT YOU SHOULD USE**

Bright lights   Water torture   Good coffee   Comfortable chairs

Sodium pentothal   Thumbscrews   Pastries   Patience

Fig. 2.2. Analysis tools.

- *Avoid personality conflicts.* Don't pit people against one another and don't let participants get away with personal attacks. You may want to segregate individuals of different levels in the corporate hierarchy so that superiors don't inhibit the remarks of their subordinates. Members of upper-level management often are less familiar with the details of a business function and have fewer insights to offer on the application than the people who will work with it every day.

- *Show concern for user needs.* Successful systems are the systems people actually use. No database designer can make a system succeed over its users' objections. Show that you are working with the users to make their efforts more productive. Responsiveness to user input increases acceptance of the system.

- *Avoid technical jargon.* Speak English to users; don't try to overwhelm them with your knowledge of computer acronyms. Be sure to define technical terms when you use them. Keep the discussion focused on data and the users' direct contact with the system rather than on technical details of implementation (memory usage, protocols, query language).

- *Write down everything.* As all bureaucrats know, the final word goes to the person who writes the memo summarizing the meeting. Assign someone the task of taking notes, translate the notes into English, and dividing them by topic to make them more readable. You may want to keep suggestions anonymous to avoid bureaucratic conflict and to keep all ideas equal for later debate. Use a tape recorder if you must, but remember that recording inhibits many participants (talk to your lawyer before you record someone without their knowledge and consent) and that listening to a tape takes as long as the original meeting.

- *Identify the decision maker.* The identity of your real client is not always obvious. Make every effort to please the person with authority over the project. If that person is you, all the better.

The Interview

With the preceding guidelines in mind, gather the participants and begin the interviews. If you have difficulty formulating your questions, the following icebreakers provide a starting point for nearly any application:

- What are your goals for building this application?

- How does your process currently work? Is it manual or computerized?

unit of information. A last name, a street address, a city, and a ZIP code are examples of fields. Attributes are represented in the database as fields, such as the field 321 in the Room column in table 2.1.

Several fields describing a particular entity combine to form a *record*. One address book entry, made up of a person's name, address, and phone number, is a record. A record appears as a row in a database table.

Distinguishing entities from attributes can be difficult. Remember that an attribute cannot exist without an entity. For instance, an invoice can exist without a date (although this condition would complicate billing), but an invoice date cannot exist without an invoice to reference. The invoice is the entity, and the date an attribute. Although a client-tracking database may contain ZIP codes, these ZIP codes (attributes) are meaningful only for this application as part of the client addresses (entities).

If you are tracking more than one entity, those entities may be related. *Relationships* describe how two entities are related to one another. In a sales application, for instance, customers may be related to purchases by a customer number, and the relationship is important if you want to break down sales by customer.

Databases are made of more than data; after you put the information into the database, you want to *do* something with it. Perhaps you want to extract information, perform calculations, or modify data. *Procedures* perform actions using database tables, such as reports, account posting, or entering orders.

A *form* is a computer screen designed to accept data entry and is analogous to a paper form. The form contains fields and text to guide the user in data entry. After you enter information in the form, the information is stored in one or more tables in the database. Forms may process data before it is stored and may contain integrity checks to validate information before accepting it. For instance, the form may check the ZIP code of an entry to see whether it falls within the ZIP code range of the state.

Finally, *menus* enable users to view and select database functions. Most kinds of software contain menus, such as the list of functions across the top of a spreadsheet or the main menu of a word processing program. Menus can contain options for entering data, running reports, or performing other database tasks. Menus help tie together all application functions and make the program simpler to use.

You can compare database elements to parts of speech. Entities, like nouns, represent concrete or abstract things. Attributes, like adjectives, modify or describe entities, much as adjectives describe nouns.

Procedures, comparable to verbs, represent actions performed on entities. A procedure can list the contents of a table or add, modify, or delete records.

Figure 2.3 shows the main elements of a database. The database consists of several entities or files (addresses, birthdays, recipes). Each file consists of one or more records (for example, Jane Doe's address). Each record in turn consists of the smallest database elements: fields. The phone number in the addresses file is a field.

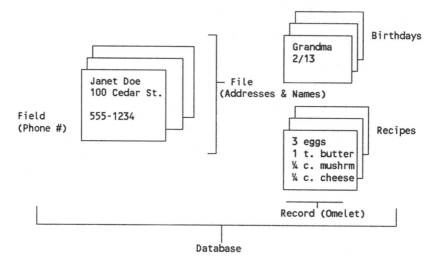

Fig. 2.3. Elements of a database.

NOTE: Some database software publishers have invented their own special terms for database elements or have distorted the meaning of standard terms as applied to their particular software. For instance, dBASE II calls a file a *database*. DataEase combines table and form creation into one step, so the DataEase term *form* is different from the common meaning of the term.

You can create *reports* by using information entered into a form. For example, a report can print the names and phone numbers of the people in your database. Reports can contain any (or all) of the fields you define in the database. You can design your reports to look any way you choose.

You use reports to retrieve data from the database, and you can send reports to the screen, a printer, or a disk file. Reports fulfill users' needs by sorting data in different ways. Reports can be routine, such as monthly sales reports to management, or for a single purpose, such as receivables for one customer. Unlike data-entry forms, reports often contain repetitive information to facilitate reading.

Reports also can contain graphics, such as line plots, bar graphs, or pie graphs. Graphics often convey a more powerful message than words or text alone. Some database packages (such as Paradox) include built-in graphics features; other packages use add-on programs or exports to specialized graphics software.

A *relational database* stores information in a number of related tables. A relational database enables you to form powerful queries from one or more tables, and its structure is easy to modify. (The characteristics of relational databases are discussed in greater detail in Chapter 14, "Choosing Database Software.") For tracking retail sales, you might create a Customers table listing your customers and their addresses and a Purchases table containing information about each purchase your customers make.

You can design one table to hold everything, but that approach may lead to problems. If one table holds all customer information, you have to enter all customer information, including name, address, and phone number, each time a customer places an order. By creating two tables, you enter most customer information only once.

Tables can be linked by a common field. For example, you can create a field called *customer number*. Assign the customer number when you enter a customer's name and address. When you enter subsequent orders, you need enter only the customer number in the order table, and the database will refer to the Customer table and read all pertinent information. The customer's address is stored only once, saving time and disk space. For reports, you can print information about the customer and then jump to the Purchases table and print information about all the purchases they have made.

Input Versus Output

To understand how a database works, imagine that it is divided into three main parts, as shown in figure 2.4.

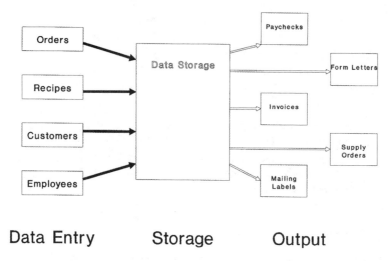

Data Entry   Storage   Output

Fig. 2.4. *The main parts of a database.*

Data-entry forms are used to capture information. In most cases, operators manually enter this information. Sometimes this data is complemented by data from other computer systems or from instruments (for example, bar code readers). The data-entry screen helps users fill in the information quickly and accurately.

The *internal storage structure* provided by the DBMS enables efficient searching and retrieval. You can build indexes for some fields so that records can be found or sorted more quickly. An *index* is a special file that points to records in the database in a sorted order (for example, alphabetical by last name). See Chapter 5, "Building Tables," for a detailed discussion of indexes.

Finally, the database is used to create *output.* Database output usually consists of reports, listings, summary reports, mailing labels, and letters, or data exports to other programs, such as word processing programs, spreadsheets, and other databases. Output is designed to be as useful to the reader as possible, containing only the information necessary for a particular purpose. Output is essentially independent of data entry. You might have a dozen different reports that use information from one data-entry form, or vice versa. The only connection between output and data entry is that reports can contain only information entered (manually or imported from another program) into the database or calculated from entered information. Nothing can come out of a database that does not go into a database.

Database Jargon

Database developers, like most computer specialists, have developed extensive jargon. The practice of software companies to coin their own catchwords when describing database functions also promotes the growth of obscure database terms. Some database vendors use different words to describe the same thing in the same database package. Symantec's Q&A, for instance, calls records both *forms* and *records*. The following table unravels the synonyms of the database world.

Term	Equivalents
Record	Row, tuple, occurrence
Field	Column, attribute
Key	Unique identifier, unique field(s)
Table	File, relation, database
Form	Screen, layout, panel
View	Subform, multiform, multitable, set
Relationship	Association, link, join
Procedure	Report, process
Domain	Legal values, program

Sampling an Interview

Returning now to the interview process, after you identify the goals for your application and define the necessary terminology, you can be more specific about what the database should contain. Identify the major elements of an application by asking questions such as the following: What are the main entities you want to track in this database? Which characteristics of each of these entities are important? How do the entities relate to one another?

Discuss with your audience the major elements of a database. The more the prospective users of the system understand about databases, the better. Do not barrage innocent users with technical terms, however. Be sure to explain the broad goals of the requirements exercise.

When first asked, users probably will not list everything that they want the database to track. Be sure to probe enough to reveal most of the entities users want included in the database and how users finally will use the data.

At the conclusion of an interview, you should be able to produce a draft of entities and attributes similar to table 2.2.

Table 2.2. Alma Mater University Entity and Attribute Listing

Entities	*Attributes*
Students	Social Security Number
	First Name
	Last Name
	Middle Initial
	Local Address
	Permanent Address
	Birthdate
Instructors	Social Security Number
	First Name
	Last Name
	Middle Initial
	Permanent Address
	Birthdate
Courses	Course Number
	Department
	Description
	Credit Hours
Course Offerings	Year
	Semester
	Course Number
	Section Number
	Instructor Name
	Building
	Room
	Dates
	Time
Student Schedule	Student Social Security Number
	Year
	Semester
	Course Number
	Section Number

Reporting Requirements

As part of the analysis process, gather samples of all printed output that the database application will produce. Many automated systems are designed to replace manual systems, so report formats often already are designed for you. For new reports, fill out a worksheet such as the one shown in figure 2.5.

```
                        REPORT WORKSHEET


Report Name: Sales Summary

Report Title:    Information Strategies, Sales Summary
                 Covering 00/00/00 to 00/00/00

Output Device: Printer      If disk output, file name:

Print Style:  Landscape, condensed

Selection Criteria:

User chooses date range at runtime; only paid orders included.

Fields to Include:

Inventory Class (in groups), Stock number, Description, Quantity
(Total), Unit Price, Extended Price (Total).

Sample Format:

Information Strategies, Sales Summary for 06/01/91 to 08/31/91


Class      Stock #    Description    Unit Cost     Qty   Total Cost


Books
           D4AL       dBASE IV Apps   39.95        100   3,995.00

Software
           WP         WordEase       250.00        10    2,500.00
           SPREAD     dSheet         534.00        10    5,340.00
```

Fig. 2.5. *A sample report worksheet.*

Use a separate sheet for each report requested. These sheets serve as checklists later in the development process.

Processing Requirements

When discussing the application with users, you may discover requirements for processing as well as storing information. You can use pseudocode to record these requirements. *Pseudocode* expresses operations systematically and step by step, much like a computer program. Pseudocode is plain English, however, not a programming language. You can translate pseudocode into programming later in the design process. The following list gives examples of processes expressed in pseudocode:

- *Procedure.* Purge inactive customers from catalog list

- *Frequency.* Quarterly

- *Description.* Deletes all inactive customers from the catalog mailing list

- *Definition.* Inactive means that a customer has ordered nothing in 12 months, total purchases are less than $100, or customer has expressed lack of interest

  If a customer is inactive, delete the customer from the catalog mailing list and transfer their information to the inactive customers list. Send them a postcard asking whether they want to continue to receive the catalog.

- *Procedure.* Monthly sales figure consolidation

- *Frequency.* Monthly

- *Description.* Consolidates sales by product categories and week and then transmits to the main office

- *Definition.* At the end of each month, generate total sales by product category by week; then dial into the corporate mainframe and transfer the file

Pseudocode is not as detailed as database code, but it provides a good basis for defining requirements so that users can discuss them with programmers. A programmer can use pseudocode to record a requirement without necessarily knowing the exact commands it will require.

Relationships

If your database tracks only one entity or several unrelated entities, you can skip the rest of this chapter. Relationships are necessary only when data from one entity relates to another. For instance, recipes, daily menus, and grocery lists for a restaurant are related, because changes in menus affect the grocery list, and menus are derived from recipes.

In the database world, a relationship is a way of tying together records from two different entities. For instance, customers can be related to invoices by the customer name. Invoices can be related to invoice line items by the invoice number.

Database relationships fall into the following three categories:

- *One-to-one.* Each record has one—and only one—related record in the second file (husbands and wives, for example, where polygamy is illegal), and vice versa.

- *One-to-many.* Each record has one or many related records in the second file (for example, students can sign up for more than one course).

- *Many-to-many*. Each record in one file may have many related records in a second file, and those related records may in turn have many related records in the first file (for example, insured cars to drivers in an insurance company's database).

Many-to-many relationships create problems for data entry and for information retrieval. One of the challenges for the database designer is to identify many-to-many relationships. For instance, an automobile insurance database may need to track drivers for insured vehicles. A family may have several drivers and several cars. Since each driver may drive more than one car, and each car may have more than one driver, these two entities have a many-to-many relationship. Chapter 4, "Organizing Your Data," explains how to handle these relationships.

To define relationships, specify the entities to be related to one another. If possible at this stage, you may want to identify the field or fields used in the relationship. A relationship statement may read "Invoices are related to customers when the customer ID in the invoice is equal to the customer ID in the customers file." Your current goal is to identify and categorize the relationships that link the main entities. Relationship statements for the Alma Mater University application follow:

- Students are related to student schedule by Social Security number.

- Student schedule is related to course offerings by year, semester, course number, and section number.

- Course offerings are related to courses by course number.

- Course offerings are related to instructors by instructor Social Security number.

Another way to show relationships is to draw a table such as table 2.3, listing all the entities and indicating a relationship with a check mark.

Table 2.3. Relationship Matrix

	Students	Professors	Courses	Course Offerings	Course Registration
Students					✓
Professors				✓	
Courses				✓	✓
Course Offerings	✓			✓	✓
Course Registration	✓			✓	

You also can use the table style used in table 2.4 to show relationships.

Table 2.4. Alma Mater U Relationship Table		
Form 1	*Form 2*	*Type*
Students	Student Schedule	One-to-many
Course Offerings	Student Schedule	One-to-many
Courses	Course Offerings	One-to-many
Instructors	Course Offerings	One-to-many

After you identify relationships, your next step is to draw a schema of the database.

Using Schemas

When planning a database, keep in your mind an overall picture of the database structure. A *database schema* is a graphic diagram of the database, identifying its major entities and relationships.

You can depict a schema in many ways. The examples in this book are simple, but sophisticated sets of symbols are available for depicting data elements in great detail. The most important goal is that your audience be able to understand the schema. Many database users learn much more from a one-page drawing of a design than from dozens of pages of narrative description.

Choose the schema format that you like best. Figure 2.6 shows a schema for Alma Mater's enrollment system.

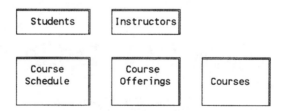

Fig. 2.6. *The Alma Mater U preliminary database schema.*

You can make your boxes large enough to contain a list of the attributes—this information will be useful during forms design. Some designers also write the approximate number of records for each entity inside the box, to help determine storage and performance requirements.

Figure 2.7 shows the schema of the Alma Mater enrollment system with relationships included.

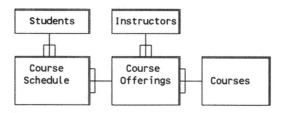

Fig. 2.7. *The Alma Mater U schema with relationships.*

The lines in the schema connect related forms. The lines are single or forked to show the relationship, with forked lines indicating the "-many" side of a one-to-many relationship.

Students to Course Schedule is a one-to-many relationship because each student may sign up for more than one course, but a single entry in Course Schedule may pertain to only one student. A record in Course Offerings may relate to only one instructor or course, but may have several records in Course Schedule (one record for each student enrolled), so its relationships are many-to-one and one-to-many, respectively.

If you change the assumptions for the database, you also must modify the schema. For instance, the structure shown in this example does not accommodate courses taught by more than one instructor, because the relationship between instructors and course offerings is one-to-many. To meet this new requirement, you must change the relationship to many-to-many, as shown in figure 2.8.

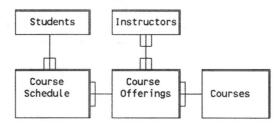

Fig. 2.8. *A schema for team teaching.*

Schemas are invaluable for working with users to refine the data model. The number of entities often grows as analysis continues.

Creating a Service Call Tracking Schema

A client at an appliance store asks for a system to track service calls. To create this automated system, you work backward from the paper form currently used to record service calls. The client shows you the current service call form (see fig. 2.9).

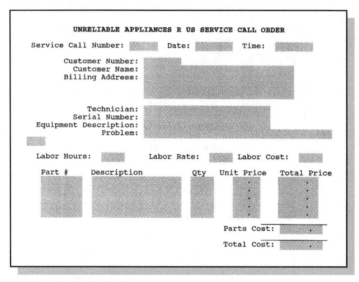

Fig. 2.9. *A service call order form.*

> USER: I want a system to track appliance service calls to print a list of all service orders at the end of each day, including the time and cost of each call.

You have identified one entity so far, *Service Calls*, as shown in figure 2.10. This entity will contain attributes such as service call number, technician number, appliance serial number, date, time, hours, spare parts, and total cost.

```
Service Calls
```

Fig. 2.10. *Service calls schema 1.*

> USER: I want to include more information on each technician, such as full name and telephone number.

To accommodate additional information about the technician, you could add to the SERVICE CALL file for technicians new fields for first name, last name, and telephone number. These new fields would create redundant data entry, however, because you have to fill them in for each and every service call, even if one technician performed many service calls. To save data entry time, you create another file to contain detailed information about each technician—information that will not change from one service call to another.

Your first addition is a second entity, *Technicians*, related to the Service Calls entity by the technician's name. Attributes for Technicians include the technician's name, Social Security number, address, telephone number, and specialty. You still have to enter something in Service Calls to identify the technician for each particular call. Although first and last names can serve this purpose, some form of code, such as a technician number or technician's initials, is shorter and quicker to enter.

The relationship in this example is a one-to-many relationship because each technician can handle more than one service call, but each service call is handled by only one technician. In figure 2.11, the line drawn in the schema is forked to show the "-many side" of this one-to-many relationship.

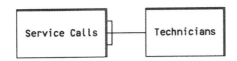

Fig. 2.11. *Service calls schema 2.*

USER: Actually, I also want to know more about the customers who call in and the repair history for a particular appliance.

Again, you can add the fields to store this new information in the SERVICE CALLS file. Adding the fields, however, creates redundant data entry, because you need to enter the customer's name and address each time that customer purchases an appliance.

Instead, you can add two entities, *Equipment* and *Customer*. You need both entities because a customer perhaps bought more than one piece of merchandise in the past, and you need to distinguish which appliance needs repair and whether it still is under warranty.

The Equipment form uses the serial number field as the unique identifier of each appliance, because you know that no two serial numbers can be identical. Additional equipment attributes include customer ID, date of purchase, warranty expiration date, type of appliance, manufacturer, and model. You can incorporate rules for calculating the warranty expiration date based on the date of purchase and the type of appliance.

The CUSTOMER file includes Customer ID and the customer's name, street address, city, state, ZIP, and telephone number. The customer ID is a field of your own contrivance, a sequential number assigned to a customer upon their first purchase.

The Customer and Equipment forms both have CUSTOMER ID fields, and the Equipment and Service Call forms both have SERIAL NUMBER fields. The link between the customer and the service call is naturally through the equipment itself. Figure 2.12 shows the new entities and relationships to track customers and equipment.

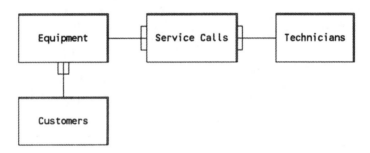

Fig. 2.12. *Service calls schema 3.*

USER: To be thorough, I want to show how the service calls affect our parts inventory.

To help monitor the spare parts inventory, you add two new entities, *Parts Used* and *Inventory*. The application will record each part used on service calls in the PARTS USED file and then subtract those parts from its total inventory through the IVENTORY file. You now have the schema shown in figure 2.13, including entities and relationships for spare parts used and inventory.

Through dialogue with users, the database designer can refine the boundaries of the application. Even in simple applications, the number of entities usually exceeds the users' original vision of the application. More complicated systems can result in dozens or hundreds of entities.

Consider distributing database schemas to potential users for their comments. Additional entities often crop up when a user reviews a new schema.

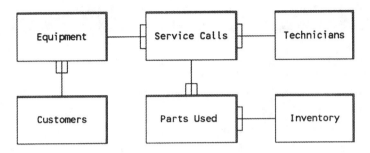

Fig. 2.13. Service calls schema 4.

Levels of Detail

As the preceding example reveals, the complexity of a database depends on the level of detail the application needs to track. Keeping a record of every single part on your car is much more complicated than storing one entry for the car itself.

You may have to compromise on the level of detail of your database. Suppose that, to improve your golf game, you decide to build an application to track your performance on the course. You want to keep a record of your score for each game you play, showing the name of the course and par, as in table 2.5.

Table 2.5. Tracking a Golf Game

Date	Course	Par	Score
4/16/88	Shady Acres	71	99
5/20/88	Low Point	71	95
5/21/88	Low Point	71	93
10/6/90	Mosquito Bend	71	89

You also could add fields to record the temperature, weather, and time of day. Table 2.5 is fine for showing your overall scores, but you also can record your score for each hole. Table 2.6 shows the front nine from Mosquito Bend.

This information is useful for determining whether you are going astray by loosing a stroke or two on each hole or making monumental blunders on just a few holes. You also can discover whether you score better on par 3 or on par 4 holes. If you enter the score for each hole, you can calculate the total score by adding together all the individual scores.

Table 2.6. Tracking a Golf Game (with hole detail)

Date	Course	Hole	Par	Score
10/6/90	Mosquito Bend	1	4	5
10/6/90	Mosquito Bend	2	3	4
10/6/90	Mosquito Bend	3	4	5
10/6/90	Mosquito Bend	4	5	5
10/6/90	Mosquito Bend	5	4	4
10/6/90	Mosquito Bend	6	3	4
10/6/90	Mosquito Bend	7	5	5
10/6/90	Mosquito Bend	8	4	4
10/6/90	Mosquito Bend	9	4	5

With another, deeper level of detail for the golf database, you can track each shot for each hole, recording information such as the club you selected, the distance to the hole, obstacles, and the result of the shot. This database would be quite detailed, holding 80 to 100 records for each game (depending on your handicap). You may decide that entering all this detail will take nearly as long as playing the game. If you compromise on the level of detail, you will have more time to go to the driving range. You may stop, therefore, with recording each hole rather than every single shot.

If this golf database seems like an extreme example, remember that you could go to even greater levels of detail. This example showed scores for only one person. You can expand the database to track the scores of a large group of people and show which golfers played together. You can modify the system for stroke or match play and can take into account the golf handicaps of the participants. As a golf course operator, you may want additional information such as the time required for the group to complete each hole.

Although golf may not be your game, business applications face similar analytical questions and compromises.

Back to the Drawing Board

After you complete the interview, grab the last cheese danish and return to your inner sanctum. Now the real work begins: you must translate the users' hopes and dreams into specific database requirements and design specifications.

If you start to feel that the analysis process is too time-consuming, remember that, compared to analysis, implementation is trivial.

Summary

To build a database, you must determine what entities to track and which of their attributes to record. The best source for database requirements is usually the users themselves. Set up user interviews early in the design process.

Use printed forms and reports from the current system to learn how the business works and how the database will fit in. As you begin to understand the database, draw graphical schemas so that users can check your progress. Above all, write down your analysis of goals and requirements to serve as a yardstick for the finished application.

Planning Your Database

The cautious seldom err.

Confucius

No scheme can succeed without a plan, and database design is no exception. This chapter explains the benefits of good project management and introduces the phases of the database design process. You can build simple databases in a relatively unstructured way, but more substantial projects demand systematic planning.

Designing a database application can be a complex process even for simple applications and especially for larger, multiuser databases. You need to make hundreds of decisions, from the length of each field to the screen colors of the data entry forms and the format of printed reports. Several people (users, managers, programmers, and others) may provide input into the project, and you must solicit, analyze, and incorporate their suggestions. As development work continues, new needs often emerge, and the original requirements may change. This complexity and change underscores the need for planning.

Fortunately, you do not have to learn all the lessons of project planning through experience. The mainframe computing community has done a great deal of research on planning. Books and courses in management information systems (MIS) cover requirements analysis, interface planning, and all types of documentation.

If you have never taken a computer science course, you are not alone. According to database vendor Nantucket's research, 70 percent of Clipper users have no formal computer science training ("Nantucket CS 101," *DBMS*, August 1990, 8). This statistic is even more striking when you consider that Clipper is one of the more difficult database programming environments to master. Imagine the same statistic for users of simpler systems such as Lotus, Q&A, or AskSam.

In place of formal MIS education, most PC developers often learn by experimenting with software firsthand and learning on the job. Their expertise often lies in the business operations for which they build applications rather than in formal computer training. As the tedium of programming is made obsolete by more intelligent database software, more and more users will be able to manage their information on their own. Their intimate knowledge of their business requirements, combined with grounding in database fundamentals, will make their applications suit their business needs.

The value of formal planning in software design has grown along with the power and importance of PC applications in business. PC-based applications once were seen as peripheral to the core requirements of businesses, and all "serious" applications were run on the mainframe. This attitude has disappeared as PC and local area network (LAN) applications support critical business needs and even replace the traditional corporate mainframe. Many PC database developers would benefit from computer science or management information systems education.

PC software applications contain the same essential elements as mainframe software. You must develop a data structure, menus, forms, and reports whether you are creating an application for yourself or for hundreds of users. Even the smallest PC database projects raise many of the same issues as large-scale applications. These issues include data integrity, security, upgrade strategies, and hardware migration (moving the system from one type of computer to another). The best way to prevent problems is through planning. This book proposes a grand strategy—a master plan—for building a database application.

Have a Master Plan

To come up with a master plan for developing your database application, you must step back and look at the big picture. Start with the business problem you want to solve and move through the decisions you must make to achieve a working computerized system.

Each step in designing a system takes you from a broader understanding of the problem to its specifics. The project may move on several levels at one time. If you start from scratch, for instance, without hardware or software, you need to define the number of users and their location to determine suitable hardware and network requirements. To estimate the size of the database, you have to choose the data elements that you want to track and decide how much detail the database will contain. The size of the database also affects the hardware you use to run it. Table 3.1 shows the levels of each step in the life of a typical computer application. The business scope calls for broad information on the goals of the application, the processes or functions it must perform, and the location of its users.

Table 3.1. Applications Life Cycle†

	A. Data	*B. Process/ Network*	*C. Hardware*
1. Business Scope	List of goals and elements important to the business	List of processes the business performs	List of locations in which the business operates
2. Business Model	Business entities and their inter-relationships	Flows between processes	Communications links between business locations
3. Information Systems Model	Model of the business data and its inter-relationships	Flows between application processes	Distribution network
4. Technology Model	Database design	System design	Configuration design
5. Technology Definition	Database schema and subschema definition	Program/ pseudocode	Configuration definition
6. Information System	Data storage structure	Finished program/ Executable code	System configuration

†Adapted from John Zachman's Information Systems Architecture (ISA) Framework, *Database Programming & Design*, June 1991, 58.

The three levels of analysis shown in table 3.1 are relatively independent of one another. The column describing data contains things. If they were a part of speech, the data would be nouns. The processes are more like verbs; they do things to the data (transactions). The hardware/network level concerns how the communication will take place; this level is like an adverb describing how the processes will reach the data. Systems that contain the same data and perform the same functions may be implemented quite differently if one system is a single-user application on a PC and another is a global network of thousands of users.

You usually start a project with several levels already complete. Perhaps you already have a computer or network to run the application. The rules of your business may already be well defined. If so, move to the rows and columns where you still have questions, starting at the highest level of analysis and moving to the lowest.

Keeping the levels of analysis separate from one another helps you understand how changes in business rules affect various components of your system. If new locations are added, communications links must be added to the network (although the database structure may not necessarily change). New products or services may introduce new data elements to track. These changes must be integrated into the business model and ultimately into the database structure and the application.

The preceding broad conceptual breakdown of project activities describes the processes used to build simple or complex information systems.

The master plan can be divided into two main parts: the analysis phase and the implementation phase. The analysis phase determines the scope of the application, relates it to business goals, and establishes a model of the data the database will track. Much of the analysis phase is spent talking, especially with future users of the system. The rest of the analysis phase is spent writing documents for review and use in the implementation phase.

During the implementation phase, you sit at the terminal or PC and turn out designs for file structure, screens, menus, and reports. If you plan properly, implementation is relatively smooth. The programmer follows the recipe provided by the analyst. You probably will play both roles.

You will make many changes to the master plan. As development proceeds, however, the cost of changes increases. Changes may affect other parts of the application. The more complete the application when a change is made, the more tables, forms, reports, and procedures that will be affected. If you add a middle initial field to the customer table, for instance, you also must add this field to the data-entry form and to all reports (such as address labels, form letters, and invoices) that include customer information. Similar effects may be caused by changing the name, length, or type of a field. Good planning can mitigate the cost of changes and protect the project against cost overruns. To encourage timely introduction of changes, consider prototyping. In prototyping, users test the application throughout development rather than waiting for a finished product.

Managing Personnel

As you can imagine, many databases are too big for one person to complete without assistance. Sometimes several specialists are called in to work on different phases of a project. Within a phase, particularly the programming phase, a team of workers may divide one task among themselves.

Be warned that the amount of time required for a project expands in proportion to the number of people involved. A project that takes one person three months to complete may take three people six months to complete. With each new participant, meetings become longer and more difficult to schedule. Testing becomes more complicated because the programming styles of several people must be taken into account. More time is spent explaining your work to other team members instead of working on the application. The slowest worker in the group can bring the schedule to its knees. Finally, group decision-making can spread responsibility so thinly that individuals no longer have the ability to act decisively. You need to monitor the progress of the project closely and lead the team members to avoid delays and indecision.

Prototyping

Prototyping is not a distinct phase of development but a technique for producing good results quickly. A *prototype* is a working version of your database application that fulfills most of the database's requirements. A prototype is not necessarily perfect, however. It may lack some minor features or need polishing. I strongly advocate the use of working prototypes to build database applications. Nothing contributes more to the accuracy and usefulness of an application than using prototypes.

The goal of prototyping is to shorten the development cycle and produce a product that best serves its users. The longer the time you need to build an application, the more likely that the application will be obsolete when you implement it. Moreover, especially if you are automating a function for the first time, you may not know at the outset what a system can and cannot accomplish, resulting in inaccurate requirement statements.

Prototypes provide immediate feedback for the database designer and enable users to evaluate how the system works. Prototypes are more interesting to evaluate than requirements documents, which are generally as boring as they are long. A working model shows users fine details of the system that are too time-consuming to describe in the requirements document.

The prototyping approach assumes that database designers are fallible and that they can learn from the users of the systems they create. With prototypes, users can provide additional input for making design compromises. Performance can be analyzed with real data to show the productivity changes introduced by a system. Prototyping also limits damage from major flaws in design or conception by bringing them to the fore early in the development cycle.

Early in the design process, give users a prototype of the application for testing and evaluation. You may need to produce two or more prototypes, depending on how closely the prototype fits user requirements. If your first prototype misses the mark, repeat the prototyping process as often as necessary to win user approval.

To make prototyping practical, you need database software that produces results quickly. A procedural language such as COBOL is not suitable for prototyping because making even minor changes in data structure, input screens, or reports requires tedious work. Prototyping usually can be done on a PC or PC-LAN. PC prototyping is faster, less expensive, and more portable than working on a mainframe. You can carry your prototype on a laptop computer for meetings with users. If you will use your system on a mainframe or minicomputer, you may want to choose software that runs on both the PC and the larger computer.

You can use different software for prototyping and production systems. DataEase, Paradox, and Alpha Four, for example, minimize unnecessary coding for fast prototypes and enable you to enter test data.

After the forms, relationships, reports, and menus are complete, present the prototype database to users for testing and evaluation. Users are the best judges of a system's effectiveness. Only users can detect the subtle problems with forms and reports. Small changes in the flow of data-entry fields can make a big difference in how quickly and easily data is entered.

When testing the prototype, encourage users to write down all problems and to make a "wish list" of new features they desire. You may want to use change order forms to keep track of changes that are requested. Figure 3.1 shows a sample change order form.

```
                          Change Order Form


  From:_____

  Company:_____

  Database Name:_____

  Instructions:  Please describe the changes in detail.   Make only one
                 change request per order form.  Be sure to specify field
                 length and type.  For reports show desired format or a copy
                 of sample.  Attach copies of form definitions or procedure
                 definitions if applicable.


  Changes requested for: Form / Report /
  Other_____ (menu, etc.)

  _____
  _____
  _____
  _____
  _____
  _____
  _____
  _____
  _____
  _____
  _____
  _____
  _____
  _____

  Date of Request  _____    Authorized by  _____
```

Fig. 3.1. *A sample change order form.*

A change order may ask for an additional line for addresses in a data-entry form or suggest a new format for a report. Each request should be listed on a separate form so that you can record when each change is completed.

Testing

A database is not fit for production use until you subject it to rigorous tests. Testing procedures vary according to your resources and the importance of the application. At the very least, enter sample data and generate reports to check for design and programming flaws. (Experienced programmers prefer not to call these problems *bugs*, a term that implies the work of a poltergeist rather than a programmer.) See Chapter 11 for a detailed discussion of the testing process.

Preparing Documentation

The final stage in designing an application is preparing documentation. The need for manuals depends greatly on the users of the system, training requirements, and corporate policies. The manuals can range from sparse to lavish. Even if you do not prepare user documentation, system documentation should describe how the application is written so that someone other than the developer can maintain it. See Chapter 12 for more information about writing documentation.

This book discusses each of these stages—requirements analysis (Chapter 2), implementation (Chapters 5 through 10), testing (Chapter 11), and documentation (Chapter 12)—in detail, and contains hints to guide you through the database labyrinth.

Keep It Simple

As a project grows more complex, avoiding unnecessary complications becomes crucial. Even seemingly simple applications can turn out to be complex by the time you finish them. Borderline cases and exceptions are often the culprits. When building a database to track product distribution, I included a table to record each driver's daily trip sheet. The original requirement specified that the driver pay be calculated by multiplying the number of miles by a fixed dollar amount per mile. When another location started using the system, someone complained that the database was not properly calculating payroll. I discovered that the second location paid drivers on an hourly basis rather than by mile. A third location paid drivers by mile and by hour, depending on the origin and destination of the particular trip. Another location paid drivers on a per-mile basis, but the pay per mile varied depending on the length of the trip. The moral of the story: things are not always as simple as they seem.

Make every effort to prevent unneeded complexity as early in the design process as possible. Keep the application focused on achieving the greatest gains in productivity for the users of the database. Remember that simple systems are easier to design, test, and maintain.

Summary

Databases, especially complex databases, demand planning to achieve the best results. How formal your planning should be depends on the size of the project and the requirements of your organization. Even if you are building a database for your personal use, planning makes your work easier.

Use prototyping to test your ideas as the project progresses. Often the prototype database spurs new ideas and reveals shortcomings in your analysis. Prototyping is especially important if you are working with first-time database users.

As much as possible, keep your database simple. If you succeed with a simple database, you will be encouraged to take on new challenges.

3

Organizing Your Data

A place for everything, everything in its place.

Benjamin Franklin

File structure—the way data is stored in fields and tables—is the heart of a database. A sound structure can provide better performance, simpler reports, and easier maintenance, whereas a poor structure can make a database inefficient, inflexible, and costly to modify. This chapter discusses the principles of setting up the logical design of database tables in a multiple-table database. The techniques discussed here translate your conceptual model of the application (created in the analysis phase) into the actual tables that will store the data.

The concepts discussed in this chapter are also important for nonrelational DBMS. So-called flat-file or pseudorelational databases (for example, Q&A, Reflex) require a logical file structure for best performance. Setting up a flat-file system requires the same understanding of which tables to create and which fields to place in each table. Even if your database software does not fully support simultaneous access of multiple files, you need to understand the optimum file structure so that you can make intelligent compromises to suit the constraints of your software.

Using Multiple Tables

Some small applications track only one entity and need only one table, but they are the exception rather than the rule. Most business databases deal with several related entities and can take advantage of multiple database tables.

I once designed a database for a telemarketing company. The company told me that they would need only one table, Prospects, to contain all the information for the database. Two days into the project I had uncovered eighteen tables in my analysis; the final system had more than twenty-five.

Using multiple tables rather than one table gives a more elegant and realistic model of the business reality you are trying to model. Using multiple tables promotes data integrity and simplifies data entry and reporting by minimizing redundant data.

Using tables also can make your database more flexible. Consider a payroll application for recording employee time sheets and calculating payroll. A table contains time sheet records for each employee for each day worked. You can handle the pay calculations in two ways.

One approach is to write an IF clause similar to the following:

```
IF EMPNAME = "Jones" then HOURS * 7.50 , IF EMPNAME = "McDougall"
then HOURS * 10.00 , IF EMPNAME = "Packard" then HOURS * 6.25
```

and so on. This statement checks the employee's last name, determines the hourly wage, and then multiplies it by the hours worked.

> **NOTE:** The preceding example is written in *pseudocode* (a simplification of computer instructions that uses words rather than symbols to describe the actions to be performed by a program). The exact syntax used varies from one DBMS to another.

A second approach is to build a table, Employees, which stores the employee name and hourly wage along with other pertinent information. The formula for calculating the payroll is similar to the following: HOURS * LOOKUP Employees Wage. This solution is much simpler to set up. More importantly, if wages change or new employees are added, you need to enter them only in the Employees table; you need not change the program for calculating payroll. Again, the mechanics of setting up such a formula depend on your database software.

Understanding the Goals of Normalization

Database experts have developed several structured, logical methods for organizing data. One method is called *normalization*, a method for reducing a relational database to its most elegant and streamlined structure for optimum performance and reliability. Two alternative methods for organizing data are discussed at the end of this chapter.

Normalization is nearly as much an art as a science, although computer aids are being developed to take some of the guesswork out of normalization. Normalization requires in-depth knowledge of the data itself—the items you are tracking—and of how the data will be used in the application.

This chapter is perhaps the most important in this book, because the penalty for failing to heed the rules of normalization is severe. An unnormalized database is error-prone and offers poor performance for developing reports and other procedures.

The goal of normalization is to reduce data to its simplest structure with minimum redundancy and maximum data integrity. The goal of the database designer is similar to that of an aircraft builder—to strip away all unnecessary elements to reveal the cleanest structure that will fly. Less is more in database design, and baroque is definitely out of fashion. Figure 4.1 shows an artist's conception of how normalization can improve the organization of your data.

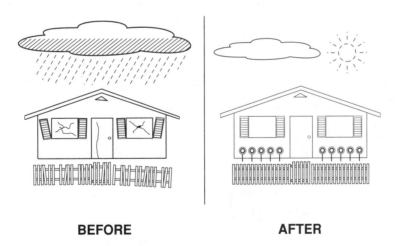

BEFORE   **AFTER**

Fig. 4.1. *Before and after normalization.*

Fortunately, normalization follows common sense. Follow the golden rule of normalization: enter the minimum data necessary, avoiding duplicate entry of information, with minimum risks to data integrity. This rule, like most golden rules, has a number of important corollaries. To be more specific, the goals of normalization are as follows:

- Eliminate redundancy caused by the following:

    Fields repeated within a file

    Fields that do not directly describe the key entity

    Fields that you can derive from other fields

- Avoid anomalies in updating (adding, editing, deleting)

- Represent accurately the items being modeled

- Simplify maintenance and retrieval of information

In addition to eliminating redundant storage, you must make sure that attributes are stored with the entities they describe, not in some other location. Normalization eliminates risks for creating anomalies in the data when records are added, modified, or deleted.

Common Normalization Problems

Failing to normalize lowers the performance and complicates the maintenance of a database. The most common mistake inexperienced developers make is to repeat fields in a file. A personnel file, for example, may contain several fields for the names of the employee's children. If the names of the children are stored in the PERSONNEL file in fields such as CHILD1, CHILD2, and so on, the first rule of normalization is broken. A one-to-many relationship (employees to children) has been obscured by making children attributes to the employee.

Using repeating fields also creates several performance problems. To search for a child by name, for example, you have to search each CHILD field. Similarly, counting the number of children requires checking each field. In a large database, these redundant passes through the file can convert a simple query into a marathon.

The children of an employee are not attributes of the employee, but constitute another entity themselves. You can create a file called CHILDREN to store their names and tie it to the PERSONNEL file by the employee's Social Security number. This example assumes that the company using this system forbids nepotism, and that only one parent is an employee at this company. If both parents work at the same company, two relationships may occur—one for the mother and one for the father.

You cannot detect all violations of the rules of normalization by looking at only one file. When data is unnecessarily stored in multiple files, attributes can be entered for the wrong entity. If, for example, the

CHILDREN file contains the parent's Social Security number and name, one field is redundant. If you know the parent's Social Security number, you can look up the name from the PERSONNEL file. Storing the name in the CHILDREN file wastes space and introduces the possibility of error.

The most subtle normalization goal is to eliminate fields that can be derived from other fields. This rule proscribes entering information that can be determined from the data already entered in the database. In a personnel database, for example, you might want to include the number of years an employee has worked for your company. You should not, however, create a field for this purpose if you already have a field for the hiring date, because you can calculate seniority by subtracting the date hired from the present date. If you store a field for years of seniority, erroneous information can be entered. You also must update the database when the anniversary of each employee's hiring date passes.

Similarly, the SALES TAX field in INVOICES might be superfluous because you can determine the amount of tax based on other fields with known values (total cost, sales tax rate, tax-exempt status of customer). You can display the value of the sales tax on-screen or in a printed report, but you should not enter or store it. Entering data in this field is a waste of time and introduces a risk of inconsistency in the data because of possible errors in data entry. Do not enter data you can determine by other means such as calculations, lookups from other database tables, and a combination of the two.

Another common normalization problem is table duplication—two or more tables that essentially track the same entity. A real estate sales system, for example, may have separate tables for office buildings, retail space, warehouses, and residential properties. All these tables really contain the same entities—properties. Keeping separate files for different types of property makes searches for a particular building more difficult. To find the property at 100 Elm Street, you may have to search all four tables (if you do not know which type of property it is). If a property is rezoned from office to retail, you have to delete the record from the office table and reenter it in the retail table. You can simplify these tasks by combining the four tables into one table and adding a new field to show the property type.

Using these rules, you can create a clean, normalized data structure that simplifies the development and maintenance of the database. You also will earn the undying respect of other database developers who see your handiwork.

The Concept of Uniqueness

To proceed with normalization, you need to know what constitutes a duplicate record. Each record in a table needs to be *unique*; that is, the table should have no two records that are the same. The fields that determine whether two records are duplicates are different depending on the nature of the data. By definition, the value in a *key field* (also called *primary key*) cannot be the same for two different records. A list of hotel rooms, for example, could use the room number as the key field. If two records have the same number, you know they are duplicates. Chapter 5, "Building Tables," discusses ways to determine the key field (or fields).

Another kind of key field is a *foreign key*, a field that is the key field for another table. If you assign sales representatives to customers by initials, the SALESREP INITIALS field in the CUSTOMERS file is a foreign key. It is not the key field for CUSTOMERS, but the key for a "foreign" table, Salesreps.

Defining Normal Forms

Database theoreticians have defined rules for rating the level of normalization in a relation or table. The pioneering relational database theoretician, E. F. Codd, defined three normal forms in the early 1970s. Since then, more advanced levels of normalization have been specified.

You can think of the normal forms as tests your database files must pass to receive the relational "seal of approval." Each normal form addresses a specific threat to the integrity of your database design. The higher the form, the more stringent the test.

Try to achieve at least third normal form, as illustrated in the following sections, for all tables in your designs. You do not need to remember which normal form is which (unless you want to impress a computer science professor), but you should learn to spot potential redundancy and inconsistency problems and wipe them out with extreme prejudice.

> **NOTE:** Some readers may be interested in the official, textbook definitions of normal forms, from C. J. Date, *An Introduction to Database Systems: Volume 1* (Reading, Mass.: Addison-Wesley, 1990) 533-536:

- *First Normal Form.* A relation is in first normal form (1NF) if and only if all underlying simple domains contain atomic values only.

- *Second Normal Form.* A relation is in second normal form (2NF) if and only if it is in 1NF and every nonkey attribute is fully dependent on the primary key.

- *Third Normal Form.* A relation is in third normal form (3NF) if and only if, for all time, each tuple [row in a table] consists of a primary key value that identifies some entity, together with a set of zero or more mutually independent attribute values that describe that entity in some way.

By definition, a relation in third normal form is also in second normal form and first normal form.

For second normal form, a relation must be in first normal form and all the nonkey fields (attributes that do not uniquely identify the record) must describe the entity itself (as represented by the primary key) rather than be dependent on each other. If the nonkey fields are dependent on one another, further breakdown of the file structure is desirable.

In third normal form, no nonkey fields depend on one another; they all depend on the key field. A *tuple* is another term for a row in a table.

More rigorous analysis has identified higher forms of normalization. These forms (Boyce-Codd Normal Form, Fourth Normal Form, and Fifth Normal Form) are not discussed here. Third normal form is sufficient for most business applications.

If this introduction whets your appetite for further knowledge of relational databases, I urge you to read the works of the originators of relational theory. Database normalization is a challenging and rewarding body of logic. For a concise introduction to normalization, see Chapter 21 in C. J. Date, *An Introduction to Database Systems: Volume 1* (Reading, Mass.: Addison-Wesley, 1990) or E. F. Codd, *The Relational Model for Database Management: Version 2* (Reading, Mass.: Addison-Wesley, 1990).

First Normal Form

To achieve first normal form, eliminate duplicate fields within a table. After you eliminate these repeat offenders, the relation is in first normal form and is considered to be *normalized*. Table 4.1 is an unnormalized table.

Table 4.1. Unnormalized Employees Table

ID	Name	Vacation
32	Powell, Bud	07/01/78
		11/24/79
		12/27/80
65	Powers, Jean	12/27/80
		07/03/81
		11/24/81
71	Sharp, Kenneth	03/12/81
		11/24/81

The column for vacations has more than one entry for each row, violating the rule for first normal form. Table 4.2 shows the same unnormalized table with a different layout.

Table 4.2. Unnormalized Employees Table with Split Fields

ID	Name	Vacation1	Vacation2	Vacation3
32	Powell, Bud	07/01/78	11/24/79	12/27/80
65	Powers, Jean	12/27/80	07/03/81	11/24/81
71	Sharp, Kenneth	03/12/81	11/24/81	

Splitting the values into separate rows makes the problem less obvious. The values are still repeating values, however, and do not conform to first normal form. Look for this type of repeating field in tables you design or inherit.

An unnormalized structure is undesirable for several reasons. Anticipating how much space is needed for vacation days is difficult. If you provide three fields for vacations, as in the preceding example, you cannot enter a fourth day. When a record fills all available fields, you need to enter a new field or clear an existing field to allow for a new entry. To store all vacation dates for a long-time employee, you may need hundreds of fields (VACATION1-VACATION400). Moreover, clearing out the fields for a certain date range is difficult because you have no way to determine how many fields have been filled for a particular person without looking at that record.

If you are generous with vacation fields to accommodate the employee with the greatest number of vacations, you waste a great deal of space in the database because the average employee probably needs far fewer fields for vacation days. On the other hand, you cannot be so stingy with vacation fields that you run out of fields for an employee. No sound basis exists for creating multiple vacation date fields in the Employees table.

Even more important than wasting space, duplicate fields make extracting data more difficult. To print a list of all employees absent on November 24, 1981, you need to look in every employee record at each individual vacation date field to find a match. To print a list of all employee vacations in chronological order, each date must be compared to all dates for that employee and for every other employee record.

You can convert the Employees table to first normal form by breaking it into the following two tables, Employees and Vacations.

Employees	
ID	*Name*
32	Powell, Bud
65	Powers, Jean
71	Sharp, Kenneth

Vacations	
ID	*Vacation*
32	07/01/78
65	12/27/80
71	03/12/81
32	11/24/79
65	07/03/81
71	11/24/81
32	12/27/80
65	11/24/81

Notice that the vacation date for each person requires a record in the Vacations table, but the Employees table has only one record per employee. Consequently, you can enter from zero to an infinite number of vacation days for an employee. To add another vacation date, you add a new record to the Vacations table; you need not add new fields to either table.

You need one common field to associate the vacations records with the employee records. In this case, the employee number works because no two employees have the same employee number.

The normalized form makes reporting much easier. Although you now have more records, the vacation date occurs in only one field. You need to examine only one field to sort all records in chronological order.

Second Normal Form

First normal form is not the end of the line. You can eliminate additional levels of redundancy and ambiguity.

To normalize further, eliminate any fields that do not give you information about the entity you are tracking. In other words, move to another table fields that depend on one another but not on the primary key.

Table 4.3 shows an insurance agent's file for policies.

Table 4.3. Insurance Policies Table

Policy #	Type	Customer	Sex	Phone
80738281	Life	Jane Redmond	F	(415) 555-4146
83792201	Health	Jane Redmond	F	(415) 555-4146
53628170	Life	Jean Greenway	F	(215) 784-6603
54228270	Life	Joan Black	F	(301) 332-4643
98732203	Health	Jean Noir	M	(803) 567-4321

This relation is in first normal form because it has no repeating fields. It does not meet the test of second normal form, however, because the sex and phone number of the customer do not depend on the policy number; rather, they pertain to the customer. Table 4.4 shows the structure in second normal form.

One indication that a file is not in second normal form is the repetition of information from one record to another. This repetition is not inherently a sign of poor design (the customer name still repeats in the POLICIES file when a customer has more than one policy), but a hint to look for more opportunities to normalize.

Table 4.4. Insurance Policies in Second Normal Form

POLICIES

Policy #	Type	Customer
80738281	Life	Jane Redmond
83792201	Health	Jane Redmond
53628170	Life	Jean Greenway
54228270	Life	Joan Black
98732203	Health	Jean Noir

CUSTOMERS

Name	Sex	Phone
Jane Redmond	F	(415) 555-4146
Jean Greenway	F	(215) 784-6603
Joan Black	F	(301) 332-4643
Jean Noir	M	(803) 567-4321

Third Normal Form

The next level of normalization is third normal form. This level of normalization eliminates fields that you can derive from existing fields in the database. The goal is to have independent attributes, all of which describe the entity.

With independence, each attribute describes the entity; the attribute does not describe or depend on another attribute. One test for independence is to determine whether changing one attribute forces changes in other attributes.

The following Sales table shows purchases (see table 4.5). The invoice number is the key field.

Table 4.5. Sales Table

Invoice	Customer	Amount	Tax	Total
0987	Acme Drugs	987.60	98.76	1086.36
0988	Acme Dogs	87.60	8.76	96.36
0989	Acme Rugs	98.60	9.86	108.46

The TOTAL field is dependent on the AMOUNT and TAX fields. If you change the amount or the tax, you also need to change the total. To comply with third normal form, remove the TOTAL field. You do not need to enter this field because you can calculate it for a report by adding AMOUNT and TAX. If you can use a formula to calculate the tax, you also could eliminate the TAX field. If, however, users must decide whether to change the tax (and these rules are not part of the database), the TAX field should remain.

Table 4.6 is not in third normal form because REGION depends on STATE, not on PARK NAME (the key field).

Table 4.6. National Parks

Park Name (Key)	State (Nonkey)	Region (Nonkey)
Death Valley	California	Western
Acadia	Maine	Northeastern
Yosemite	California	Western
Yellowstone	Wyoming	Western
Shenandoah	Virginia	Mid-Atlantic

Assuming that each state belongs to only one region, you can determine the region by the state; therefore, you should not have a field for the region in this table. Instead, you can create a separate table for states so that you can tag each state with the region to which it belongs.

Many database designers are content to stop the normalization process at third normal form. For most purposes, you have eliminated the worst sources of database error when you reach this point in the normalization process.

Reaching Normalization

Unfortunately, the world is not laid out in a normalized way. As your analysis probably has revealed, most business forms contain references to several entities, and many contain redundant fields. Your job is like that of a sculptor chipping away excess material to free the underlying shape.

Normalization consists of two main activities: integration and decomposition. *Integration* is the process of combining two or more tables into one table. *Decomposition* is the process of breaking one table into two or more tables without losing the meaning of the fields.

Integration

The data integration process is like organizing your closet; the first step is to group similar items together. In your closet, you may want to store all shirts in one place, all slacks in another place, and jackets in another place. You may create groupings of clothing with similar functions, hanging belts and suspenders together, or consolidating neckwear (ties, bow ties, and mufflers).

In the database, the process is similar but more abstract. Look at all the items you need to track and group them together into tables. You can group items together in many ways, some of which are not obvious. In a banking application, for example, you probably want to group all deposits together because they contain the same fields (account number, date, amount). You may want to store all checking account debits in another table, with fields for account number, date, amount, check number.

You can combine these two tables, however, into one file, TRANSAC-TIONS. This file includes all the fields in either table, using a positive dollar amount for deposits and a negative amount for checks, with the check number left blank for deposits (or the number on the deposit slip entered rather than a check number). Combining these files enables you to determine total debits and credits by running a query in only one table.

A common mistake is to maintain separate tables for items that are fundamentally the same. I have seen cases where several apparently identical tables with only subtle differences existed in the same database. I once saw, for example, an application with separate tables for three different "To do" lists: urgent tasks, important tasks, and routine tasks. The user had to scan through three files to assemble a complete "To do" list. Changing the priority of an item required deleting it from one table and adding it to another. The solution is to combine the three tables, adding a new field to show the priority of the task.

One of the best ways to check for duplicate tables is to compare the key fields. If the key fields are the same, the two tables are candidates for integration. A department store, for example, may keep mailing lists for preferred customers, Christmas Club members, board members, and direct mail advertising. All these files contain information about people. The key field may be the same in all cases—the person's name. You can combine these tables into one table with a new field or fields to show to which group a person belongs.

Another way to find duplicate entries is to check the table names for adjectives describing the entity. A sales tracking database, for example, may have tables called Men's Clothing Mailing List, Appliances Mailing List, Women's Shoes Mailing List, and so on. These duplicate entities beg to be combined.

Why combine these files? Updates are simplified when all customers are in the same file. If a customer moves, you may have to change the address in several tables, increasing the risk of inaccurate data. Combining the files also simplifies searches. If the store receives a change of address card that does not indicate which list to update, you may have to search and update each table.

I came across a fund-raising database with separate tables for each type of donor based on the fund-raising campaign to which the donor first responded and on the size of the donation. The database had tables for the wealthiest donors, donors who attended ground-breaking ceremonies, charter donors, real estate donors, and other categories. Unfortunately, when donors sent in a change of address, they did not include the name of the table where they could be found. To update the record, all the database tables had to be searched.

Combine two tables when the contents are identical in structure but the name of the table conveys an additional attribute. A common mistake is to create separate tables for January invoices, February invoices, and so on. With such a fragmented structure, summary reports for periods longer than a month become quite difficult to write. To correct this normalization error, add a field to the table showing the date and then merge all the tables.

Exceptions to this rule do exist. The department store probably keeps a file on another group of people—its employees. This table should not be integrated with the mailing list table because it contains much more detailed information (salary, hire date, title, and so on) that does not apply to customers. The best key field for the personnel table is the employee's Social Security number—information that probably is not available for all the store's customers.

Another exception may be based on performance. Some companies keep huge lists of sales prospects to use for advertising and telemarketing. The prospect list can be many times larger than the client list. To speed processing of client records, the design may be compromised to keep clients separate from prospects. Although the system might need this type of structural change to achieve acceptable performance, you might want to wait until later in the design process to find out exactly how the system performs with each configuration before you choose one. More importantly, be sure to remember the implications of the compromise for searching and updating: searching, updating, and deleting at times will involve searching in two files rather than one, considerably complicating data security.

After you have properly integrated the entities, you are ready to continue the normalization process.

Decomposition

Although the word *decomposition* conjures up images of rotting leaves (or worse), decomposition is not an unpleasant process in the context of database design. By following the well-trodden path of normalization, you can break down a file structure to its most basic elements. Figure 4.2 shows an unnormalized file structure.

```
┌─Classes──────────────────────────────────────────────────┐
│                                                           │
│  Name: _____,_____ __  SSN:___-__-____ │
│              Last            First    MI                  │
│                                                           │
│  Graduation Year: __   Sex:_____  Birthdate: __/__/__    │
│                                                           │
│  Classes                                                  │
│          Year  Semester   Course Number   Hours   Grade   │
│   Class1:__   _____   _____   __    ___       │
│   Class2:__   _____   _____   __    ___       │
│   Class3:__   _____   _____   __    ___       │
│   Class4:__   _____   _____   __    ___       │
│   Class5:__   _____   _____   __    ___       │
│   Class6:__   _____   _____   __    ___       │
│   Class7:__   _____   _____   __    ___       │
│   Class8:__   _____   _____   __    ___       │
│   Class9:__   _____   _____   __    ___       │
│   Class10:__  _____   _____   __    ___       │
│   ....etc....                                             │
└───────────────────────────────────────────────────────────┘
```

Fig. 4.2. *An unnormalized form for recording classes.*

To ensure that students do not run out of course fields before completing their studies, the table shown in figure 4.2 contains multiple fields for each class a student takes, to accommodate the maximum possible number of classes any student may take. This table violates the first rule of normalization (no repeating fields).

Table 4.7 shows another example of an unnormalized file structure.

Table 4.7. An Unnormalized File Structure

Student SSN	Name	Course/ Section	Semester/ Year	Room	Instructor
112-45-6789	Grey, Zane	0100/01	Spring90	1125	Williams, Ted
222-33-4455	Flintstone, Wilma	0100/01	Spring90	1125	Williams, Ted
333-45-6789	Banshee, Sousie	0100/01	Spring90	1125	Williams, Ted
444-33-4455	Jung, Victor	0100/01	Spring90	1125	Williams, Ted
555-45-6789	Young, Lester	0100/01	Spring90	1125	Williams, Ted
666-33-4455	Perry, Noelle	0100/01	Spring90	1125	Williams, Ted
777-45-6789	Baker, Christine	0100/01	Spring90	1125	Williams, Ted
888-33-4455	Edison, Tina	0100/01	Spring90	1125	Williams, Ted
222-33-4455	Flintstone, Wilma	0200/03	Spring90	5130	Mead, Margaret
333-45-6789	Banshee, Sousie	0200/03	Spring90	5130	Mead, Margaret
555-45-6789	Young, Lester	0200/03	Spring90	5130	Mead, Margaret
666-33-4455	Perry, Noelle	0200/03	Spring90	5130	Mead, Margaret

This table represents the relationship between two other files—STUDENTS and COURSE OFFERINGS—showing all the classes for which each student has registered. Although this table does not have repeating fields, it has many repeating values. Some students have signed up for more than one class, and each instructor has more than one student. This table violates the third normalization rule; several fields do not belong in this file because you can derive them from the main file.

Because this table includes the Social Security number of the student, a unique entity, you can derive the student's name by looking it up from STUDENTS. Similarly, although course, section, semester, and year are necessary to indicate precisely the class in which the student is registered, you do not need to enter the room and instructor's name; you can derive this information from Course Offerings.

The unnormalized approach results in several performance penalties. First, to find all the students who have taken a given class, you have to perform a search on each field because you have no way to determine in advance which of the sixteen fields was used. The query is complicated and takes longer to execute. For more complicated queries, the penalty is even greater. To determine which students have taken both English 101 and Introduction to Databases, for example, you have to formulate a query that accounts for every possible combination of those values in each of the class fields—a programmer's nightmare.

Second, each record is larger than necessary because it must contain the maximum number of classes any student can attend, whether these fields are used or not. Most students will not use all the fields. In particular, transfer students and dropouts use few of the possible fields. Consequently, the file wastes disk space and slows down every search on that file. You have to keep indexes for each class code field so that you can search them efficiently, wasting additional disk space.

Third, as the needs for the application change, requiring a change in the number of class fields for each student, these changes affect all reports and procedures for the file, requiring a great deal of reprogramming and debugging.

Fourth, speeding searches by indexing every field of an unnormalized table is not practical. Separate indexes require extra time to maintain, and they cannot boost performance as much as one index for one field.

In general, the benefits of normalization outweigh any disadvantages. Good file structure is an essential part of a well organized database.

Unfortunately, no database development tool can ensure that you normalize your data structure properly. A badly organized structure does not result in error messages. The screen does not flash, nor does the bell sound when you break even the holiest of relational design rules. (Perhaps this oversight will be corrected in future software releases.) The structure works, in some manner at least, but it can never perform as well as a normalized structure.

To normalize the student enrollment table, divide the fields into two separate files, one file to store a record for each student, the other file to store a record for each class in which each student enrolls. Figure 4.3 illustrates the resulting normalized structure.

The STUDENTS file contains all the attributes that relate to the student: date of birth, year of graduation, sex, and so on. The CLASS ENROLLMENT file contains all the attributes for each enrollment of a student in a class. The two files are related by the student's Social Security number, which is a field unique for each student.

The relationship between STUDENTS and CLASS ENROLLMENT is a one-to-many relationship. Each record in CLASS ENROLLMENT can have only one matching record in STUDENTS, but STUDENTS may have an infinite number of matching records in CLASS ENROLLMENT.

The normalized structure is simpler and more efficient than the unnormalized structure. To search for all students who have taken a given class, you search only one field—the course number. The data is saved more compactly because no empty fields are stored; a record is written only when a student enrolls in a class.

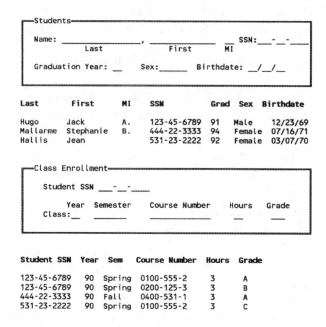

Last	First	MI	SSN	Grad	Sex	Birthdate
Hugo	Jack	A.	123-45-6789	91	Male	12/23/69
Mallarme	Stephanie	B.	444-22-3333	94	Female	07/16/71
Hallis	Jean		531-23-2222	92	Female	03/07/70

Student SSN	Year	Sem	Course Number	Hours	Grade
123-45-6789	90	Spring	0100-555-2	3	A
123-45-6789	90	Spring	0200-125-3	3	B
444-22-3333	90	Fall	0400-531-1	3	A
531-23-2222	90	Spring	0100-555-2	3	C

Fig. 4.3. *A normalized student enrollment file.*

Figure 4.4 shows another example of duplicate fields in a system for tracking donors' attendance of fund-raising events.

Last	First	SSN	Event1	Location1	Event2	Location2
Smith	Joan	123-45-6789	12/31/89	Marriott	10/31/90	Holiday Inn
Somers	Jamie	987-65-4321	12/31/89	Marriott	02/14/90	Dream Inn
Jones	Jean	777-66-5555	12/31/88	Hilton	10/07/90	Old Point Inn
Goh	Kim	887-22-8765	01/01/91	Radisson	--------	------------

Fig. 4.4. *Fundraiser Tracking with duplicate fields.*

The fund-raiser tracking system stores the name of each attendee (donor) along with four events attended. This structure can benefit from normalization by creating a new file for events. The fields pertaining to the donor remain in the main donor file; a second file captures the information for each fund-raiser attended (see fig. 4.5).

```
┌─Fundraising──────────────────────────────────────────────┐
│  Name: _____ , _____   SSN: ___-__-____     │
│             Last              First                      │
└──────────────────────────────────────────────────────────┘

┌─Event Attendance─────────────────────────────────────────┐
│                                                          │
│  SSN: ___-__-____                                        │
│                                                          │
│  Event Attended:                                         │
│          Date              Location                      │
│          _____           _____                  │
└──────────────────────────────────────────────────────────┘
```

Fig. 4.5. *Fundraiser Tracking, normalized.*

The new and improved fund-raiser tracking system enables you to enter an infinite number of fund-raisers for each donor. To find all the people who attended a particular fund-raiser, you search only the EVENT ATTENDANCE file.

The disadvantage of normalization is that the data is no longer stored in one file. You cannot view all fund-raiser information by looking at a single record, and queries must take account of this structure. Many DBMS (such as DataEase and Paradox), however, minimize this effect by enabling several tables to appear (to the user) as one. By using views and subforms, you still can enter the data from one screen (see Chapter 7). Fear of multiple tables is no reason to avoid normalizing.

Avoiding Overnormalization

In most applications, normalization is less than complete. Despite its benefits, you should not carry normalization to an extreme.

In an address file, for example, a dependency exists between the ZIP code and the combination of city and state. If you know the ZIP code, you can determine the city and state. You therefore could argue that the database design can be made more efficient by eliminating the city and state fields from the file and adding a reference table to store ZIP codes along with their corresponding city and state. A *reference*, or *lookup*, *table* contains a list of possible values for a field. A reference table for states, for instance, would contain all valid state abbreviations. To print labels, the data entry operator enters just the ZIP code, and the database refers to the lookup table for the city and state. Unfortunately, this method cannot work in all cases. For addresses without a ZIP code (foreign addresses, for example), recording the city and state is impossible. Consequently, most designers compromise, leaving all three fields in the table.

Breaking attributes of an entity into different files can go too far. In its extreme form, overnormalization may result in a structure with one attribute per file (see fig. 4.6).

```
┌──Students' Last Names────────────────────────────────┐
│                                                       │
│   Last Name: _____     SSN:___-__-____    │
│                                                       │
└───────────────────────────────────────────────────────┘

┌──Students' First Names───────────────────────────────┐
│                                                       │
│   First Name: _____    SSN:___-__-____    │
│                                                       │
└───────────────────────────────────────────────────────┘

┌──Students' Birthdates────────────────────────────────┐
│                                                       │
│   SSN:___-__-____      Birthdate: __/__/__            │
│                                                       │
└───────────────────────────────────────────────────────┘
```

Fig. 4.6. Overnormalized files.

The table structure shown in figure 4.6 breaks the rules of normalization because all the attributes that describe an entity should be together in one table. This structure is difficult to use for data entry, viewing, or reporting. One of the warning signs of overnormalization is the proliferation of forms with one-to-one relationships.

Examine one-to-one relationships carefully. If one record always exists on each side of the relationship, you should consolidate the tables.

Consider a less obvious example. The file shown in figure 4.7 appears to have a structure similar to the fund-raiser example in figure 4.4.

```
┌──Enrollment Tracking─────────────────────────────────┐
│  Name: _____,_____  SSN:___-__-____     │
│             Last          First                       │
│                                                       │
│            Date        Phone/Mail      Handled by     │
│  Applied:_____    _____   _____   │
│  Accepted:_____   _____   _____   │
│  Notified:_____   _____   _____   │
│  Enrolled:_____   _____   _____   │
└───────────────────────────────────────────────────────┘
```

Fig. 4.7. Enrollment Tracking.

Like the donor tracking system, you can divide this file into two, with the second file storing the key dates in the enrollment process along with the event (application, acceptance, notification, or enrollment), the means (phone or mail), and the name of the person who handled the transaction.

This structure is different from the Donor table, however. In the Donor table, the values of the repeated fields are interchangeable because you can list a fund-raiser in any of the four fields. In the Enrollment Tracking table, the fields are not duplicates because they each refer to a different action. These fields, therefore, should not be broken off into another file even though they seem quite similar.

In sum, let moderation be your guide to normalization. After wrestling with many applications, you will develop your own instincts for how much to normalize.

Using Alternatives to Normalization

Other database design methodologies lead to the same results as normalization. They require the same knowledge of the data itself but build the structure in different ways. The following sections briefly discuss two such methodologies: entity-relationship modeling and the Date-Wilson technique.

Entity-Relationship Modeling

Entity-relationship modeling (E-R modeling) starts with a list of entities and their relationships, such as the list of entities you created in Chapter 2, and builds them up to tables by adding nonkey attributes (fields). E-R modeling uses diagrams to depict the entities, attributes, and relationships. Several standard sets of symbols depict the various database elements: entities are shown as squares, relationships as diamonds, and attributes as circles. More sophisticated notation can be added to show subtler characteristics, such as conditional or required relationships.

The E-R approach assumes that the analyst can separate the entities from the attributes accurately. If the E-R diagram is well executed, creating the database tables is straightforward. If problems arise during the design process, E-R modeling can be used in combination with normalization techniques.

The Date-Wilson Technique

A second alternative to the normalization approach was developed by Chris Date and Max Wilson, pioneering database researchers at IBM. The Date-Wilson technique is a hybrid of E-R and normalization. It assumes that the designer understands entity types, foreign keys, and so on. The Date-Wilson technique is as follows:

1. Start with a list of entities.

2. Add attributes to appropriate entities.

3. Add foreign keys for one-to-many relationships.

4. Add weak entities for many-to-many relationships.

Using Normalization Exercises

The best way to learn normalization is to apply it to practical cases. Suppose that a major movie studio has retained your firm to catalog its holdings. The resulting database will be made available to video distribution companies and film scholars.

The first task is to identify the major entities that you will track. The most obvious entities are the movies and the key personnel involved in producing the movie (actors, directors, producers, and so on). Table 4.8 shows a preliminary list of entities.

Table 4.8. Preliminary Entity List for a Movie Catalog

Entities	Key	Attributes
Movies		
		Title
		Year
		Format
		Language
		Video Available
Directors		
	Name	
		DOB
		Death
		Nationality

Entities	Key	Attributes
Producers		
	Name	
		DOB
		Death
		Nationality
Actors		
	Name	
		DOB
		Death
		Nationality
Writers		
Award? Movie		
	Award	
		Year
Film Formats		
	Format	

4

You next need to formulate questions to get a better list of entities and attributes. Be sure to raise the following issues in your interview with the movie studio representative:

- People with one person performing multiple jobs (such as acting and directing)

- Movies with the same titles (remakes)

- People with the same name

Identify the entities and attributes and draw a schema showing how the entities are related. Proceed with the normalization process as described in this chapter.

The files for actors, producers, writers, and directors all contain the same fields, creating possible redundancy in the database. Barbra Streisand and Woody Allen, for example, may appear in all four files, making up-dating more difficult, because a correction would require searching all four files.

To eliminate this redundancy, you can combine actors, producers, writers, and directors into one file called CAST & CREW. Each person has one entry regardless of the role in the movie.

To show the role a person fills in a particular film, a new entity must be created, ROLE ASSIGNMENT. This file connects all the cast and crew to the movies on which they have worked, identifying their specific job.

You can find normalization exercises all around you. You may want to start with a genealogy application to track your family tree, a database of baseball statistics, or a system to chart the growth of your garden. One of the greatest rewards of database theory is that it changes much more slowly than the mercurial computer industry. Like the logic and semantic theory on which it is based, relational design philosophy is of enduring usefulness, with a beauty all its own.

Summary

Nothing is more important to the success of your database than a sound file structure. Normalization is a process by which you reduce data tables to their simplest structure to minimize redundant data entry and maximize data integrity. Normalization is based on common sense rules about data.

This chapter has outlined the rules of normalization, along with samples of unnormalized and normalized data structures. By applying these techniques, you can make your database easier to build, maintain, and operate. The benefits of normalization are as follows:

- Better performance

- Easier queries

- Easier maintenance

If you fail to normalize, you may run into dead ends during database design, and entering and retrieving data might not be as easy as you would like. These structural problems become progressively more difficult to fix later, after data has been entered.

To find out whether your structure is normalized, check it against the following warning signs. Then follow the step-by-step normalization procedures outlined in this chapter. Only when normalization is complete should you proceed with building forms, reports, and menus. The warning signs of poor normalization are as follows:

- Duplicate fields in a file
- Duplicate field values in related files
- Proliferation of one-to-one relationships
- Fields that can be calculated from other fields
- Blank fields in many records

4

Building Tables

*In anything at all, perfection is finally attained not when there is no longer
anything to add, but when there is no longer anything to take away, when a
body has been stripped down to its nakedness.*

Antoine de Saint-Exupery

Tables are the building blocks of a database. They describe the entities that the
database tracks and are the source for reports and other database output. A *table*
consists of rows for each record and columns for each field. Tables also have
some special properties, discussed later in this chapter.

Although some simple databases contain only one table, most databases contain
several. Some database software packages (notably dBASE and compatible programs) refer to tables as "databases." In this book, a *database* consists of one or
more tables, grouped together to make up an application. Table 5.1 is a sample
table from a publication sales database.

Table 5.1. Publication Inventory

Stock Number	Title	Publication Date	Pages	Qty On Hand
12344	The Sixties Generation	12/01/76	268	500
456221	A Better Mousetrap	05/20/87	308	12
33309	Blue and Green	09/01/91	168	76
834121	Glass Houses	03/30/66	176	19

You build database tables after designing the database schema. Analysis and the
normalization process help you determine which entities (things) to track; by
building tables, you organize and structure the specific data you need to store for

each entity. Begin by consulting the entity and attribute listing you created during analysis (as described in Chapter 4), noting the field type, method of entry, and field length. The more planning you have done, the easier the tables will be to create.

In most database software or spreadsheets, you create the table structure in one step and design data-entry forms (the subject of Chapter 6) in another. Visually oriented packages, such as DataEase, perform both functions in one step. As you build a data-entry form, the software automatically builds the table structure behind the scenes. The trend toward integrated table and form design will continue with graphically oriented Windows and OS/2 DBMS. Graphical user interfaces encourage users to translate common office objects into computer applications with a minimum of programming. The most common office object that represents a database is a paper form, such as an invoice or personnel application. With Windows applications, you can come close to duplicating the form on-screen and as printed output. The trend is away from traditional procedural programming (with languages such as BASIC, COBOL or dBASE) toward visual programming techniques that enable the user to manipulate database objects directly on-screen. If you can use your software to build tables and forms at the same time, you may want to read this chapter and the next before starting up the PC.

Field Characteristics

Fields are the primary building blocks of database tables. Fields are the smallest meaningful units of information, the atoms of the database universe. Tables consist of one or more fields.

By definition, a field cannot contain more than one value. In practical terms, this means that the database should accept only one entry in one field. A field for interests, for example, should not contain the entry *sailing,golf,tennis*; enter each interest in a separate field (or as a separate record). Fields with more than one value make searches difficult. The database cannot identify the entries *sailing,golf,tennis* and *golf,sailing,tennis* as equal, although they are synonymous.

> **TIP:** If you are creating your database in a spreadsheet program such as 1-2-3 or Quattro, be sure to use the same data type for the entire data column. Don't mix text labels in the middle of a column of numeric values, for example.

To create a table, you must answer a number of questions about each field you define, such as the field type, name, and length. The following section discusses field characteristics.

Field Types

The most common database field types are *text* (alphabetic, numeric, and punctuation characters accepted), *numbers* (for example, integer, fixed point, floating point), *numeric strings* (only numeric characters, such as phone numbers), *date*, and *time*. Some software packages support other specialized field types.

A *text field* (called *alphanumeric* in some packages) is the most general field type and can contain all types of characters, including letters, numbers, and spaces. EMPLOYEE NAME and STREET ADDRESS are examples of text fields.

> **NOTE:** Throughout this book, field names are capitalized to set them apart from text. This does not mean that you have to capitalize field names in databases you create. Acceptable field names vary depending on the DBMS. Some packages force the field names to all capital letters, while others accept upper- or lowercase names. Some accept spaces and other punctuation marks in field names; others do not. This book uses longer, more descriptive field names to make explanations more readable. Depending on the database you choose, you may be able to use more or fewer characters for field names.

Use a *number field* when the data is a quantity or value to be used for calculations. Three commonly supported types of number fields are integer fields, fixed point fields, and floating point fields. Use an *integer* field for whole numbers, positive or negative. In a *fixed point* field, you define the number of digits to the left and right of the decimal point. In a *floating point* field, the number of digits on each side of the decimal point can vary within a maximum number of characters for the field. Table 5.2 shows the three types of number fields.

> **NOTE:** Most database software does not calculate fractions (such as 1/4, 13/16) properly in a text field, so you need to convert fractions into their decimal equivalents. You can set up the conversion in the database by creating separate integer fields for the numerator and denominator of the fraction and convert them to decimals later in reports or other procedures.

Table 5.2. Database Number Field Types

Type	Example	Use
Integer	175, 20	Quantities, counts
Fixed point	1.75, 20.00	Dollar or other currency, grade point average
Floating point	1.75, 20.0016	Where precision is required

Not all numbers represent quantities or are used for calculation. Use numeric string fields to store identification numbers, such as Social Security numbers, phone numbers, or serial numbers. Numeric string fields accept only numbers, but you can build other characters into the format. Unlike number fields, numeric strings insert zeros into unfilled digit spaces. A value of 1624 is stored as 001624 in a six-digit numeric string field, as 1624 in a text field, and as 1,624 in a number (integer) field.

Some DBMS provide format options for Social Security numbers or phone numbers, so that you can create your own formats. dBASE IV and Paradox have no numeric string field type; you must use the alphanumeric (text) field type. The data-entry form can be programmed to limit entry to numerals only.

Date fields are formatted with slashes to accommodate dates. Some database packages support several date formats, including MM/DD/YY (month, day, year), DD/MM/YY (standard international format), DD-MON-YYYY (with month written as 3 alphabetic characters), and YY-MM-DD (metric format). Q&A, for instance, uses 20 different date formats.

Use date fields to validate entries against a calendar and to perform calculations on dates. Date fields do not accept entries for dates that don't exist, such as June 31 or February 29, 1990. In calculations, you can use date fields to calculate the turnaround time for an order (in days) by subtracting the date of shipment from the order date. You also can use date fields to convert dates to text (9/01/67 becomes September 1, 1967) or to the day of the week (Saturday).

Time fields separate hours, minutes, and seconds by colons, and work in 24-hour clock time. You can use time fields to perform calculations to show elapsed time. A lawyer, for example, can use time fields to log hours for billing clients by deducting ending time from starting time.

If a DBMS does not support a particular field type, you may be able to work around that restriction in the programming. dBASE IV, for instance, does not have a time field type. You can enter the time as a number, however, which dBASE then converts to the number of seconds and uses for calculations, as shown in the following listing.

```
@ 7, 10 SAY "Enter starting time: " GET mbeg_time PICTURE
"##:##:##"
@ 9, 10 SAY "Enter ending time:  " GET mend_time PICTURE "##:##:##"
READ
mbeg_secs = (VAL(LEFT(mbeg_time,2))*3600) + ;
  (VAL(SUBSTR(mbeg_time,4,2))*60) + (VAL(RIGHT(mbeg_time,2)))
mend_secs = (VAL(LEFT(mend_time,2))*3600) + ;
  (VAL(SUBSTR(mend_time,4,2))*60) + (VAL(RIGHT(mend_time,2)))
mdiff = mend_secs - mbeg_secs
STORE 0 TO mhours, mminutes, mseconds

IF mdiff > 0
    mhours = INT(mdiff/3600)
    mdiff = mdiff - mhours*3600
    mminutes = INT(mdiff/60)
    mdiff = mdiff - mminutes*60
    mseconds = MOD(mdiff,60)
ENDIF
mhours = RIGHT(STR(mhours+100,3),2)
mminutes = RIGHT(STR(mminutes+100,3),2)
mseconds = RIGHT(STR(mseconds+100,3),2)
@ 12, 10 SAY "The time difference is " + mhours + ":" + mminutes + ":" ; + mseconds
```

You can record times in dBASE as integer values for hours, minutes, and seconds. To perform calculations on time values, record the values as seconds and then convert the result back to standard time format. To perform the calculations correctly, be sure to use the 24-hour clock (military time). To perform calculations on time values that extend from one day to another, you need a more complicated formula than the preceding.

Time calculations can be tricky. Suppose that you are calculating hours for people working the late shift. If employees start work at 8:00 PM and end work at 4:00 AM, the calculation (in 24-hour clock time) subtracts 20:00 from 4:00, equalling –16 hours. Losing credit for 16 hours by working eight does not make employees happy. You have to find a way to fix the problem.

The following example comes from a time sheet system in DataEase. This system provides a way to work with employee hours that may start before midnight and end after midnight.

```
if ( end time > 0 and end time not < start time ,
( end time - start time ) / 3600 ,
    if ( end time > 0 and end time < start time ,
(( 1440 - (start time/60))+end time/60)/60,
blank )
```

The preceding derivation formula has three parts; the use of each part is conditional, depending on the values in the START TIME and END TIME fields. The IF statements tell the program which calculation to perform for each condition. To calculate elapsed time, the user must enter a starting time and an ending time.

The first condition is that an ending time has been entered and that it is a higher number than the starting time (a normal condition for a time sheet). If this condition is met, the starting time is subtracted from the ending time (end time - start time). The result of this calculation is expressed in seconds. The result is divided by 3,600 (the number of seconds in an hour) to convert it to hours, because worker pay is calculated by the hour rather than by the second.

The second condition is that an ending time has been entered and that it is a lower value than the starting time, which happens if an employee starts work late in the evening and finishes after midnight. To correct the calculation, the system adds 24 hours to the ending time (expressed as 1,440 minutes), subtracts the starting time, and converts the final result to hours.

If no ending time is entered, the third condition applies and the field remains blank. If the derivation does not include this condition, errors result when a starting time is entered with no corresponding ending time.

Some databases support additional field types such as memo fields, logical fields, choice fields, variable length text, or graphic images. Each of these exotic field types fills a special application requirement. Many of these field types are derived from the basic field types listed at the beginning of this section.

Use a *memo field* to store lengthy text remarks with a database record without adding a series of long text fields to the table. Due to their special properties, memo fields handle data entry differently than do plain text fields and can include features such as word wrap or a spelling checker. The memo field itself does not store the text, but points to another file (independent of the table data), which holds the contents of the memo. dBASE IV supports memo fields; it automatically tracks which memo files go with which database tables.

A *logical field* stores a yes/no or true/false value and limits the user to these two choices. Logical fields are suitable for storing survey results or checklists.

Use *choice fields* to define a list of possible values. Choice fields are stored as one-byte fields pointing to the list of choices. Choice fields help reduce operator error and save storage space, but use them only where the choice of values truly is finite. (In some database software, choice fields go by other names. Alpha Four, for instance, calls choice fields *lookup tables*.)

A choice field for titles that include only Mr., Mrs., Miss, and Dr. will be unusable if you need to list people with the titles Ms, Honorable, Princess, Reverend, or Rabbi. Before you create a choice field, be sure that the choices are finite and stable. Even then you may want to add an extra option for Other, so that you can enter unusual records without reprogramming.

Variable length text fields expand or contract to fit the size of the information entered. Variable length text fields are handy for dealing with full text or extensive excerpts from documents.

Currency or *dollar fields* contain monetary values and are formatted to store currency amounts. The currency field type is not available in all DBMS, but is equivalent to a fixed point number field. You simply choose the proper number of decimal places (usually two to the right of the decimal point) for the type of currency you will enter.

Most DBMS now integrate *graphics fields*, which store graphic images. Like memo fields, graphics fields may point to files outside the DBMS. Sometimes the graphics field contains the name of the graphics file, although the program may not display this name to the user. You can view the graphics files during record entry. Graphics fields are useful for a wide range of applications, from parts inventory to personnel.

Unfortunately, graphics files are quite large, consuming as much as a megabyte or more for a detailed drawing. Graphics files quickly use up disk space and can create a need for high-capacity storage systems such as optical disks (similar to audio compact disks). Databases do not yet support direct search of graphic files contents, so you must cross-index files with text entries. For this reason, on-line document storage is a costly process.

When choosing field types, remember that each type is sorted differently, even when fields store the same value. A sorted text field, for example, lists 1642 before 2, because text fields are alphabetized from left to right and 1 comes before 2. Number fields, however, are sorted in ascending order by number, with negative numbers appearing before positive numbers. Date and time fields are sorted in chronological order.

Choosing Field Types

Choosing the right field type for the job is not always easy. Some field types contain several options, each with their own advantages and disadvantages. The following example shows how to determine field types for a typical database table.

In this example, your goal is to automate a medical office. The first step is to capture information on all new patients. During their first visit, each new patient completes the following patient intake form:

Office of Joseph Giovinco, M.D. F.A.C.S. P.A.
Tampa, FL

Name
Date of Birth
Sex
Address

Phone   Home   Work
Occupation
Employer Name
Employer Address

Social Security Number
Primary Insurance Company
Policy Holder's Name
Policy Number
Supplemental Insurance Company
Policy Number
Reason for Visit

A user enters the information from the patient intake form into the computer, where the information becomes part of the patient's permanent record for use in billing and insurance claims. Many businesses that keep

close tabs on their clients use similar information. My favorite haber-
dasher keeps file cards with each customer's name, clothing sizes, and
style preferences.

Now, back to the doctor's office. The first field in the patient intake form,
for the patient's name, must be a text field so that you can enter letters.
You can split up name fields in many ways. You can create one field, for
example, long enough to hold the longest possible patient name—perhaps 35 characters. You can enter names in a single field as follows:

> NAME
> Ms Jane Quinn-Pierpoint
> Ben Geronimo, Jr.
> Ms Bess Truman
> Smith, Mr. George D.
> J.R.R. Tolkien

You can enter names in single fields in almost any format, with or without titles, with first or last name appearing first. This setup may work
well enough for printing address labels (although last name first is a bit
awkward on an envelope), but it presents problems when you try to sort
patient records alphabetically. The preceding list of patients sorts as
follows:

> NAME
> Ben Geronimo, Jr.
> J.R.R. Tolkien
> Ms Bess Truman
> Ms Jane Quinn-Pierpoint
> Smith, Mr. George D.

The names are in alphabetical order, but this is not the sorting you had
in mind. You should have sorted on the last name rather than the title or
first name. A sort on last name is difficult, however, because all parts of
the name have been entered in one field.

Alphabetical sorting is easier if you break NAME into two fields: LNAME
for last name and FNAME for first name. If you use this system to enter
the names, your have the following list:

FNAME	LNAME
Ms Jane	Quinn-Pierpoint
Ben	Geronimo, Jr.
Ms Bess	Truman
Mr. George D.	Smith
J.R.R.	Tolkien

Now the records are easier to sort alphabetically. Dividing the name into separate fields also has other benefits. You can isolate the first or last name to search or print in reports.

You can break down names into more fields, for title, name suffixes (such as Jr. or Esquire), or middle initial—entities that are not part of the first or last name. The separate fields make a form letter with a personalized salutation easy to print. Figure 5.1 shows a sample letter that uses field names rather than data from the table.

```
TODAY'S DATE


TITLE FNAME MI LNAME SUFFIX
ADDRESS
ADDRESS2
CITY, STATE ZIP

Dear TITLE LNAME:

You've been chosen for a very special introductory offer, available for a limited
time only. For only $19.95 a month, you can subscribe to the new video series,
"Learning to Play the Pan Flute for Fun and Profit."

Not available in stores, the series offers in-depth musical training from the world's
leading Pan flautists. Act now to reserve your copy.

Sincerely,
```

Fig. 5.1. *A sample form letter.*

Another way to handle names for form letters is to create a SALUTATION field to contain the name as it should appear in the salutation of a letter (Mr. Jones or Billy Bob). The SALUTATION field may default to title (Mr., for example) combined with the last name. Users can override this default to personalize letters to people they want to address on a first-name basis.

Next, you need to create the address fields. You usually should include more than one line for the address to accommodate suite numbers and post office boxes. If you intend to print mailing labels, each address line should be no wider than a standard mailing label (usually 40 characters).

Some specialized applications separate the address into two fields, one for street numbers and one for street names. With this arrangement, the system can look up map grid coordinates from another database table that stores all the street names for a city or town. Although this application is great for pizza delivery services, you usually don't need to slice the address (pardon the pizza pun) that finely.

The third line in the address block should have separate fields for city, state, and ZIP code to facilitate searching and sorting. Sorting by ZIP code is especially important for mass-mailings because the postal service has lower rates for presorted mail. To use extended ZIP codes (ZIP +four), you can lengthen the ZIP code field or create a second field to store the extra four digits. I recommend creating a second field, so that the user does not have to fill in unknown extended ZIP codes with zeros to complete a nine-digit field. Using separate fields also helps prevent records without ZIP codes from printing on mailing labels and other reports. If you work with foreign addresses, you can add another mailing code field to accommodate letters and numbers.

The capability to check ZIP codes by state is a handy addition to any application that uses names and addresses. ZIP code checking requires a table containing the state abbreviations and the minimum and maximum ZIP codes for that state. When you relate this table to the address table, you can set the ZIP code field to reject entries that fall outside the specified range. You also can add a table of all United States ZIP codes and their corresponding cities and states. This system automatically fills in the city and state when the user enters a ZIP code. The United States ZIP code file is quite large, however, and needs frequent updating.

The phone number field is relatively simple. Remember that you are interested only in the numbers themselves, not in punctuation marks such as parentheses or hyphens. If your database has a numeric string field type, use it. Remember that a numeric string is like a text field in which you can enter only numerals. For dBASE-compatible software, make the field a text field and create a template in the form to show punctuation and prevent entry of alphabetical characters. Chapter 6, on building forms, describes the use of the edit mask. Do not use a number field for phone numbers, Social Security numbers, and other strings of numbers not used in calculations. Foreign phone numbers need space for extra digits. You can create separate fields for domestic and foreign numbers so that they will be formatted properly.

The sex field has only two valid choices—male and female. If your database supports choice fields, you can set up choices for these two values. Otherwise, use the abbreviations M and F and limit field entry to those characters. Do not create a six-character text field in which users can enter whatever they want. If you do not restrict entry, you may end up with invalid responses such as *man*, *woman*, *other*, or *often*. In addition to protecting data integrity, a choice field or single-character field conserves record space by using only one byte of storage per record.

5

The Social Security number is a string of digits separated by hyphens. As with the phone number, you should store in the database only the numbers themselves and not the punctuation.

The spouse and employer information fields use the same field types and lengths as the patient name and address fields. You can copy the field lengths to make them consistent for all address fields within the database. Using consistent lengths saves you time when you write reports: you know how much space an address requires and need not flip from one table to another to make sure that you choose the correct field length.

> **TIP:** When you work with numeric fields, be generous with field lengths for dollar amounts, quantities, and related numbers. When you design a system, providing for six-digit invoice totals costs nothing. If you make a five-digit field and then need to enter a $100,000 invoice, you have to make quite a few changes in tables, forms, and reports. Always use the same unit of measure in a field. You will have trouble performing calculations if the same measurement is entered in meters, inches, feet, and miles. You can add a conversion routine to the data entry form to handle alternative units, but you should store the information only once.

Using Codes for Fields

Fields for insurance information need special attention. If you mimic the paper form and provide long text fields for the name of the insurer (for example, *Blue Cross/Blue Shield of Northern California*), you may limit your ability to group patients by insurer's name. Any variation in a user's spelling of an insurer's name throws off the grouping. The database interprets *Blue Cross/Blue Shield* as a different company from *BCBS*, although the two are equivalent. If you use a special code for each insurance company, the distinction between companies will be clear.

One way to assign codes is to create a short abbreviation or acronym for each company, such as the following:

BCBS	Blue Cross/Blue Shield of Northern California
AETNAS	Aetna San Francisco
EQUIT	Equitable
STATE	State Farm

In addition to making grouping easier, insurance company codes are easier to enter because they have fewer characters to type and take less storage space than do full company names. You can protect against bad data entry by allowing users to enter only valid company codes. Users can look up the code from a table that stores all the insurance company names and codes.

Rather than alphabetic codes, you can use numeric codes such as the following:

00001	Blue Cross/Blue Shield of Northern California
00002	Aetna San Francisco
00003	Equitable
00004	State Farm

Numeric codes have some of the same advantages as alphabetic codes and are shorter than text fields. The numbers are more difficult to remember, however, than meaningful abbreviations. Numeric codes may be better for recording a large number of insurance companies because alphabetic codes are difficult to create for so many records. For this reason, numbers are useful in creating quick ways to retrieve transactions such as invoice or policy numbers. Reports sorted in numeric code order may not be as pleasing as those sorted by alphabetic codes, however, because alphabetic codes resemble company names more closely than do numeric codes.

Although codes have certain advantages, especially for database design, be careful not to use codes that make the information less understandable to the user. Early in my career, I was shown an impressive application that stored demographic characteristics of the Soviet elite and performed sophisticated statistical reporting and analysis of that data. Users entered all data in codes. An individual might be represented as something like A657H33K992JH234FG3922, denoting a blonde 5' 11" Eastern Orthodox left-handed cabinetmaker of Georgian descent with a slight limp (I'm making these details up, but the database really existed). Analysts actually learned these codes (after months of working with the system) and were able to interpret them directly. The codes helped speed computer processing. With the processing power available at that time, storing the same information as text would have resulted in much slower statistical analysis. Although processing codes is still faster than processing long text, readability is crucial to database users; so when you develop coding schemes, be sure to keep your database easy for users to understand.

5

How Fields are Filled

You can enter and store data in three different kinds of database fields. Most fields are *user fields*, where data is entered by a user from a data-entry screen and stored in a table. *System-derived fields* are filled by the system without input from the user. Time and date stamps, for example, are often attached automatically to transactions by recording the date and time from the computer's clock. System-derived fields save time for the user (calculating sales tax, for example) and keep the data precise.

Finally, *virtual* or *lookup fields* show data that is not stored in tables. These fields are for display purposes only. Virtual fields can look up values from related tables to help the user. Virtual fields, for instance, can display a customer's name and address when the user enters the customer number in an invoice. Customer data (except for the customer number) is not stored in the invoice record, because it is kept in the customers table. The user can check the customer data display to verify that the correct customer number has been entered. Virtual fields also are used to calculate values that do not need to be stored, such as subtotals in a database table that will be recalculated when you run a report. On-screen displays of subtotals help the user.

You can define fields and data-entry forms that deny users access to fields by *preventing data entry*. This practice is useful for derived fields such as calculations, current information (user name, date, and so on), and virtual fields. Be sure to note which fields the user may not enter. With most database packages, you can control access to the field when you are designing data-entry forms.

Integrity Checks

Many fields are designed for specific values. DBMS offer several types of integrity checks. *Range validation*, for example, sets limits on the values that you can store in a field. You can set limits for each field type. These limits may refer to constants or may be derived from other database values. You can limit a percentage field to numbers between 0 and 100, for example. You can use variables in range validation. You can assign an upper limit of the current date to a birth-date field to prevent the entry of information on people who are not yet born. You also can use calculations to determine upper and lower limits. A business, for example, may limit customer credit to twice the amount of a customer's outstanding bill. The database should not accept a new order on credit that exceeds this amount.

Another type of integrity check performs a lookup into another table to ensure that an entry is valid. You can set the CUSTOMER NUMBER field in a table containing invoices to accept only customer numbers that also are entered in the Customers table.

In some DBMS, you can define integrity checks at the field level; in systems, you must wait until form design to put the integrity checks in place. Table-level integrity checks are better than form level validation, because they protect the data no matter how it is accessed.

Table and Field Security

Because keeping the integrity data in any database is essential, you may need to restrict user access to certain forms and fields. Many DBMS, such as dBASE and Paradox, control security at the field level only through data-entry forms. This means that any user who directly accesses a table (without using a form) has virtually unlimited ability to add, edit, or delete data. With some DBMS, you can restrict access at the field level. DataEase, for instance, provides security options for viewing and entering data. *View/write security* options establish the security levels needed to view and to change data in the field. These security levels can be different so that all users can view data, for example, but only certain users can enter data.

Required Fields

Required fields contain information that is essential to the record and that must be entered before a record can be saved. In a personnel record, for instance, a Social Security number field may be a required field, because the Social Security number is essential for payroll, taxing, and medical benefits. The primary key field is always a required field, because if it is left blank, duplicate records can be entered. The primary key field is the field used to establish uniqueness, such as the Social Security number in a personnel table. Rules for determining key fields are discussed in the section "Primary Key Fields," later in this chapter.

Before you designate a required field, be certain that you can fill it in every case.

The Field Definition Screen

You have learned about your options in defining fields. This section shows you how tables are built in some PC DBMS. Figure 5.2 shows the questions you answer when you define a field in dBASE.

```
  Layout    Organize    Append    Go To    Exit                    4:16:46 pm

                                                Bytes remaining:       3725
  ┌─────┬────────────┬────────────┬───────┬─────┬────────┐
  │ Num │ Field Name │ Field Type │ Width │ Dec │ Index  │
  ├─────┼────────────┼────────────┼───────┼─────┼────────┤
  │   1 │ LNAME      │ Character  │  20   │     │   Y    │
  │   2 │ FNAME      │ Character  │  15   │     │   Y    │
  │   3 │ MI         │ Character  │   1   │     │   N    │
  │   4 │ COMPANY    │ Character  │  30   │     │   N    │
  │   5 │ TITLE      │ Character  │  35   │     │   N    │
  │   6 │ DEPARTMENT │ Character  │  40   │     │   N    │
  │   7 │ ADDRESS    │ Character  │  40   │     │   N    │
  │   8 │ ADDRESS2   │ Character  │  40   │     │   N    │
  │   9 │ CITY       │ Character  │  15   │     │   N    │
  │  10 │ STATE      │ Character  │   2   │     │   N    │
  │  11 │ ZIP        │ Character  │   5   │     │   N    │
  │  12 │ ZIP_EXT    │ Character  │   4   │     │   N    │
  │  13 │ PHONE      │ Character  │  10   │     │   N    │
  │  14 │ FAX        │ Character  │  10   │     │   N    │
  │  15 │ ENTERED    │ Date       │   8   │     │   N    │
  └─────┴────────────┴────────────┴───────┴─────┴────────┘

Database C:\dbase\CLIENTS              Field 1/15
              Enter the field name. Insert/Delete field:Ctrl-N/Ctrl-U
     Field names begin with a letter and may contain letters, digits and underscores
```

Fig. 5.2. *The dBASE field definition screen.*

dBASE requires three pieces of information about each field: name, type, and length. You need not specify length for field types with set lengths, such as date fields.

Other DBMS require similar information for field definition, although the mechanics of choosing the field characteristics are different.

Figure 5.3 shows the DataEase field definition screen. Notice that many of the questions are similar to those in figure 5.2, but that DataEase combines building the table and the data-entry form in one step.

Indexed Fields

One way to speed up database searches is to use *indexes*. The database keeps a special file containing a list of the records arranged by the value in the indexed field. Indexes speed up grouping, sorting, and checking for duplicates.

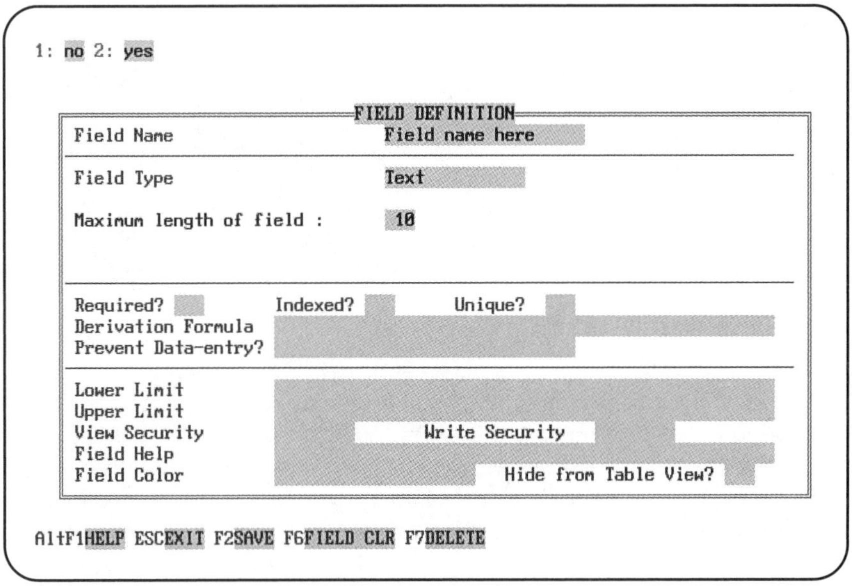

```
 1: no 2: yes

                            ┌FIELD DEFINITION┐
          Field Name              Field name here

          Field Type             Text

          Maximum length of field :    10


          Required?        Indexed?        Unique?
          Derivation Formula
          Prevent Data-entry?

          Lower Limit
          Upper Limit
          View Security            Write Security
          Field Help
          Field Color                      Hide from Table View?

      AltF1HELP ESCEXIT F2SAVE F6FIELD CLR F7DELETE
```

Fig. 5.3. *The DataEase field definition screen.*

A database index works much like a book index. You refer to a book's index rather than read the entire book to find the topic you seek. The index does not contain the topic information itself, but has a *pointer* (the page number) that tells you where to find the information. The index also tells you how many references to the topic the book holds. If your topic is not listed (and the index is thorough), you know that your topic is not in the book and you can save yourself the trouble of reading it.

In the example shown in figure 5.4, records are stored in the order in which they were entered rather than by part number or invoice date. The user has to examine each record individually, from the top of the table to the bottom, to locate a specific part or invoice date. The index file speeds searches by creating a new file in the same order as the field being indexed; the index file, therefore, is easier to scan. The index file's pointers to records (a record number in this example, although the disk location is often used) enable you to access the record in the main file. The index file, therefore, is always in the proper order (alphabetical, numerical, or chronological). When searching for invoices dated October 12, 1991, the DBMS scans the index until it finds that date and uses pointers to read the records with that target date. The search is complete when the DBMS reaches the next date (October 13, for example). You need not read the rest of the index file because it contains only dates greater than October 12, 1991.

Part # Index		Invoices Table			Date Index	
Record	Part#	Record	Part#	Qty	Date	Record Date
6	A09	1	A12	500	12/31/90	2 07/16/90
2	A12	2	C71	750	07/16/90	1 12/31/90
1	C71	3	J67	880	03/03/91	3 03/03/91
3	C71	4	C71	950	10/12/91	4 10/12/91
4	H24	6	A09	200	11/16/91	7 10/13/91
7	J67	7	H24	175	10/13/91	6 11/16/91

Fig. 5.4. *Using an index for faster searching.*

Of course, you can sort the file so that it appears in a specific order. In dBASE, the SORT command (for example, SORT ON PARTNUM TO PARTNUM) creates a data table sorted in order by the specified field. Sorting is not as flexible as indexing, however. You cannot sort the parts file shown in figure 5.4 simultaneously by date and by part number, because the correct order for each of the fields is different. Sorting is attractive only for tables that rarely change and that need to be sorted by only one field, such as reference tables (a list of states and their ZIP codes, for example).

Most database software uses index files. Packages differ widely in the amount of control they give the user over indexes. With some packages, the user can control how indexes are built and maintained; other systems manage these tasks without user control. Software with query optimizers (such as Paradox or Q&A) may build temporary indexes without notifying the user, to speed up the query. Spreadsheets, however, do not use index files for their database features.

Special index files combine (*concatenate*) two or more fields and index all records by all fields at once. You can build a combined index on LASTNAME + FIRSTNAME in a personnel database to retrieve all records in order by both fields. Combined (or *clustered*) indexes yield faster searches than do single indexes in some applications. Another type of special index is a *multilevel index*—an index file based on another index file. The database searches one index file, which directs it to the proper location in a second index file, which then points to the data file itself. Several levels of indexing are possible with this technique.

Another special index type is a *conditional index*, an index for records that meet certain criteria. The index contains some, but not all, of the records from the table. In essence, you are performing a search when you build the index. If you use a conditional index in a search, the search only looks at those designated records. Not all database software supports conditional indexes.

You also can use indexes for sorting and grouping records in reporting. The index enables the database to scan the data file in indexed order rather than in the data's physical order on the disk. When you browse an indexed table in dBASE or FoxPro, for instance, the records are displayed in index order.

Despite their benefits, indexes require disk space and time for updating as data is entered, modified, or deleted. If you are working with the data shown in figure 5.4 and you change a part number in the invoices table, you also must change it in the part number index; otherwise the index will not to point to the correct invoice record. If you update the part number, you need to resort the index to put all the index items in alphabetical order. Similar index maintenance is required if you add or delete a record in the table. If you have 50 fields in a table and index every field, you have to update 51 files (the data file and the 50 index files) when you add, edit, or delete information. Calculating and writing all these files to the disk takes time. How do you know when to use an index?

Deciding When to Index

Indexing is one of the best ways to tune a database for optimum performance. Indexing has few hard and fast rules, because the particular demands of an application greatly affect index performance. The one hard and fast rule is to index all primary key fields. Index performance chiefly depends on three factors: the number of records in the table, the length (in characters) of the indexed field, and the number of indexes for the table. Use the following broad guidelines to determine when to index.

First, the larger the table, the more you need indexes to achieve results in an acceptable period of time. For a small table (about a dozen records), a sequential search can be performed so quickly that you do not necessarily need an index to boost performance. Building and maintaining an index on a small table takes little time or disk space, however, so you do no harm by creating indexes for it, especially to provide for growth.

Second, indexes work best on short fields (12 characters or less). An index on a longer text field takes more time to build, occupies more disk space, and works more slowly than an index on a shorter field. In a personnel file, an indexed Social Security number of 9 characters helps you find a record more quickly than does an indexed name field of 30 characters.

Third, the time needed to maintain indexes increases with the number of indexes that you designate for the table. Before you create excessive indexes, be sure that you really need to search or sort on the fields you want to index. If your database slows after additions or while the indexes are updated, you may want to remove some indexes.

Index primary key fields. The key field is the field (or combination of fields) that uniquely identifies a record. The phone number, for example, may be the key field for a telemarketing database, because each entry should have a different (unique) phone number.

If you use combined indexes (as in dBASE), be sure to use the TRIM function to remove trailing spaces. Otherwise, the index for a partially empty text field will refer to the spaces at the end of the field (for example, SMITH   JOHN rather than SMITHJOHN). These extra blank spaces make the index file larger and make your searches more complicated. In most cases, you can write a program to combine the first and last names without inserting blanks to pad the last name to its full length.

Do not index fields that you seldom or never will use for searching or sorting. Excessive indexes waste disk space, and their maintenance slows down operations. In a sales application, you probably will not search for a particular invoice amount, so only index the invoice number, date, or customer number.

Maintaining an Index

To keep your indexes useful, you must update them when you add, delete, or modify database records. Some DBMS automatically update indexes; others leave this task up to the programmer. Alpha Four, for instance, permits up to seven indexes to be "attached" to each table and automatically updates indexes to reflect changes.

You occasionally may see an error message that warns of an "inconsistent" index. This message means that the index and table no longer match, and that you must rebuild or update the index. An inconsistent index can occur if the power fails or if you shut off the PC while your database files are open. Be sure to heed the error message, because an inconsistent index can produce inconsistent results in your queries.

Primary Key Fields

As discussed in the preceding chapter, a fundamental rule of relational database design is that the users must not be able to enter duplicate rows in a table. Duplicate records clutter the database and harm the integrity of the data.

The field (or field combination) used to detect and prevent duplicate records is the *primary key*. You must designate a primary key in every file to prevent users from accidentally entering duplicate records. The Social Security number field, for example, can be the primary key in an employee directory file (assuming that no employee will be listed twice).

In many cases, more than one field may be eligible to serve as the key. Each potential key field is a *candidate key*. In a personnel file, the employee name, Social Security number, and home address each can work as a key field. To choose between candidate keys, apply the following criteria:

- The key field must never be blank (or null). If you use the Social Security number field, you must enter the Social Security number for every record. If you leave the key field blank in a record, you risk duplication. Differentiating two records with the key left blank is impossible.

- The key field should be as short as possible. Shorter fields boost database performance because their index files are smaller and therefore quicker to search and sort.

- The key field should be meaningful. It should describe the entity.

Every table must have a key field. Using a personnel file as an example, apply the preceding criteria to select a primary key field. Every employee record in the personnel file includes the following fields: Social Security number, name (last, first, middle initial), position, address, and phone number. Because each Social Security number is unique, select that as the key field in the field definition.

Determining the key field is not always easy. Using a person's name as a key field is particularly risky. Databases do not detect legitimate variations on a name (such as Bob for Robert or Jack for John) as duplicates. If a person changes their name, the database records the new entry as a different person. Celebrity names can pose particular problems; do you enter Cher and Madonna as first or last names?

5

One field is often not enough to establish uniqueness. A toothpaste company, for example, sends an invoice to a drugstore. A simple invoice record includes fields for invoice date, drugstore name, and quantity of tubes shipped. The unique field cannot be drugstore name alone, because the toothpaste company probably will send many invoices to that drugstore over time. The date alone cannot create a unique field either, because several invoices may be sent out on the same day to many customers.

How do you make an invoice record unique? By combining invoice date and customer name, you establish a unique designation that enables you to distinguish individual records. This analysis assumes, of course, that the toothpaste company would never send more than one invoice to the same drugstore in the same day.

You also can use codes as key fields. You can use a numeric string field for invoice numbers, for example; this field increases the number by one with each new invoice. Numeric strings are useful as key fields in applications for transaction processing that creates student and employee identification numbers and other types of codes. Unless the codes are meaningful, however, be careful when you use them to establish uniqueness. An arbitrary customer number, for instance, may not establish uniqueness because the user unknowingly may assign several codes to the same customer (by entering the customer as a new customer more than once). That is the reason why you can receive several copies of a catalog from the same company, based on addresses gathered from different purchases you made or different mailing lists. A Social Security number, on the other hand, is meaningful because the U.S. Social Security Administration assigns it to only one person.

Even if you don't use identification numbers to establish uniqueness, you can use them to speed lookups and create compact links to other files. Airline reservation systems, for example, assign a reservation number to each passenger on a flight. The reservation number code refers to passenger name, flight number, and date, and gives you quick access to flight information (if you know the reservation number).

Using a student's Social Security number as the primary key field in the STUDENT file guarantees that no two records will be saved with the same Social Security number, and thereby safeguards against duplicates. Assigning a key field can be more complicated because not all data contains inherently unique fields. A customer table, for example, probably will not contain a Social Security number, so you must use more than one field (such as first name, last name, and company) to establish uniqueness.

In a relational database, you designate a primary key field so that the DBMS can check for uniqueness and enforce *entity integrity*. In DataEase, for instance, the field menu (displayed in field definition) has a yes-or-no field labeled Unique. You designate a unique field by selecting Yes for primary keys (and primary keys only). In Paradox, an asterisk next to the field indicates a key field. In Paradox and DataEase, you can designate more than one field as unique. In both databases packages, if a user attempts to enter a duplicate record, an error message is displayed and the duplicate is not accepted. Duplicate records in Paradox are written to a special exception table where they may be corrected or deleted.

DBMS that do not support this relational rule depend on the application to check for uniqueness of rows—you must write a program to enforce uniqueness. dBASE, for example, has no simple way to designate a unique field. A user can enter duplicates in a dBASE table, and the database provides no special option to indicate the primary key. The user can check for duplicates before a new record is written, however, by modifying a data-entry routine using a form. The following example shows how a source code prevents a duplicate entry by checking the customer identification number (the unique field).

```
PROCEDURE New_cust
USE Customer ORDER Cust_id
CLEAR
DO WHILE .T.
    mcust_id = SPACE(6)
        @ 8, 10 SAY "Customer ID Number for new customer" ;
        GET mcust_id PICTURE "999999"
    READ
    IF " " = TRIM(mcust_id)
        RETURN
    ENDIF
    IF SEEK(mcust_id)
        ?? CHR(7)
        @ 9, 10 SAY "Customer " + cust_id + " exists-retry."
    ELSE
        EXIT
    ENDIF
ENDDO
APPEND BLANK
REPLACE cust_id with mcust_id
EDIT NEXT 1
RETURN
```

The preceding program prompts the user to enter a customer ID and then checks the ID against the CUSTOMERS file. If the customer ID already exists, the program displays an error message. If the ID does not already exist, the program appends to the end of the CUSTOMERS file a new record with the ID number that the user just entered, and the user can continue editing. If you use a dBASE program to check for duplicates, you must be sure that users cannot access the table directly to add or modify records. If users can add or edit data without running the program, your uniqueness checks will be circumvented.

dBASE IV contains another method for assigning uniqueness within a table. If you use the Unique option for the INDEX command, only the first record with the key field is included in the index. Commands using the index to find records, therefore, only find the first record and skip duplicates. The INDEX Unique command does not prevent entry of duplicate records, however, and the first record may not be the record you want to view. Consequently, this technique is a slender reed on which to depend for entity integrity.

In Paradox, defining the key fields in a table ensures that the program will check entries for uniqueness. If the user enters a duplicate record, Paradox writes the record to a special table called KEYVIOL. The user then can edit duplicate records and merge them back into the table or discard them.

DataEase works in a similar fashion. If you choose Yes for Unique on the field definition screen, the program uses that field to check uniqueness. You can designate more than one field as unique in the same DataEase form (known also as table). If a user tries to save a duplicate record, an error message indicates that the record already exists. The user then must change or discard the record.

Derivation Formulas

In many cases, the contents of a field may be dependent on other fields. You can derive a salutation field for generating form letters by combining a title field with a last name field. An invoice subtotal field can be the sum of all line item amounts, which in turn can be the product of quantities multiplied by unit prices. Such derived fields may be user fields, system fields, or virtual fields. As you are listing fields, make a note of any fields which are derived. Using derived fields can save you time, because you avoid unnecessary data entry and thereby avoid making mistakes.

Some fields have *default values*, typical values that are valid in most cases, but which the user may override. Vassar University, for instance, may set a sex field to default to Female, because most of the university's students are women. The sex field would then automatically say Female unless the user filled it in as Male.

If a field has a default value, you can use a derivation formula to calculate the value of a field. In some databases, you can enter the derivation formula when you create the field. Derivation formulas in DataEase, for instance, may contain up to 2,000 characters and can be quite complex.

Field Names

You should use fields of the same type and length in all tables in an application. Use the same field names, if possible. Do not use the same name, however, if a field has different meanings in the context of different tables.

Make field and table names as descriptive as possible with the naming requirements of your DBMS. Avoid using acronyms and jargon when legitimate words will suffice. CUSTOMER_NAME reads better than CSTNM. If you use descriptive words, you probably will have fewer misspellings in your program later in the development process.

Punctuation can cause problems in field names. Using commas in a field name creates conflicts if the query language has a special use for the comma (as a separator for an IF clause, for instance).

> **TIP:** Because spreadsheet databases enable users to enter duplicate labels, make sure that you define unique column headings that are not names of other spreadsheet elements, such as ranges. Don't separate the row of field names from the first data record by any rows.

Force yourself to be consistent with all field names within an application and from one application to another. Decide, for instance, what field names you will use for a person's first and last names. Do you prefer FNAME, First_Name, FIRST, or FN? You will create unnecessary complications if you use several variants and then forget which you used in a particular file.

5

Reserved Words

Although the database designer has poetic license in most aspects of database design, special restrictions on naming database elements exist. All programs reserve certain words for commands, and these reserved words are off-limits for use in naming tables, fields, views, indexes, or memory variables.

If you use reserved words, the program will have a difficult time distinguishing commands from database objects. You are bound to have unpredictable results if you use reserved words in vain.

Be sure to consult your software documentation for a full list of reserved words. Table 5.3 lists reserved words from page 6-2 the dBASE IV manual.

Table 5.3. dBASE IV Language Reference

SQL Reserved Words

ABS	DECIMAL	LOG	SHOW
ACOS	DECLARE	LOG10	SIGN
ADD	DELETE	LOGICAL	SIN
ALL	DELIMITED	LOWER	SMALLINT
ALTER	DESC	LTRIM	SOUNDEX
AND	DIF	MAX	SPACE
ANY	DIFFERENCE	MDY	SQRT
AS	DISTINCT	MIN	START
ASC	DMY	MOD	STOP
ASIN	DOW	MONTH	STR
AT	DROP	NOT	STUFF
ATAN	DTOC	NUMERIC	SUBSTR
ATN2	DTOR	OF	SUM
AVG	DTOS	ON	SYLK
BETWEEN	EXISTS	OPEN	SYNONYM
BLANK	EXP	OPTION	TABLE
BY	FETCH	OR	TAN
CDOW	FIXED	ORDER	TEMP
CEILING	FLOAT	PAYMENT	TIME
CHAR	FLOOR	PI	TO

SQL Reserved Words			
CHECK	FOR	PRIVILEGES	TRANSFORM
CHR	FROM	PUBLIC	TRIM
CLOSE	FV	PV	TYPE
CLUSTER	FW2	RAND	UNION
CMONTH	GRANT	REAL	UNIQUE
COS	GROUP	REPLICATE	UNLOAD
COUNT	HAVING	REVOKE	UPDATE
CREATE	IN	RIGHT	UPPER
CTOD	INDEX	ROLLBACK	USER
CURRENT	INSERT	ROUND	USING
CURSOR	INT	RPD	VAL
DATA	INTEGER	RTOD	VALUES
DATABASE	INTO	RTRIM	VIEW
DATE	KEEP	RUNSTATS	WHERE
DAY	LEFT	SAVE	WITH
DBASEII	LEN	SDF	WKS
DBCHECK	LIKE	SELECT	WORK
DBDEFINE	LOAD	SET	YEAR

The preceding list does not include all the dBASE commands themselves, which are also reserved words.

I have often traced mysterious software "bugs" to conflicts created by database naming. You can avoid using reserved words by misspelling words that sound like they might be database functions. Many programmers, for example, use "kounter" instead of "counter" to avoid confusing the DBMS.

Using the Data Dictionary

Most database programs contain a special table called a *data dictionary*, which stores the names, lengths, and other characteristics of fields used throughout the database. The data dictionary provides consistency from one form to another and speeds the table-building process by enabling you to copy the elements.

Data dictionaries can be active or passive. *Active dictionaries* are dictionaries that the DBMS automatically updates to reflect changes in table structure. The system catalog in SQL Server is an active data dictionary. The developer, however, must update a *passive data dictionary* to show structural changes. DataEase, for instance, has a passive data dictionary that comes stocked with standard fields for business use. A number of stand-alone dictionary programs are available separate from the DBMS. These programs have detailed information on all data elements and their relationships, and can work with most DBMS.

As you build each form, you may want to add all the fields to the data dictionary. The data dictionary stores commonly used field definitions that you can copy when you create new tables. The data dictionary ensures that field types and lengths match from one table to another.

If you build many applications, consider installing your personal data dictionary in each application you design, to ensure that you use consistent field names, types, and lengths in all applications. You can add to the data dictionary as you go along. A well-stocked data dictionary can speed up table design by cutting the time needed to define a field.

If your DBMS does not have a data dictionary, create your own. Build a table containing all the fields you commonly use, showing the field name, meaning, type, and length. Maintain your personal data dictionary by adding fields as you create tables. You can install this table into any new application and use it as a permanent data dictionary across applications.

You also can build additional tables to store the names of all tables used in the application and the relationships among the tables. You end up with four tables: Tables, Fields, Fields Used, and Relationships. The Fields Used table contain records for each field in each form, and the Relationships table contains the names of the related forms along with the fields that relate them. Table 5.4 shows an example of a data dictionary.

Most database packages have commands to copy the structure of one table to another. In Paradox, for instance, you can use the BORROW command to retrieve the structure of another table (or tables) when defining or restructuring a table.

Table 5.4. Do-it-Yourself Data Dictionary

Tables

Varieties
Vineyards
Vintages

Fields

Name	Type	Length
CITY	Text	15
COLOR	Choice	5
NOSE	Text	20
SHELF LIFE	Number	5
STATE	Text	2
VARIETY	Text	12
VINEYARD NAME	Text	30
YEAR	Numeric Str.	4

Fields Used

Table	Field
Varieties	VARIETY
Varieties	COLOR
Vineyards	CITY
Vineyards	VINEYARD NAME
Vintages	VINEYARD NAME
Vintages	VARIETY
Vintages	YEAR
Vintages	NOSE
Vintages	COLOR

Relationships

Table1	Table2	Field1	Field2
Vineyards	Vintages	VINEYARD NAME	VINEYARD NAME
Vintages	Varieties	VARIETY	VARIETY

5

Table 5.5 shows a sample data dictionary that includes many common database fields. Field names are restricted to ten characters so that they can be used for dBASE-compatible DBMS and Paradox. If your DBMS supports longer field names, you can make the names more descriptive.

Table 5.5. Sample Data Dictionary

Description	Field Name	Type	Length
Social Security Number	SSN	Numeric String	9
Title (Mr., Ms, and so on)	TITLE	Text	6
First Name	FNAME	Text	15
Last Name	LNAME	Text	20
Middle Initial	MI	Text	1
Salutation	SALUT	Text	27
Position (Corporate Title)	POSITION	Text	40
Company	COMPANY	Text	40
Address	ADDRESS	Text	40
Address (second line)	ADDRESS2	Text	40
City	CITY	Text	20
State Abbreviation (U.S.)	STATE	Text	2
Zip Code (U.S.)	ZIP	Numeric String	5
Zip + 4 Extension	ZIPEXT	Numeric String	4
Country	COUNTRY	Text	30
Province	PROVINCE	Text	20
Postal Code (non-U.S.)	POSTCODE	Text	12
Posted (flag for posting routines)	POSTED	Logical (Y/N)	1
Invoice Number	INVNO	Numeric String	6
Telephone Number (U.S.)	PHONE	Numeric String	10
Facsimile Telephone Number (U.S.)	FAX	Numeric String	10
Quantity	QTY	Number	6
Date of Birth	DOB	Date	6
Comments	COMMENTS	Text	60

You must decide whether to embed spaces in table and field names. If your data will be moved to a client-server Structured Query Language (SQL) system, do not embed spaces or use strange characters in field names, because you will have to rename them. To improve readability, you can embed underscore characters (_) or hyphens in field names instead of spaces.

Table 5.6 shows field characteristics for the Alma Mater University enrollment system.

Table 5.6. Alma Mater University Field Characteristics

Field	Type	Length
1. **Students**		
SOCIAL SECURITY NUMBER	Numeric String	9
FIRST NAME	Text	10
LAST NAME	Text	15
MIDDLE INITIAL	Text	1
LOCAL ADDRESS	Text	30
LOCAL ADDR CITY	Text	15
LOCAL ADDR STATE	Text	2
LOCAL ADDR ZIP	Numeric String	5
PERMANENT ADDRESS	Text	30
PERM ADDR CITY	Text	15
PERM ADDR STATE	Text	2
PERM ADDR ZIP	Numeric String	5
BIRTHDATE	Date	6
RACE	Choice	
2. **Instructors**		
SOCIAL SECURITY NUMBER	Numeric String	9
FIRST NAME	Text	10
LAST NAME	Text	15
MIDDLE INITIAL	Text	1
LOCAL ADDRESS	Text	30
LOCAL ADDR CITY	Text	15
LOCAL ADDR STATE	Text	2
LOCAL ADDR ZIP	Numeric String	5
PERMANENT ADDRESS	Text	30
PERM ADDR CITY	Text	15
PERM ADDR STATE	Text	2
PERM ADDR Zip	Numeric String	5
BIRTHDATE	Date	6

continues

Table 5.6. Continued		
Field	*Type*	*Length*
3. **Courses**		
COURSE NUMBER	Numeric String	6
DEPARTMENT CODE	Numeric String	3
DEPARTMENT NAME	Text	12
DESCRIPTION	Text	20
CREDIT HOURS	Integer	2
4. **Course Offerings**		
YEAR	Numeric String	2
SEMESTER	Choice	
COURSE NUMBER	Numeric String	6
SECTION NUMBER	Numeric String	2
INSTRUCTOR SSN	Numeric String	9
BUILDING	Text	8
ROOM	Text	6
DAY	Integer	1
TIME	Time	
5. **Student Schedule**		
SOCIAL SECURITY NUMBER	Numeric String	9
YEAR	Numeric String	2
SEMESTER	Choice	
COURSE NUMBER	Numeric String	6
SECTION NUMBER	Numeric String	2

Required Fields

Required fields are fields that must be filled for a record to be entered in the database. A required field prevents incomplete information from being stored.

When you write a field list, indicate which fields the user must enter to make the record complete. For personnel files, Social Security number and name are the obvious choices to designate as for required fields. Always make all key (unique) fields required, to provide for comprehensive checks for duplicates.

Be careful not to make too many fields required. Although you want to ensure that the full name is entered in a personnel file, for instance, do not make the middle initial field required, because not everyone has a middle initial. Be sure that users do not sidestep required fields by entering N/A or some other invalid entry. Mailing labels look bad with names such as *John N/A Smith*. If the field has no legitimate value, the program should permit users to leave the field blank.

Style Standards

If you are the only user of a database application you develop, creating consistent forms, reports, or menus is not important. If, however, you develop applications that others will use or if you develop more than one application, you need to establish standards for your database style.

Database style standards resolve in advance many decisions that arise during applications development and give you more time to address the challenges unique to the application. The principles of clean database design make a system easier to use, maintain, modify, and document.

Summary

Tables are at the heart of a relational database, and coming up with a good table structure is an essential step toward a healthy application. Start by working from the lists you prepared during the analysis process. Create a table for each of the entities you identified, and list all the attributes as fields. Choose the appropriate field type from those offered by your particular database software. Next, add the special characteristics of the fields (primary key, required, indexed, and so on).

The most challenging field characteristic to determine is whether a field is a primary key field. With rare exceptions, every table should have a primary key field to prevent duplicate entries. You might need to use more than one field as a primary key. Be sure that you create indexes for all primary key fields.

You might create new fields that you did not identify during your analysis. One field might need another to help describe the entity better. You also might create alphabetic or numeric codes to speed entry where appropriate. In most cases, you also need to build a reference table where codes are used, to contain the valid entries for the field.

Try to follow consistent conventions for naming tables and fields. Write down your standards as you go along, and keep the same standards from one database to the next. By using consistent field names, you save yourself a great deal of time when creating forms and reports later in the development process.

Building Forms

What we do is never understood but always merely praised and blamed.

Friedrich Nietzsche

After the table structure is in place, you can build forms. Forms are screens that enable users to add, view, or delete database records. Forms are the typical means of accessing database information. In fact, most database designers prevent users from direct access to database tables and use forms exclusively to control what users can see and access.

Forms have several special features that tables do not. With forms, you have more control over the appearance of the screen. You can change the order fields in the form and add descriptive text labels and background text instructions to explain what information goes where. You can highlight fields in your form with a bright color or draw boxes around important areas. With databases written for Windows and other graphical interfaces, you can add graphics and even business graphs to forms. With most DBMS, you can add fields that are for display only, and are not stored in data tables. A good form can make data much easier to understand.

Forms help protect the integrity of the database. You can use forms to restrict users from seeing or modifying certain fields. Forms can contain sophisticated error checking that validates each field as it is filled.

You can create special forms, called *views*, that contain fields from several tables at once. Chapter 7 discusses the creation and use of views.

Although, strictly speaking, you do not need forms to enter information in a database, using forms offers a number of compelling advantages. If you enter information directly into a table, fields might not appear in the order you expect. With a form, you can change the order of fields to match the flow of data entry. The field names used in a table, or even the table name itself, may not be sufficiently clear to the user. Unclear field names are especially common with DBMS such as dBASE, which accept only ten characters for each field name. By using forms, you can enter longer, more descriptive field names, and background information on how the form is to be used. Finally, direct entry into tables, at least in some DBMS, limits your capability to verify data and increases the chance that you will enter invalid data. dBASE field types, for instance, do not provide for defining a text field that accepts only numeric values, such as a telephone number or a ZIP code. In dBASE, you can perform this kind of validation in a form.

Most users prefer to enter information into forms rather than tables because on-screen forms resemble the paper forms with which users are familiar. An on-screen form can emulate a paper form so closely that users can enter data without even looking up at the screen. With operating systems that use graphical interfaces (such as Microsoft Windows), you can use scaled typefaces and images to make database forms look even more like their paper counterparts. Windows databases also resemble paper forms more than character-based applications because they typically use dark characters on a white background.

This chapter outlines form design step-by-step, and suggests guidelines for developing forms to make your applications easier to build, use, and maintain.

Learning Form Design

Good form design gives immediate rewards. Everyone who uses your database notices the style of its data entry forms (and menus) more than any other component. The user interface is the means by which the user interacts with an application, using input and output devices such as the screen, the keyboard, and the mouse. When you create a database application, you are building a interface for your users. Make the interface as attractive and easy to use as possible. Because forms are such an important part of the interface, they are worth a great deal of consideration and care.

An interface should make the user's time more productive. To this end, the interface must be easy to learn and, equally important, easy to use. Many people will use an application during its lifespan. If the application is too difficult to learn, users will be discouraged and may fall back on other ways of getting the job done, even if this means abandoning the computer. For organizations with high turnover, ease of learning is especially important. Make your forms self-explanatory, with plenty of on-screen help to guide data entry. Be certain that the overall purpose of the application and the meaning of each function is obvious to the user.

Field Colors

In most DBMS, you can set different field colors within a form. Although you should not undervalue color's aesthetic value, use field colors conservatively and strategically. Users spend a great deal of time staring at forms and menus, so make yours as comfortable on the eyes as possible. (Note that the current versions some databases, such as Q&A, do not support colors.)

You can use colors to highlight field types. You can make all required fields white on a red background, for example, to remind users to fill those fields before saving the record. I prefer to make display-only fields a different color than fields that the user enters. This color difference helps the user know where the cursor can and cannot go. You can use complex color schemes to differentiate primary key fields, fields looked up from other tables, calculated fields, and so on.

Colors can emphasize screen text. Bright colors grab the user's attention and can warn of impending danger when used for error messages or hazardous procedures that delete data. Blinking or flashing colors are even more powerful, but have certain disadvantages. Although blinking text demands attention like nothing else, it is the most tiring display you can place on-screen. Before you use flashing text, be sure that you really need it to deliver your message. I never use blinking fields or messages in applications.

You can choose from among many pleasing color combinations. Remember that users must sit through extensive data-entry sessions while looking at the colors you have chosen. Don't go overboard with wild color combinations that will tire the user. A friend of mine wrote an application with color combinations such as green letters on a pink background and flashing purple text on light gray. He called his palette *psycho*, and with good reason. Any user saddled with my friend's system would not find it humorous for long.

You can adopt the colors used by your favorite database software. Table 6.1 lists the default colors used in several popular PC DBMS.

Table 6.1. Standard Screen Colors

Type	dBASE IV	Paradox	R:base	DataEase
Background	Blue	White on gray	Blue	Black
Menu	White on black	White on cyan	White on blue	White and blue on black
Menu highlight	Yellow on cyan	White on blue	Blue on gray	White on blue
Error messages	Gray on black	Flashing white on red	White and red	Red
Record entry background	Blue	Cyan	Blue	Black
Record entry fields	Black on cyan	N/A. Fields do not show. Black on gray	Blue on gray	Blue
Prompt line	Blue on gray	White on cyan	Black on gray	Yellow on red
Message	White on black	White on red	Black on cyan	Red and/or purple
Function key list	White on black	N/A	Red	Yellow on red

The preceding colors may change in future software releases, but they provide a reference for setting up your own color scheme. Choose colors that suit the DBMS you are using and that create a familiar environment for your users.

Don't forget that many users work with monochrome monitors. Test your selections in monochrome to make sure that they have the proper highlighting and contrast without the use of colors. Testing is particularly important if you are building an application for distribution, because you cannot predict what types of monitors will display your work. You can allow users to choose their own color preferences, by offering options for color monitors, monochrome, and monochrome with color display cards (common on laptop computers).

In most DBMS, you can change the colors for all screens or for individual screen elements such as text, fields, and menu prompts. In dBASE, you can use the Tools menu to change colors globally. To change the colors of an individual field, follow these steps:

1. Move the cursor to the field and press F6 to select the field.

2. Press F10 to reveal the Words menu. Choose the Display option and press Enter.

3. A menu showing all the color combinations appears (see fig. 6.1). Move the cursor to the desired foreground color. As you move through the colors menu, the color of the column headers changes to show your color choice.

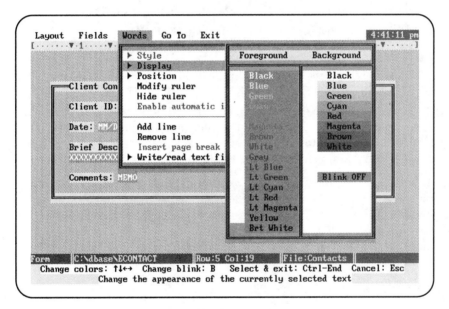

Fig. 6.1. *dBASE menus for selecting field color.*

4. Choose the background color by moving the cursor to the right and then selecting the desired color.

5. Press Ctrl-End to save your color choices.

dBASE and similar languages have commands in their programming languages that control the colors of screen elements. Table 6.2 contains a summary of these commands for dBASE IV.

Table 6.2. dBASE IV Screen Color Commands

Screen Element	Command
Entire form	SET COLOR TO
@...SAYs	@...SAY...GET...COLOR
GET fields	SET COLOR OF FIELDS
Error messages, message line	SET COLOR OF MESSAGE
Help messages	SET COLOR OF MESSAGES
Lines, Borders	@...TO COLOR
Interior of Boxes	@...FILL TO...COLOR
Text inside box or window	SET COLOR OF NORMAL
Window border or interior	DEFINE WINDOW...COLOR
Pop-up menus, dialog boxes	SET COLOR OF BOX
Selected menu options	SET COLOR OF HIGHLIGHT
Clock, status bar	SET COLOR OF INFORMATION

You can even change the color of a field based on its value, by writing a program that sets the field color after checking the value in that field. For a financial database, for example, you could show negative account balances in red and positive balances in black.

As with all screen elements, be consistent in your color choices. Find a pleasing palette and use it throughout the application (and all your applications, if possible). Don't use different colors for two screens that perform essentially the same function. Use the same color scheme, for example, for all menus, and the same scheme for all data-entry forms.

Screen Layout

Screen layout is the most aesthetically demanding area of database design. Over the life of an application, users will spend far more time staring at the data-entry screens than you spend building the entire database, so don't give users something that will bore them. Make screens as interesting as possible. Figure 6.2 shows an uninspired, boring form layout.

Although the fields in figure 6.2 are laid out in the order in which they are to be entered, much space is wasted because each field is on a line by itself. The screen will flow better if the designer reformats it to resemble a mailing label or address-file card (see fig. 6.3).

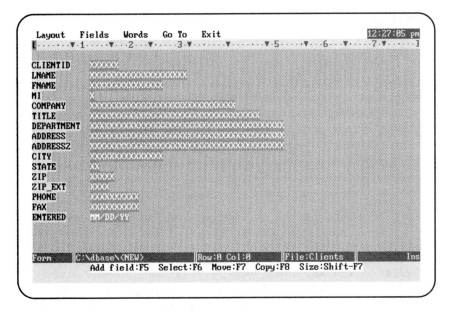

Fig. 6.2. A dBASE clients form.

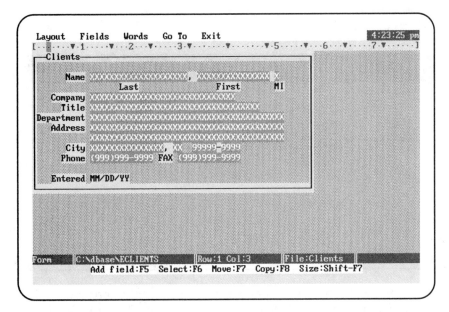

Fig. 6.3. An improved dBASE clients form.

Field Labels

Background text on the data-entry screen helps the user understand how to fill in fields. In addition to words, background text can include boxes, shadowing, and other graphic effects.

Don't use ambiguous words for labels and choices. The label NAME is not specific enough. You can interpret it to mean customer name, product name, or user name, and it does not tell the user the proper format for entering the name. CUSTOMER NAME (LAST, FIRST MI), is a better field label because it indicates the type and order of the names the user will enter (customer names, last name first). YEAR is another ambiguous label, if used for a field that stores fiscal year or academic year.

Even if your field names are too short to be descriptive, you can use labels to explain fields. LAST ORDER DATE is a better label than the field name LSTORDT.

Abbreviations can be useful in form design because they save screen space. Be certain, however, to use only abbreviations that are widely understood in the context of your application. Many abbreviations work in nearly all business applications. Other abbreviations are specialized for use in specific industries, such as MILSPEC for military specification. Table 6.3 shows some common business abbreviations that many users will recognize.

Table 6.3. Useful Business Abbreviations

Term	Abbreviation
Account	Acct
Building	Bldg
Department	Dept
Division	Div
Number	No., Num, or #
Room	Rm
Social Security Number	SSN
Telephone	Phone or Ph

Don't use field labels for system-derived fields except to prevent ambiguity (such as tax and total fields for dollar amounts). The meaning of a system-derived field often is obvious without a label, as with customer address fields displayed on an invoice when the customer number is entered.

Be consistent in your use of capitalization. Choose all capital letters, mixed case, or even all lowercase (for that e.e. cummings look), and use the same choice for every form.

Use the same label to refer to the same field in all forms. You create confusion if you change the label of a field from COURSE ID in one form to COURSE CODE in another. Even though you know that both labels mean the same thing, users invariably will look for some subtle distinction between the terms.

Make your labels long enough to be meaningful (and grammatically correct) but concise enough to conserve screen space. If fields require more explanation, many DBMS enable you to enter instructions to the user in *field help* (see the section "Adding Field Help," in this chapter). Some fields do not need labels. You rarely need to label a field ADDRESS2 if it is situated unambiguously in an address block. Placing STATE and ZIP after CITY makes these fields obvious without any label at all.

Even if field names contain punctuation, don't embed numbers or punctuation in labels themselves, unless doing so makes the labels more meaningful. Punctuation can set labels off from their fields. If you choose to use colons between the field labels and the fields, use a colon with every field and use consistent spacing. You can use dollar signs to highlight fields in which users will enter dollar amounts. To draw attention to screen text, use special characters such as < or * (as in <<< WARNING--DO NOT PROCEED >>>). Most form design programs enable you to use characters other than those in the alphabet. The extended ASCII character set includes exotic fields such as ☺ (001), ◆(004), ☼(015), and ▌(219). Consult your software documentation for instruction on using extended ASCII in form design. You typically enter these characters by simultaneously pressing the Alt key and the number on the numeric pad. Many software manuals, including those that come with word processing programs, contain an ASCII character chart as an appendix.

Figure 6.4 illustrates many of the principles of good form design. This sample form starts with a title to orient the user. The box highlights the fields, which appear in their order of entry. The name fields are on one line, and each has a label to show what part of the name it holds. The END label in the bottom border shows that the data-entry form is only one screen long. If additional screens were available, the bottom label might be Press PgDn for More.

6

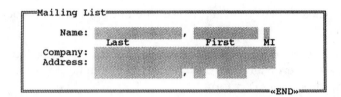

Fig. 6.4. *A sample form.*

Field Order

The order in which fields appear on the form greatly affects the speed of data entry. An awkward field order can slow down even the best operator. If you place the telephone number field between the last address line and the city field, for example, the user must visually skip ahead and then back to copy information from a paper form.

If printed forms are used to collect data, arrange the fields on the database form in the same order as the fields appear on printed forms. If practical, consider clustering numeric fields together in a group. Touch typists can enter data quickly from the numeric key pad, and their speed falls when they move back and forth from text to numbers.

Typical Form Design

When possible, lay out fields in columns to align the beginning of a field on one line with the beginning of a field on the next line. You can follow the field labels with a colon and a space without justifying the beginnings of the labels. Figure 6.5 shows columnar field layout.

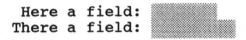

Fig. 6.5. *Columnar field layout.*

A columnar field layout enables the user to follow cursor movement easily. Having the fields in line with one another is more important than having the background text follow a straight line, because the cursor moves through aligned fields in an even, vertical fashion.

Do not scatter fields on the screen in no apparent pattern (see fig. 6.6). Forms of this fashion are disconcerting to the user.

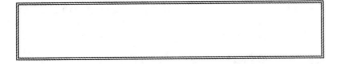

Fig. 6.6. *Crazy quilt form design.*

If you use of boxes or borders, make them consistent from one form to another. Leave a margin of two spaces between the box and the fields or labels. You can label the form above, below, or directly on the box. Figure 6.7 shows a simple box design.

Fig. 6.7. *A plain box.*

Some screen designers create a shadow box effect, as shown in figure 6.8. Designers create this effect by using the screen color commands to place a contrasting border on two sides of the form.

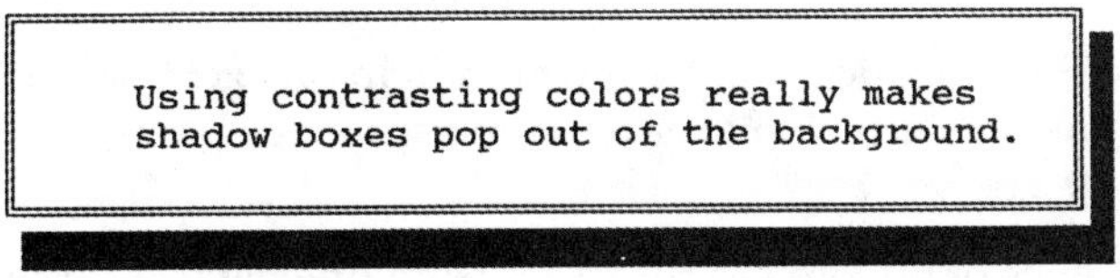

```
Using contrasting colors really makes
shadow boxes pop out of the background.
```

Fig. 6.8. *A shadow box.*

If you use more than one box on a screen, be sure to make the boxes the same width. I prefer to surround the entire screen with a single box, then use additional lines to subdivide special screen areas, grouping fields within the areas by subject, as shown in figure 6.9.

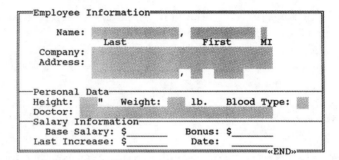

Fig. 6.9. *Fields grouped by subject.*

Label the end of each page to alert the user that more fields follow (PgDn for more, for example) or that they have reached the end of the form (END). You can save space by typing the text directly on the box.

Adding Function Key Help

An explanation for commonly used functions, such as saving, modifying, and deleting records, is an extremely useful element to include in your data-entry forms. Telling the user how to exit from the form is even more important. You can give the user this information by including a line at the top or bottom of the form as follows:

Exit—ESC   F2—Save   F10— Modify   F8—Clear   F1—Help

Some DBMS automatically place function help on each form. If this is true for your software, don't waste screen space repeating the function key help.

The mechanics of building forms varies from one database product to another. In some DBMS, such as DataEase and Q&A, you build the form and the table at the same time. Figure 6.10 shows the first step in building a Q&A form. The designer types the field names followed by a colon. A bracket (>) shows the last character space for the field.

Choosing the field types is your next step. Q&A defaults to text fields, so you must change any nontext fields (numbers, dates) to the appropriate type, as shown in figure 6.11.

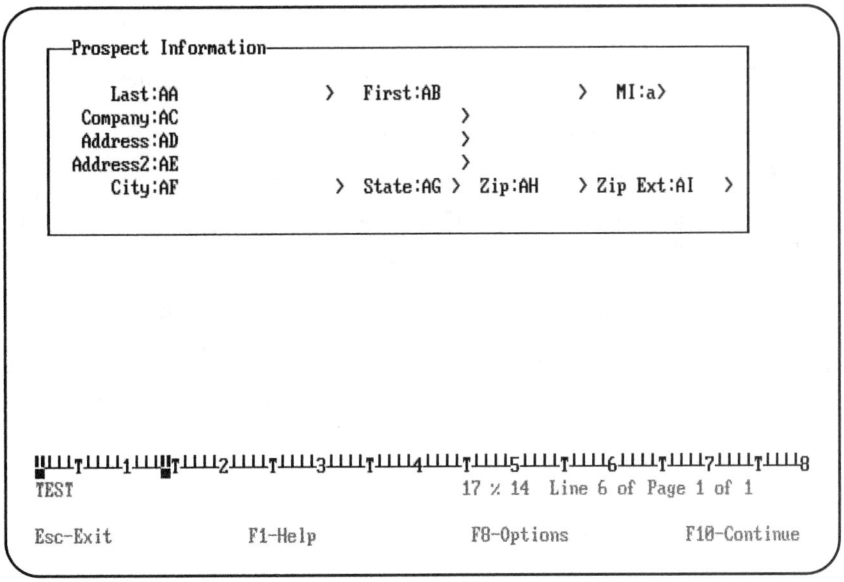

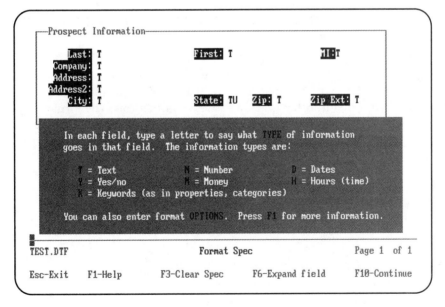

Fig. 6.10. Q&A form definition, step 1.

Fig. 6.11. Q&A form definition, step 2.

After you sketch out the form design and determine the field types, you may enter data in the form, as shown in figure 6.12. Note that Q&A automatically shows how the function keys are used in record entry.

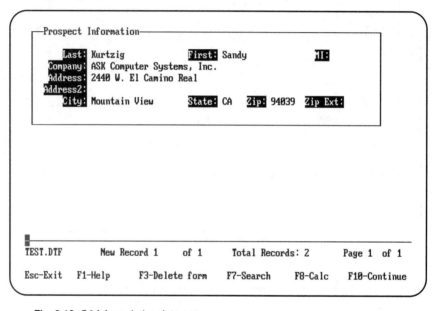

Fig. 6.12. *Q&A form during data entry.*

With other DBMS, you create tables (described in Chapter 5) in a separate step before you design forms. The dBASE IV Command Center has a form generator that quickly creates custom forms. The form in figure 6.13 was generated by the dBASE IV Command Center, and includes a number of data-entry validation checks. Behind the scenes, dBASE generated the following code to paint the screen and handle record entry. Generating code is an excellent way to prototype an application. It provides a handy basis for further customizing by giving you the basic code, which you can edit further for advanced features.

```
*********************************************************************************
*-- Name.......: ECLIENTS.FMT
*-- Date.......: 6-23-91
*-- Version....: dBASE IV, Format 1.1
*-- Notes......: Format files use "" as delimiters!
*********************************************************************************
```

```
*-- Format file initialization code -------------------------------------------

*-- Some of these PRIVATE variables are created based on CodeGen and may not
*-- be used by your particular .fmt file
PRIVATE lc_talk, lc_cursor, lc_display, lc_status, lc_carry, lc_proc,;
        ln_typeahd, gc_cut

IF SET("TALK") = "ON"
   SET TALK OFF
   lc_talk = "ON"
ELSE
   lc_talk = "OFF"
ENDIF
lc_cursor = SET("CURSOR")
SET CURSOR ON

lc_status = SET("STATUS")
*-- SET STATUS was ON when you went into the Forms Designer.
IF lc_status = "OFF"
   SET STATUS ON
ENDIF


*-- @ SAY GETS Processing. -----------------------------------------------------

*--   Format Page: 1
@ 0,0 TO 13,57
@ 0,0 TO 13,57
@ 0,3 SAY "Clients"
@ 2,7 SAY "Name"
@ 2,12 GET Lname PICTURE "XXXXXXXXXXXXXXXXXXXX"
@ 2,32 SAY ", "
@ 2,34 GET Fname PICTURE "XXXXXXXXXXXXXXX"
@ 2,49 SAY " "
@ 2,50 GET Mi PICTURE "X"
@ 3,18 SAY "Last"
@ 3,38 SAY "First"
@ 3,50 SAY "MI"
@ 4,4 SAY "Company"
@ 4,12 GET Company PICTURE "XXXXXXXXXXXXXXXXXXXXXXXXXXXXXXX"
@ 5,6 SAY "Title"
```

continues

Continued

```
@ 5,12 GET Title PICTURE "XXXXXXXXXXXXXXXXXXXXXXXXXXXXXXXXXX"
@ 6,1 SAY "Department"
@ 6,12 GET Department PICTURE "XXXXXXXXXXXXXXXXXXXXXXXXXXXXXXXXXXXXXXX"
@ 7,4 SAY "Address"
@ 7,12 GET Address PICTURE "XXXXXXXXXXXXXXXXXXXXXXXXXXXXXXXXXXXXXXX"
@ 8,12 GET Address2 PICTURE "XXXXXXXXXXXXXXXXXXXXXXXXXXXXXXXXXXXXXXX"
@ 9,7 SAY "City"
@ 9,12 GET City PICTURE "@A XXXXXXXXXXXXXX"
@ 9,27 SAY ", "
@ 9,29 GET State PICTURE "@A! XX"
@ 9,33 GET Zip PICTURE "99999"
@ 9,38 SAY "-"
@ 9,39 GET Zip_ext PICTURE "9999"
@ 10,6 SAY "Phone"
@ 10,12 GET Phone PICTURE "@R (999)999-9999"
@ 10,26 SAY "FAX"
@ 10,30 GET Fax PICTURE "@R (999)999-9999"
@ 12,4 SAY "Entered"
@ 12,12 SAY Entered
*-- Format file exit code --------------------------------------------------

*-- SET STATUS was ON when you went into the Forms Designer.
IF lc_status = "OFF"  && Entered form with status off
   SET STATUS OFF     && Turn STATUS "OFF" on the way out
ENDIF
SET CURSOR &lc_cursor.
SET TALK &lc_talk.

RELEASE lc_talk,lc_fields,lc_status
*-- EOP: ECLIENTS.FMT
```

The complexity of the preceding code illustrates why having dBASE generate codes is easier than entering them by hand. Writing all the SAYs and GETs is time consuming, and you can lose track of screen coordinates when you move fields and labels around the screen.

When you generate a dBASE form, start with a default form having one field per line. Figure 6.13 shows the default form generated by dBASE for the Clients table. After you move the screen elements around, dBASE will regenerate the program as you save the form with Ctrl-End.

The form in figure 6.13 has some obvious shortcomings. You can improve it quickly by adding background text and using the Select and Move functions.

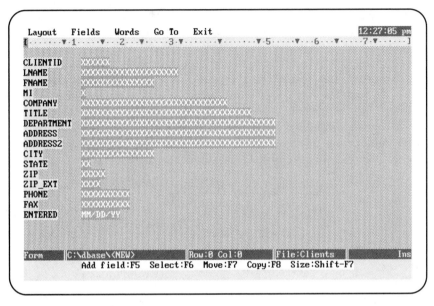

Fig. 6.13. *A default form in dBASE.*

The form shown in figure 6.14 uses fewer field labels and relies on grouping to convey the meaning of each field. The user can seek field help for an explanation of how to fill a less-than-obvious field.

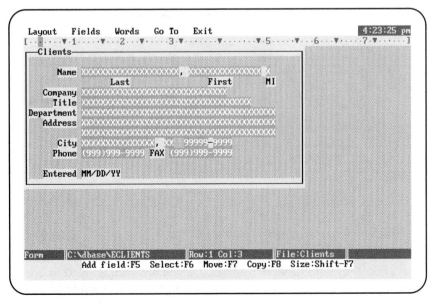

Fig. 6.14. *The improved Clients form in dBASE.*

The same design principles are used in all DBMS. Figure 6.15, for instance, shows a form designed in DataEase. This figure shows a Students form designed for a university enrollment system. The form uses white space (blank lines) to separate the fields and roughly centers the fields on the screen. Unlike a crowded layout, this arrangement helps the eye move through the form. Use white space to create room between screen borders and text or fields. You can superimpose the screen title on the border, as shown here, to save space. Figure 6.15 shows the DataEase form definition printed by the program. Below the form itself, DataEase lists the field names, types, lengths, and other characteristics.

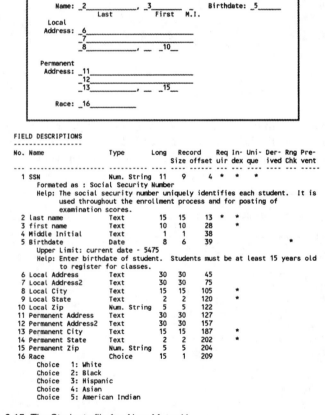

Fig. 6.15. *The Students file for Alma Mater U.*

Don't be stingy with data-entry screens. If you are struggling to fit everything on one screen, use another. Users generally do not mind pressing an arrow key or PgDn to make their work space less cluttered. Figure 6.16 shows a screen overcrowded by a lengthy form. Figures 6.17 through 6.19 show the same form divided among three screens. Users work more comfortably with easy-to-read layouts.

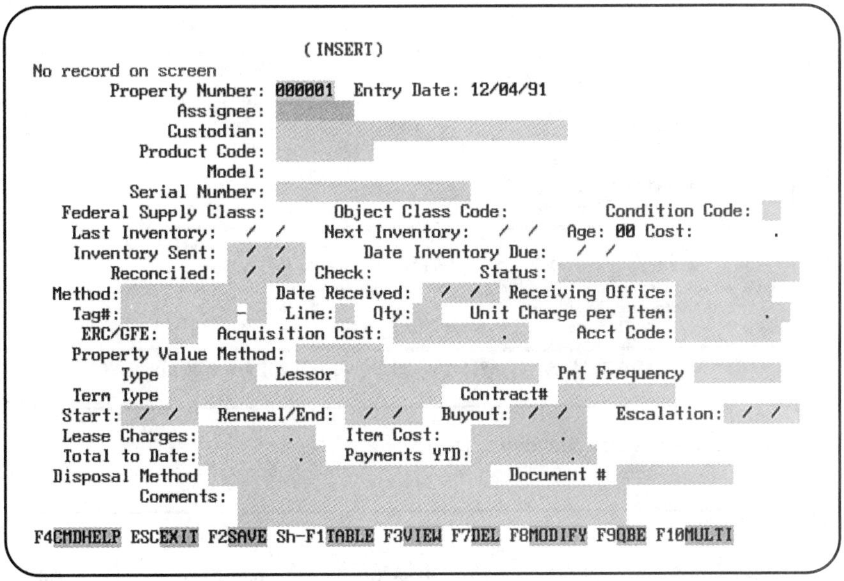

```
                          ( INSERT)
No record on screen
          Property Number: 000001  Entry Date: 12/04/91
                 Assignee:
                Custodian:
             Product Code:
                    Model:
            Serial Number:
      Federal Supply Class:     Object Class Code:      Condition Code:
          Last Inventory:  /  /    Next Inventory:  /  /  Age: 00 Cost:
          Inventory Sent:  /  /     Date Inventory Due:  /  /
              Reconciled:  /  /  Check:          Status:
Method:               Date Received:  /  /   Receiving Office:
   Tag#:         -    Line:    Qty:    Unit Charge per Item:          .
   ERC/GFE:       Acquisition Cost:          .      Acct Code:
Property Value Method:
          Type            Lessor              Pmt Frequency
   Term Type                         Contract#
   Start:  /  /   Renewal/End:  /  /    Buyout:  /  /     Escalation:  /  /
   Lease Charges:      .     Item Cost:       .
   Total to Date:      .   Payments YTD:        .
Disposal Method                       Document #
          Comments:

F4CMDHELP ESCEXIT F2SAVE Sh-F1TABLE F3VIEW F7DEL F8MODIFY F9QBE F10MULTI
```

Fig. 6.16. *A crowded screen.*

Validating Data

Forms should contain checks to promote high-quality data entry. You can apply several kinds of integrity checks in a form. You can validate each field, for example, or look it up in a reference table to ensure that it is the correct type of entry. You can use special "templates" to check the format of the entry.

Templates

In dBASE field, you can use templates to perform special validation and formatting on each field in a form. In figure 6.20, the ID code in the Client form was defined as a text field, but accepts only numbers. It was not defined as a number field because it will not be used in calculations and should not be punctuated with commas and decimal points as a number would. You can use a template to restrict entry in the CLIENT ID field to only numbers.

```
                          ( INSERT )
No record on screen
┌Office Equipment Inventory═══════════════════╤═Property Number: 000033═┐
                                               │      Entry Date:    /  /
         Assignee: ▓▓▓▓▓▓▓▓
        Custodian: ▓▓▓▓▓▓▓▓▓▓▓▓▓▓▓▓▓▓▓▓▓▓▓▓
       Product Code: ▓▓▓▓▓▓▓
                                                      Model:
      Serial Number: ▓▓▓▓▓▓▓▓▓▓▓
 Federal Supply Class:        Object Class Code:
     Condition Code: ▓
             Age: 00                    Cost:           .
═Inventory Information═════════════════════════════════════════════
    Last Inventory Date:   /  /    Next Inventory Date:   /  /
    Date Inventory Sent:   /  /    Date Inventory Due:    /  /
       Date Reconciled:   /  /              Check:
                Status:
F4CMDHELP ESCEXIT F2SAVE Sh-F1TABLE F3VIEW F7DEL F8MODIFY F9QBE F10MULTI
```

Fig. 6.17. *A less crowded form, screen 1.*

```
                          ( INSERT )
1: New - Purchased 2: New - Leased 3: Transfer 4: Donation/Other    F1MORE
┌Acquisition Information═══════════════════════════════════════════════
Method ▓▓▓▓▓▓▓▓      Date Received   /  /   Receiving Office ▓▓▓▓▓▓
  Tag# ▓▓▓▓▓▓▓▓ - ▓  Line ▓   Qty ▓   Unit Charge per Item ▓▓▓▓▓    .
  ERC/GFE ▓                           Acquisition Cost ▓▓▓▓▓▓    .
Accounting Code ▓▓▓▓▓▓   Property Value Method ▓▓▓▓▓▓
═Lease Information═════════════════════════════════════════════════
       Type ▓▓▓▓▓▓  Lessor ▓▓▓▓▓▓▓▓      Pmt Frequency ▓▓▓▓▓
  Term Type ▓▓▓▓▓▓          Contract# ▓▓▓▓▓▓▓▓
  Start Date   /  /   Renewal/End Date   /  /
 Buyout Date   /  /   Escalation Date    /  /
 Lease Charges ▓▓▓▓▓    .  Item Cost ▓▓▓▓▓    .
 Total to Date ▓▓▓▓▓    .  Payments YTD ▓▓▓▓▓    .
F4CMDHELP ESCEXIT F2SAVE Sh-F1TABLE F3VIEW F7DEL F8MODIFY F9QBE F10MULTI
```

Fig. 6.18. *A less crowded form, screen 2.*

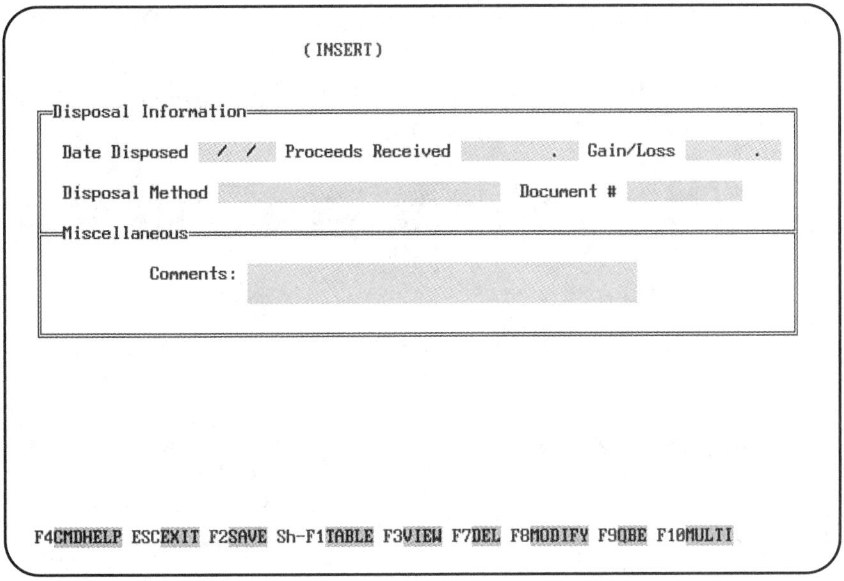

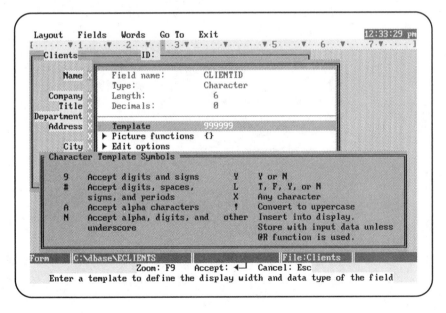

Fig. 6.19. *A less crowded form, screen 3.*

6

Fig. 6.20. *Using a template for CLIENT ID.*

In figure 6.20, 999999 was used as the template for Client ID. Notice the list of valid template characters at the bottom of the menu.

Table 6.4 lists dBASE IV template functions, including examples of how each template is used.

Table 6.4. dBASE IV Template Functions

Character Template	Description	Example
9	Accepts only digits and signs (+,–). Does not accept commas or decimal point.	ZIP code, phone
#	Accepts digits, space, period, or signs (+,–)	Any positive or negative number, with or without decimal places
A	Alphabetic characters only	First name, last name
N	Alpha or numeric but no spaces or punctuation	Parts serial number (EA76521)
Y	Accepts Y or N. Converts *y* or *n* to uppercase.	To use text field as logical field.
L	Accepts T, F, Y, N	To use text field as logical field.
X	Any character	Any character
!	Converts alphabetic characters to uppercase	*abc* to ABC
.	Position of decimal for numeric field	Dollar amount
,	Position of comma for numeric field	Dollar amount
*	Shows leading zeros as * for numeric field	$365.00 becomes ***365.00 (useful for check writing)
$	Shows leading zeros as $ for numeric field	similar to *
Other	Other symbols included literally	Hyphens for Social Security number 123-45-6789

Picture Functions

dBASE provides picture functions that offer an additional level of control over how fields are displayed. You can use picture functions to select from a number of options for displaying numeric fields in the form, as well as convenient conversions for text fields. You can use picture functions by themselves or with template functions. Table 6.5 lists the dBASE IV picture functions.

Table 6.5. dBASE IV Picture Functions

Picture Function	Numeric Fields	Input	Displayed As
C	Display CR after a positive number	500.00	500.00 CR
X	Display DB after a negative number	−50.00	50.00 DB
(	Enclose negative numbers in parenthesis	−50.00	(50.00)
L	Display a number with leading zeros	7	000007
Z	Display blanks if the value is zero	0	
$	Display a currency symbol before a number	78.00	$78.00
^	Display a number in exponential format	12,000	1.2E4
T	Remove all leading and trailing blanks	N/A	
J	Right align data in the template width	10	10
I	Center the data within the template	10	10

Picture Function	Text Fields	Explanation
A	Accept only alphabetic input	No spaces, punctuation or numbers accepted
!	Convert all letters to uppercase	FoxPro becomes FOXPRO
R	Literal characters not stored in database	(212)555-1212 stored as 2125551212
S	Horizontal scrolling within the template	Allows scrolling in form template shorter than length of field
M	Multiple choice	Allows you to define list of valid choices for field

6

Picture functions are often more convenient than templates, because they do more with fewer keystrokes. Setup is quicker, for example, when you use the picture option to convert all letters to uppercase rather than create a template of all exclamation mark symbols. The option not to store these formatting characters (also called literals) also saves space by not storing characters that are not significant for search or sorting. You need not enter or store parentheses and dashes in phone numbers or dashes in Social Security numbers, for example, because all phone numbers and Social Security numbers are formatted identically. The only purpose for the literal characters is to make the display easier to read.

Choose picture options carefully to avoid unintended results. If, for example, you program a city name field with the Accepting Only Alphabetic Input picture option, users cannot enter names containing spaces (such as New York). Make field entry as restrictive as you need to, but not too restrictive, and always check your validation techniques with sample data.

Choice Fields

You may want to restrict some fields to a limited number of possible values. You can accomplish this by creating choice fields. You may be working on a sales application, for instance, that contains a field for method of payment. Rather than use a text field in which the operator can enter any character, you can set up a one-character choice field limited to the options shown in the following table.

Character	Method of Payment
$	Cash
C	Check
A	American Express
V	VISA
M	MasterCard

As mentioned in Chapter 5, some DBMS, such as DataEase, directly support a choice field. The database designer enters the choices while defining the field. Although you can choose entire words or phrases in choice fields, only the choice number is stored in the data table.

dBASE does not offer a choice field per se, but you can use the picture function to check entries against a list of valid characters. The Contacts form shown in figure 6.21 illustrates this technique. You want to use the Contacts form to categorize each client contact by type—phone, mail, visit, or other. Create a one-character field for contact type and designate these types by single characters (to keep choice fields as short as possible). Use the picture function to enter the list of acceptable values, as shown in figure 6.21.

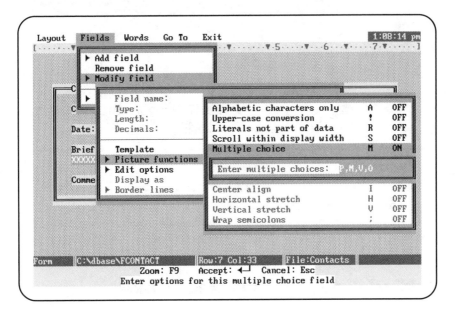

Fig. 6.21. *A choice field for contact type.*

After reaching this field, the user can scroll through the choices by using the space bar. The Contact field will not accept any character other than P, M, V or O.

The final step in designing your choice fields is to let the user know which fields to use. You can accomplish this by adding background text adjacent to the field to list the choices. Alternatively, you can put this information in the MESSAGE field of the template. Text in the MESSAGE area is displayed when the cursor is in a particular field. You also can use background text to explain how to use a choice field, as shown in figure 6.22.

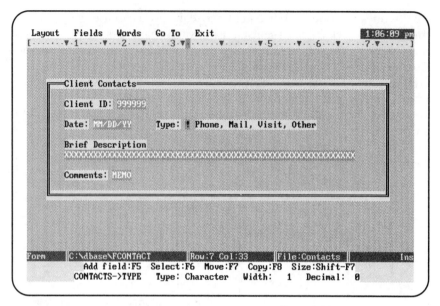

Fig. 6.22. *Choice field background text.*

In addition to maintaining data integrity, choice fields have the benefit of being quicker to enter than text fields. A skilled operator can make fast work of a screen filled with one-letter choices.

Adding Virtual (Calculated) Fields

You often want to display a field that is calculated or looked up from some other part of the database, but don't want to store the field in the table you are currently using. Suppose that you are working with a Pay Increases table that stores employee promotions and salary increases. You do not want to reenter employee names and addresses in this table, because that information, along with employee Social Security numbers, is already stored in the Personnel table. You can use Social Security numbers to relate the Pay Increases table to the Personnel Table. The Pay Increases table might look like the example in table 6.6.

Table 6.6. Pay Increases Table

SSN	Date	Title	Old Salary	New Salary
222-33-4456	09/12/89	Supervisor	20,000	22,000
123-45-6789	09/12/89	Deputy Chief	44,000	48,400
321-54-9876	03/15/90	Comptroller	37,999	42,800
222-33-4456	03/15/90	Acct. Mgr.	31,900	36,000
765-08-6221	09/13/90	Sales Rep.	40,000	41,000
617-99-0022	09/13/90	Director	48,000	51,000

Although you should not store the employee name in this table (because it is redundant and would have to be updated if it were changed elsewhere), you do want to see the employee name when you view the employee's salary history. You can satisfy both needs by creating a lookup field on the data entry form that displays the name field from the Personnel table but does not store it in the Pay Increases table. A lookup field uses a relationship between two tables to "look up" a value from another table.

Fields that are displayed but not stored are called *virtual fields* (as opposed to *real fields*), because they only appear to exist in the table. The mechanics for creating virtual fields vary from one DBMS to the next.

In some DBMS, such as DataEase, you can create a virtual field as easily as any other field. You enter a derivation formula `lookup personnel lastname`, for example) and specify that the field is virtual.

In dBASE, you can create virtual fields in forms and in views (also known as *queries* in dBASE). Figure 6.23 shows a table for tracking all contacts with clients. The contacts file records the client ID, date, type, and description of each contact. In this case, a contact may refer to a phone call, letter, meeting, or other interaction with a client.

To add the virtual field, edit the data-entry form. Place your cursor at the location of the new field and press Alt-F to open the fields menu; or press F10 to activate the top menus and scroll to field option. Highlight the Add Field option and press Enter (see fig. 6.24). Choose <create> from the Add field menu and then enter a name and optional description for the field. Enter the formula for calculating the field in the Expression option. You can use any dBASE expression to derive the field. As with other fields on the form, you can use templates and picture functions with a derived field (see fig. 6.25).

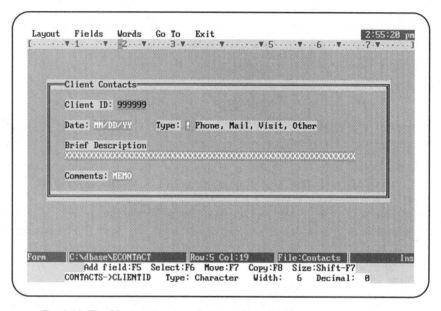

Fig. 6.23. *The Client contact form (without virtual fields).*

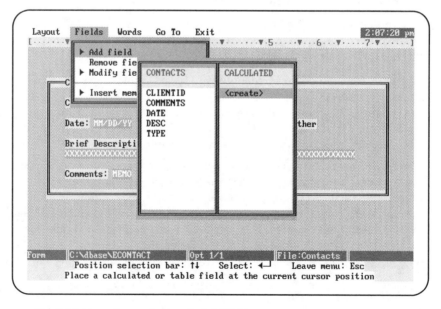

Fig. 6.24. *Menus for creating a calculated field.*

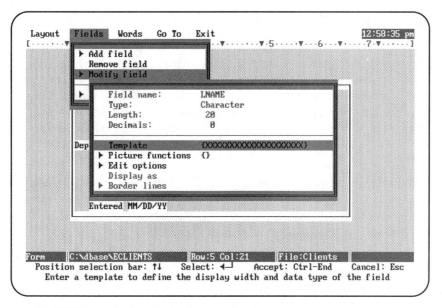

Fig. 6.25. A new field menu showing formula, picture, and template.

In many cases, the meaning of a virtual field is obvious and a field label is unnecessary. If the meaning is unclear, be sure to add background text to the form to explain the field.

Adding Field Help

Field help is text displayed during record entry when a user presses the help key. With many DBMS, you can define special help associated with each field and file. Use consistent grammar in all help messages. Decide at the outset whether you will use complete sentences (This field contains the aircraft serial number), short phrases (aircraft serial number) or commands to the user (Enter aircraft serial number here). When writing help messages, try to imagine why the user may ask for help on a particular screen. If necessary, offer the option of additional help, or provide an example of a valid entry.

Testing the Form

After you build the form, test it by entering a few sample records. Make sure that the field lengths accommodate your data, and that the flow of the form and field colors are pleasing. Watch for any error messages that appear during record entry.

Using a Style Guide

If you plan to create more than one application, set standards and conventions in the beginning and use them in the design of all applications. Using consistent field names, types, lengths, form layouts, border styles, and other features, makes each new application easier to build than the last. You save time by using standards because you don't have to make the same stylistic decisions each time you create a form. You even can borrow tables and forms from old applications to get a head start on a new project.

Standards are only worthwhile if you write them down. A good database style guide has sections devoted to naming all database elements, as well as sections recording the appearance of all screens. The following is a sample table of contents for a database style guide:

I. Tables
   Naming conventions
   Use of capitalization
II. Fields
   Naming conventions
   Use of capitalization
III. Forms
   Naming conventions
   Field color
   Background text format
   Error message list
IV. Reports
   Data-entry screens (same as forms)
   Format conventions
   Error message list
V. Menus
   Menu type (bar, pop-up, pull-down, full screen)
   Function naming conventions
   Use of capitalization
   Option color

Write down your style preferences for all the areas listed in the preceding style guide. Table 6.7 summarizes important form style issues.

Table 6.7. Form Style Issues

Do	Don't
Use colors to differentiate field types	Create psychedelic record-entry forms
Organize fields logically in rows and columns	Waste space with only one field per line, unless the table is quite short
Standardize capitalization throughout	Use cryptic field labels
Standardize data-entry forms for reports	Create reports without data-entry forms
Use boxes to make forms more readable	Use labels for obvious fields
Use the data dictionary	Vary type or length of a field from one form to another
Record your style decisions	Change standard function key assignments without good reason

If you adopt a personal or corporate style, your applications will stand out from the crowd and will be easier to use and maintain. The results are greater productivity for you as a database designer and applications that showcase your development skills. Standards are essential when more than one developer contributes to an application or when you design a database for distribution to others. Commercial applications are more successfully marketed and supported if they conform to standards.

When you write a style guide, you capture and institutionalize all that you learned while developing applications. You can use a style guide to train new developers and to evaluate design efforts. Like all planning activities, database style consistency pays off greatly in the long run.

Summary

Forms are the windows into your database world. They provide you with more control over the way data appears than is available in tables. With forms, you can change the order of fields, the contents of field labels, and screen colors.

6

Lay out fields in a logical order for efficient data entry. Be sure to allow adequate space ("white space") between screen elements so that the layout is not busy or confusing to the user. Special graphic elements such as lines or boxes can make the form easier to read.

Above all, make your forms consistent. Use the same field label for a field wherever it occurs in your application. If you use colors to highlight fields, be consistent about the meaning of colors from one screen to another. Use the same abbreviations or words throughout the application.

Users spend more time looking at data-entry forms than any other part of the database, so you should devote serious attention to making forms as pleasant as possible. You will be judged by the quality of your forms more than any other element of your application. Most users cannot appreciate fancy programs and do not see them anyway, but they all have opinions about the way forms should look. If you follow the guidelines described in this chapter, you can make your work and your applications easier and more productive.

Using Views

We don't live in a world of reality, we live in a world of perceptions.

J. Gerald Simmons

Although you may need to use many files for efficient storage and processing, the most efficient file structure may be too fragmentary for users to understand easily. For instance, for most efficient operation, you store customer information, invoice information, and inventory information in separate tables. Users, however, are accustomed to seeing information from all three tables combined, as the information appears on a paper invoice.

As a result, any single table may be difficult to understand by itself; for example, invoices with no customer or inventory description may be confusing. Furthermore, entering an invoice in three separate tables is awkward.

Most DBMS provide techniques for displaying information from multiple tables on one screen. This chapter discusses the use of *views*—special forms or data-entry screens that display selected fields from one or more tables or database files—to make your application even easier to use. (See fig. 7.1 for a sample view, which shows information from the Trips table and from the Trip Legs table.)

As a database designer, you should examine the users' data-entry forms to determine the best means for viewing data. Users often want to view repetitive or redundant information, even though you do not want to store the information more than once.

When editing a class registration file, for instance, users may want to see a student's name. You, however, have used the Social Security number (rather than the name) as the field linking students to class registration records. Perhaps users want to view data from more than one file at a time. A user of a personnel application, for example, may want to see records of an employee's promotions, pay raises, vacations, and disciplinary actions on one form, even though this information is stored in multiple tables in the database.

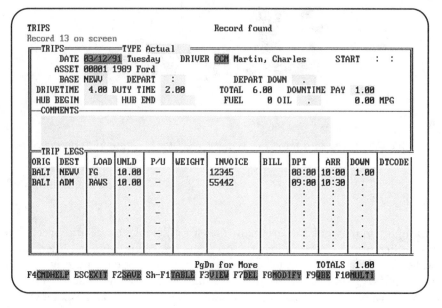

Fig. 7.1. *A sample view.*

You can use views to display selected rows or columns from a table and thereby provide security by denying unauthorized access to certain fields or records. You can grant supervisors access to the personnel files of their employees, for example, but not to the files of employees in other departments. You can create several views with different filter conditions so that each user sees only the appropriate records.

You also can create special views of data to make data-entry forms resemble the paper forms used to gather information. As you learned from the analysis process discussed in Chapter 2, these paper forms do not necessarily reflect the optimal, normalized storage structure of the database.

Using Single-Table Views

You can use a view based on one table to restrict the number of fields that the user may access. This technique streamlines data entry and on-screen queries because only the fields that a particular user needs appear on-screen.

Suppose that a company uses telemarketing to identify potential customers. For inbound telemarketing (calls from prospects to the company), you can arrange the fields in the order in which the user enters them (name, company, address, phone, screening questions). For outbound telemarketing (the company calling sales prospects), you can rearrange the fields to highlight the telephone number at the top of the screen. The original screening questions can be replaced by follow-up questions.

I used single-table views for a shipping and receiving operation. For each scheduled truckload, a record existed to detail the truck, driver, and load. The security guard at the gate, however, needed to know only the vehicle number and anticipated arrival or departure time for each truck. Rather than display all the fields from the entire table on a form, I created for the guard a view showing only the pertinent information. The view simplifies the operation by removing extraneous fields.

Restricting access to certain fields is beneficial for system security. A medical or personnel file, for example, may contain confidential information. A view gives users access only to the fields they need.

Using Multitable Views

You can use a view to access from the same screen records in two or more database files. Some DBMS call this feature a *subform,* because the main record (or *parent record*) has one or more subrecords (or *children*) in another, related table. You can use a subform to enter invoices and line items into their respective tables (see fig. 7.2).

Subforms are useful particularly for adding and viewing data when a one-to-many relationship exists between two forms. Unlike unnormalized structures, which have fields on the main form for several lines of information, subforms enable a user to enter an infinite number of records in the related file.

The following sections offer examples of multiforms that combine tables for clients and contacts. To use multiforms yourself, however, you first must create the tables. See Chapter 5 for detailed instructions on creating tables.

Each DBMS vendor has a slightly different approach to multitable views. DataEase, for example provides two principal ways to integrate fields from multiple forms: by using a virtual field or by using subforms. A *virtual field*, which displays a value from another file, is for display purposes only and is not stored in the file. Each time you view a record, the virtual field is looked up anew.

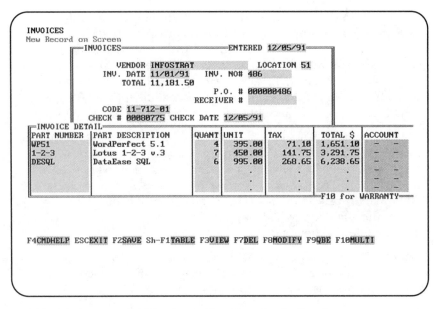

Fig. 7.2. *A parent record (Invoices) with subform (Invoice Detail).*

Although you can create multitable views in most DBMS, the methods used to create them may be different. dBASE provides several techniques for creating multitable views. The simplest approach is to use the Command Center to create a Query, as described in the following steps:

1. From the Main menu, go to the Queries column and select <create> to start a new view.

2. Select the tables that you want to use in the view (two tables in this example, but you can use three or more at a time).

3. Press F10 to activate the Layout menu and select Add file to query, as shown in figure 7.3.

4. Choose the CLIENTS file. The program displays the file as a table at the top of the screen.

5. Repeat steps 1 through 4 to add the second file, CONTACTS.

6. To select the fields to include in the view, position the cursor on the field you need (CLIENTID) and then press F5. An arrow appears next to the field label to show that the field has been selected.

    To select all the fields, press F5 at the beginning of the table. You then may remove the fields you do not want to include, one at a time. In this example, all fields are chosen except CLIENTID in Contacts, which would be redundant (see fig. 7.4).

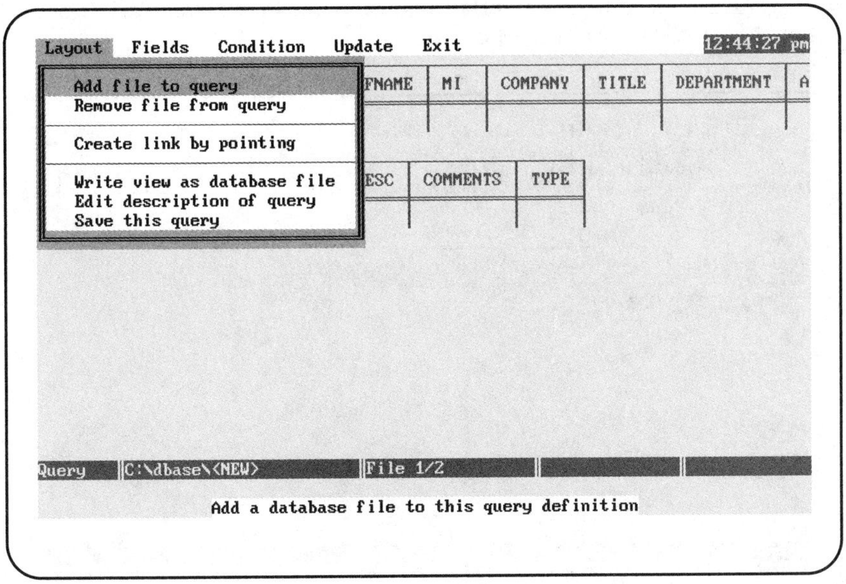

Fig. 7.3. The pull-down menu to add a file to a query in dBASE.

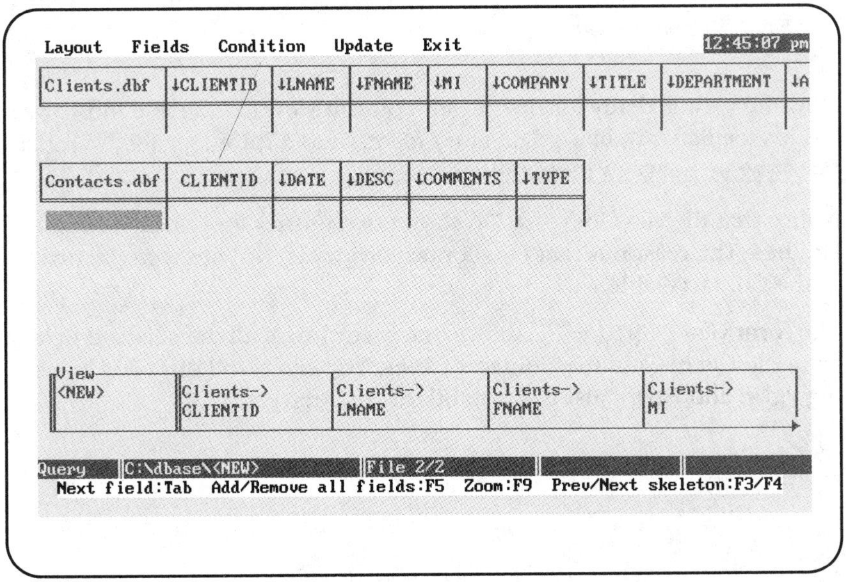

Fig. 7.4. Fields selected with F5.

Next, you link the two tables with a common field. In this case, the tables are related by the client number. Place the cursor in the CLIENTID field of Clients and type *LINK1*. Repeat for the Contacts table (see fig. 7.5). If you are using more than one relationship, you can designate additional link fields (LINK2, LINK3, and so on).

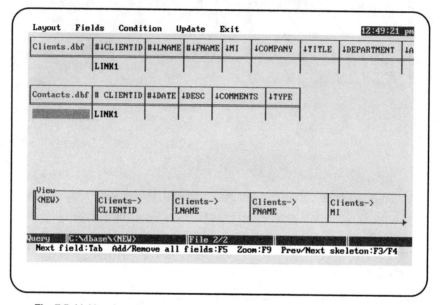

Fig. 7.5. Linking the tables.

Now the view is ready for operation. You can view it as a table in Browse Mode (see fig. 7.6), like a data-entry form, or as a form (see fig. 7.7). Use F2 to toggle between these modes.

Notice that the view in figure 7.6 shows two entries for Oliver Wendell Holmes. The reason is that two contacts with Mr. Holmes were recorded in the Contacts table.

The form view in figure 7.7 shows one record with all the selected fields from the Clients and the Contacts tables. You can scroll this view by using PgUp and PgDn, just like a standard data-entry form.

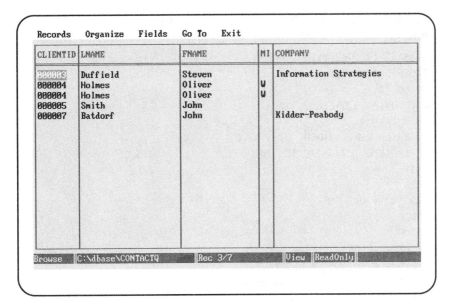

Fig. 7.6. *The results of a multitable query in table view.*

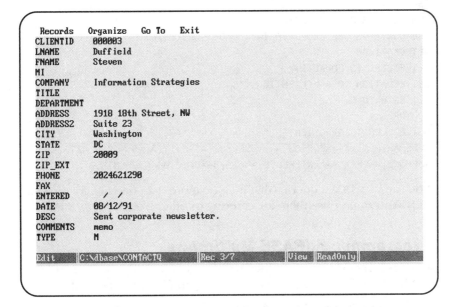

Fig. 7.7. *The results of a multitable query in form view.*

7

The following code is the dBASE code generated for the preceding query:

```
* dBASE IV .QBE file
CLOSE DATABASES
SELECT 2
USE CONTACTS.DBF
QBE__CT = 1
DO WHILE LEN(TAG(QBE__CT)) <> 0
IF TAG(QBE__CT) = "CLIENTID"
EXIT
ELSE
QBE__CT = QBE__CT+1
ENDIF
ENDDO
IF LEN(TAG(QBE__CT)) = 0
USE CONTACTS.DBF EXCLUSIVE
INDEX ON CLIENTID TAG CLIENTID
ENDIF
RELEASE QBE__CT
CLOSE DATABASES
SELECT 1
USE CLIENTS.DBF NOUPDATE
USE CONTACTS.DBF NOUPDATE IN 2 ORDER CLIENTID
SET EXACT ON
SET FILTER TO FOUND(2)
SET RELATION TO A->CLIENTID INTO B
SET SKIP TO B
GO TOP
SET FIELDS TO A->CLIENTID,A->LNAME,A->FNAME,A->MI,A->COMPANY,A->TITLE,A;
->DEPARTMENT,A->ADDRESS,A->ADDRESS2,A->CITY,A->STATE,A->ZIP,A->ZIP_EXT,A;
->PHONE,A->FAX,A->ENTERED,B->DATE,B->DESC,B->COMMENTS,B->TYPE
```

You can use dBASE queries that include more than one file, for viewing only. You cannot use them for entering or editing data.

Programming dBASE Multiforms

Besides creating views with the Query generator in the Command Center in dBASE, you can integrate views directly in your program code.

You can use the template language to create a routine for multiple-field editing with little programming. An example of such a program, INVOICES2.PRG, is included in the dBASE IV Developer's Edition sample files.

Although the template language makes this program easier to generate, using the language is definitely not for the faint of heart. To test the program, you need a thorough knowledge of all the dBASE commands used. Because you can damage the integrity of your data in many ways when you use a program such as this one, let caution be your guide.

The following program, CONTACTQ.PRG, is an example of a dBASE program that enables data entry into the Clients and Contacts tables from the same screen. Figure 7.8 shows the screen created by this sample program.

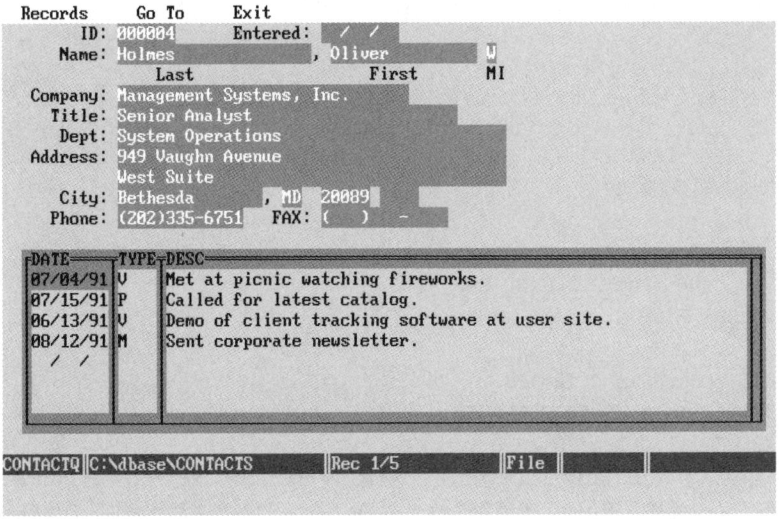

Fig. 7.8. *A sample dBASE multiform.*

```
*****************************************************************************
*-- Name....: CONTACTQ.PRG
*-- Date....: 7-16-91
*-- Version.: dBASE IV, Format 1.0
*-- Notes...: Format files use "" as delimiters!
*****************************************************************************


CLEAR WIND
CLOSE DATABASE
SAVE SCREEN TO Contactq
CLEAR
```

continues

Continued

```
DEFINE WINDOW Pause FROM 15,00 TO 19,79 DOUBLE
DEFINE WINDOW Cont_hlp FROM 3,00 TO 21,79 DOUBLE
ON ERROR DO Pause WITH "Line number in program "+Program()+": "+LTRIM(STR(LINE()))


IF EOF()
  SKIP -1
ENDIF


IF SET("TALK")="ON"
   SET TALK OFF
   lc_talk = "ON"
ELSE
   lc_talk = "OFF"
ENDIF
lc_escape = SET("ESCAPE")
lc_cursor = SET("CURSOR")
SET CURSOR OFF


*-- Imported code from C:\DBASE\CONTACTQ.QBE
* DBASE IV .QBE FILE 8
SELECT 1
USE CONTACTS.DBF ORDER CLIENTID
USE CLIENTS.DBF IN 2 ORDER CLIENTID
SET RELATION TO A->CLIENTID INTO B
SET FIELDS TO A->CLIENTID,A->LNAME,A->FNAME,A->MI,A->COMPANY,A->TITLE,A;
->DEPARTMENT,A->ADDRESS,A->ADDRESS2,A->CITY,A->STATE,A->ZIP,A->ZIP_EXT,A;
->PHONE,A->FAX,A->ENTERED,B->DATE,B->DESC,B->COMMENTS,B->TYPE
*----------------------------------------------------------------------------
GO TOP


lc_status = SET("STATUS")
*-- SET STATUS was ON when you went into the Forms Designer.
IF lc_status = "OFF"
   SET STATUS ON
ENDIF


gc_messg = "F9:Line items ¦ PgDn:Next ¦ PgUp:Previous ¦ Ctrl-PgDn:Bottom ¦ Ctrl-PgUp:Top


DEFINE WINDOW Table FROM 12,2 TO 20,78
```

```
ON KEY LABEL F1 DO Cont_hlp
ON KEY LABEL F9  KEYBOARD CHR(23)+"L" && Send Ctrl-W + L for lineitem
ON KEY LABEL F10 KEYBOARD CHR(23)+"M" && SEND CTRL-W + M FOR MENU

DO Defnmenu

gc_mdx = MDX(1)
gc_alias = ALIAS()

*-- Set up lineitem (BROWSE) workarea-----------------------------------------

gn_sele = IIF(SELE()=10, SELE()-1, SELE())
SELE (gn_sele)
USE CONTACTS ORDER TAG CLIENTID
SET FIELDS TO CLIENTID, DATE,TYPE,DESC,COMMENTS
SET CARRY TO CONTACTS->CLIENTID


*----------------------------------------------------------------------------

SELE &gc_alias.
gn_gorec = 0                       && Var for goto record option
gc_search = SPACE(200)             && Var for forward and backward search
gc_seek = SPACE( LEN( CLIENTID))   && Var for seeking records
gl_newrec = .f.                    && Var for appended record
gl_chgrec = .t.                    && Var for testing if record position changed
gl_extloop = .f.
gl_rollbck = .f.
@ 23,0
@ 23,CENTER(gc_messg,80) SAY gc_messg

DO WHILE .NOT. gl_extloop
   gn_recno = RECNO()
   gl_lineitm = .T.
   BEGIN TRANSACTION

   DO WHILE gl_lineitm
      IF gl_chgrec
         *-- Paint Say's & Get's on screen
         DO Show_get
      ENDIF

      *-- Show matching Browse Table data
```

continues

Continued

```
DO Showbrow
*-- Back to suddo edit

*-- Edit Get's
DO Edit_get

SET CURSOR ON
READ
SET CURSOR OFF

gn_inkey = INKEY()
gn_readkey = READKEY()
gc_readvar = VARREAD()
gl_lineitm = .F.

ACTIVATE SCREEN
DO CASE
    CASE gn_inkey = 76
        *-- KEYBOARDed IN "L"
        DO Lineitem
        gl_lineitm = .T.
  CASE gn_inkey = 77
    *-- KEYBOARDed IN "M"
    ACTIVATE MENU Editmenu
  CASE gn_readkey = 6 .OR. gn_readkey = 262 .OR. gn_readkey = 260 ;
      .OR. gn_readkey = 4
    *--  Pgup or Up arrow
    IF .NOT. BOF()
      SKIP -1
    ENDIF
  CASE gn_readkey = 7 .OR. gn_readkey = 263 .OR. gn_readkey = 5 ;
      .OR. gn_readkey = 261
    *-- PgDn or Dwn arrow
    SKIP
    IF EOF() .AND. .NOT. gl_newrec
        CLEAR GETS
        SET DELI OFF
        @ 23,0
      @ 23,25 SAY "===> Add new records (Y/N)?" GET gl_newrec PICT "Y"
      READ
      SET DELI ON
      CLEAR GETS
```

```
                 @ 23,0
                 @ 23,CENTER( gc_messg, 80) SAY gc_messg
              ENDIF
              IF gl_newrec
                 DO Recappnd
              ELSE
                 IF EOF()
                    SKIP -1
                 ENDIF
              ENDIF
           CASE gn_readkey = 34 .OR. gn_readkey = 290
              *-- Ctrl-PgUp
              GO TOP
           CASE gn_readkey = 35 .OR. gn_readkey = 291
              *-- Ctrl-PgDn
              GO BOTTOM
           CASE gn_readkey = 12   .or. gn_readkey = 270
              *-- Esc
              gl_extloop = .T.
              EXIT
        ENDCASE
        *
        gl_chgrec = IIF(gn_recno = RECNO(), .F., .T.)  && See if record # changed
        *
        IF gl_rollbck                && If user picked ROLLBACK option from menu
           gl_rollbck = .F.          && Reset rollback variable
           ROLLBACK
        ENDIF
     ENDDO
     *
     END TRANSACTION
     *
     IF .NOT. ROLLBACK()
        DO Pause WITH "Undo not successful"
        ACTIVATE SCREEN
     ENDIF
     DO Chkdele
  ENDDO

*-- Clean-up exit
*-- SET STATUS was ON when you went into the Forms Designer.
IF lc_status = "OFF"  && Entered form with status off
   SET STATUS OFF     && Turn STATUS "OFF" on the way out
ENDIF
```

continues

Continued

```
SET CURSOR &lc_cursor.
SET TALK &lc_talk.

ON KEY
ON ERROR

SELE 1
CLOSE DATABASE

RELEASE MENU Editmenu
RELEASE POPUPS records, go_to, exit
RELEASE WINDOWS table,pause,seek,search,bsearch,Cont_hlp
RESTORE SCREEN FROM contactq
RELEASE lc_talk,lc_fields,lc_status,lc_escape
RELEASE SCREEN contactq
RETURN

PROCEDURE Show_get
   @ 1,8 SAY "ID:"
   @ 1,12 GET Clients->Clientid PICTURE "XXXXXX"
   @ 1,24 SAY "Entered:"
   @ 1,33 GET Clients->Entered
   @ 2,6 SAY "Name:"
   @ 2,12 GET Clients->Lname PICTURE "XXXXXXXXXXXXXXXXXXXX"
   @ 2,32 SAY ","
   @ 2,34 GET Clients->Fname PICTURE "XXXXXXXXXXXXXX"
   @ 2,50 GET Clients->Mi PICTURE "X"
   @ 3,16 SAY "Last"
   @ 3,38 SAY "First"
   @ 3,50 SAY "MI"
   @ 4,3 SAY "Company:"
   @ 4,12 GET Clients->Company PICTURE "XXXXXXXXXXXXXXXXXXXXXXXXXXXXXX"
   @ 5,5 SAY "Title:"
   @ 5,12 GET Clients->Title PICTURE "XXXXXXXXXXXXXXXXXXXXXXXXXXXXXXXXXXXX"
   @ 6,6 SAY "Dept:"
   @ 6,12 GET Clients->Department PICTURE "XXXXXXXXXXXXXXXXXXXXXXXXXXXXXXXXXXXXXXXX"
   @ 7,3 SAY "Address:"
   @ 7,12 GET Clients->Address PICTURE "XXXXXXXXXXXXXXXXXXXXXXXXXXXXXXXXXXXXXXXXXXX"
   @ 8,12 GET Clients->Address2 PICTURE "XXXXXXXXXXXXXXXXXXXXXXXXXXXXXXXXXXXXXXXXXXX"
   @ 9,6 SAY "City:"
   @ 9,12 GET Clients->City PICTURE "XXXXXXXXXXXXXX"
   @ 9,27 SAY ","
```

```
      @ 9,29 GET Clients->State PICTURE "XX"
      @ 9,33 GET Clients->Zip PICTURE "XXXXX"
      @ 9,39 GET Clients->Zip_ext PICTURE "XXXX"
      @ 10,5 SAY "Phone:"
      @ 10,12 GET Clients->Phone PICTURE "@R (999)999-9999"
      @ 10,28 SAY "FAX:"
      @ 10,33 GET Clients->Fax PICTURE "@R (999)999-9999"
      CLEAR GETS
RETURN

PROCEDURE Edit_get
      @ 1,12 GET Clients->Clientid PICTURE "XXXXXX"
      @ 1,33 GET Clients->Entered
      @ 2,12 GET Clients->Lname PICTURE "XXXXXXXXXXXXXXXXXXXX"
      @ 2,34 GET Clients->Fname PICTURE "XXXXXXXXXXXXXX"
      @ 2,50 GET Clients->Mi PICTURE "X"
      @ 4,12 GET Clients->Company PICTURE "XXXXXXXXXXXXXXXXXXXXXXXXXXXXXX"
      @ 5,12 GET Clients->Title PICTURE "XXXXXXXXXXXXXXXXXXXXXXXXXXXXXXXXXXX"
      @ 6,12 GET Clients->Department PICTURE "XXXXXXXXXXXXXXXXXXXXXXXXXXXXXXXXXXXXXXXX"
      @ 7,12 GET Clients->Address PICTURE "XXXXXXXXXXXXXXXXXXXXXXXXXXXXXXXXXXXXXXXX"
      @ 8,12 GET Clients->Address2 PICTURE "XXXXXXXXXXXXXXXXXXXXXXXXXXXXXXXXXXXXXXXX"
      @ 9,12 GET Clients->City PICTURE "XXXXXXXXXXXXXXX"
      @ 9,29 GET Clients->State PICTURE "XX"
      @ 9,33 GET Clients->Zip PICTURE "XXXXX"
      @ 9,39 GET Clients->Zip_ext PICTURE "XXXX"
      @ 10,12 GET Clients->Phone PICTURE "@R (999)999-9999"
      @ 10,33 GET Clients->Fax PICTURE "@R (999)999-9999"
RETURN

PROCEDURE Showbrow
      SELE CONTACTS
      SET FILTER TO
      SEEK &GC_ALIAS->CLIENTID
      IF EOF()
         APPEND BLANK
         REPLACE CONTACTS->CLIENTID WITH &GC_ALIAS.->CLIENTID
      ENDIF
      SET FILTER TO &GC_ALIAS.->CLIENTID = CONTACTS->CLIENTID
      GO TOP
      KEYBOARD CHR(27)
      DO Browseit
      SELE &gc_alias.
      ACTIVATE SCREEN
RETURN
```

7

continues

Continued

```
PROCEDURE Lineitem
   ln_key = INKEY()
   DO Keykill
   SELE CONTACTS
   APPEND BLANK
   REPLACE CONTACTS->CLIENTID WITH &GC_ALIAS.->CLIENTID
   GO TOP
   DO Browseit
   ACTIVATE SCREEN
   DO Keyset
   *-----------------------------------------------------------------------
   *-- Could put code here to SUM the order balance and replace in a total field
   *-- Example:
   *-- SUM ALL extended TO m->extended
   *-- REPLACE &gc_alias.->Total_bill WITH m->extended
   *-----------------------------------------------------------------------
   SELE &gc_alias.
RETURN

PROCEDURE Browseit
SET CURSOR ON
BROWSE;
   FIELDS DATE,TYPE,DESC,COMMENTS,CONTACTS->CLIENTID /R;
   WINDOW table COMPRESS NOMENU NOCLEAR
SET CURSOR OFF
RETURN

PROCEDURE Keyset
   ON KEY LABEL F1 DO Cont_hlp
   ON KEY LABEL F9  KEYBOARD CHR(23)+"L"
   ON KEY LABEL F10 KEYBOARD CHR(23)+"M"
RETURN

PROCEDURE Keykill
   ON KEY LABEL F1 DO Nothing
   ON KEY LABEL F9 DO Nothing
   ON KEY LABEL F10 DO Nothing
RETURN

PROCEDURE Nothing
   ln_key=INKEY()
RETURN
```

```
PROCEDURE Chkdele
   IF DELETED()
      DEFINE BAR 4 OF records PROMPT "   Clear deletion mark";
      MESSAGE "Mark/unmark this record for deletion"
   ELSE
      DEFINE BAR 4 OF records PROMPT "   Mark record for deletion";
      MESSAGE "Mark/unmark this record for deletion"
   ENDIF
RETURN


PROCEDURE Recappnd
   *-------------------------------------------------------------------
   *-- Could put code here to advance the invoice number, etc.
   GO BOTT
   morder = ORDER_ID
   APPEND BLANK
   REPLACE order_id WITH SUBSTR(morder,1,3) + LTRIM(STR(VAL(SUBSTR(morder,4))+1))
   *-------------------------------------------------------------------
RETURN


*-- The following procedures handle the selections of the edit menu --------
PROCEDURE Get_recs
   *-- Get the user selection & store BAR into variable
   gn_pick = BAR()  && Variable for bar testing
   DO CASE
      CASE gn_pick = 1
         *-- Prepare variable for rollback operation on return
         gl_rollbck = .T.
      CASE gn_pick = 3
          DO Recappnd
      CASE gn_pick = 4
         *-- Delete/recall record
         IF DELETE()
            RECALL
            SELE CONTACTS
            RECALL ALL
         ELSE
            DELETE
            SELE CONTACTS
            DELETE ALL
         ENDIF
         SELE (gc_alias)
      CASE gn_pick = 5
         *-- Blank record
```

continues

Continued

```
    ENDCASE
    DO Chkdele
    DEACTIVATE MENU
RETURN

PROCEDURE Get_goto
    *-- Get the user selection & store BAR into variable
    gn_pick = BAR()  && Variable for bar testing
    mpict = REPLICATE("9", LEN( LTRIM( STR( RECCOUNT()))))
    gc_search = gc_search + SPACE( 200 - LEN(gc_search))
    gc_seek = gc_seek + SPACE(LEN( CLIENTID) - LEN(gc_seek))
    DO CASE
       CASE gn_pick = 1
          *-- Go to top of file
          GO TOP
       CASE gn_pick = 2
          *-- Go to bottom of file
          GO BOTTOM
       CASE gn_pick = 3
          *-- Go to a specfic record
          @ 4,39 GET gn_gorec RANGE 1, RECCOUNT() PICTURE mpict
          READ
          gn_gorec = IIF( gn_gorec=0, RECNO(), gn_gorec)
          GO gn_gorec
        CASE gn_pick = 4
          *-- Skip a certain number of records
          skiprec = IIF( RECCOUNT() > 9, 10, 5)
          SET DELI OFF
          @ 5,39 GET skiprec PICTURE mpict
          READ
          SET DELI ON
          SKIP skiprec
          IF EOF()
            SKIP -1
          ENDIF
        CASE gn_pick = 6
          ACTIVATE WINDOW seek
          *-- Seek on key field
          IF "" = ORDER()
             tempmdx = TAG(1)
             SET ORDER TO TAG &tempmdx.
          ENDIF
          @ 0,1 SAY "Enter search string for"
```

```
    @ 1,1 SAY TAG(1)+":" GET gc_seek PICT "@S20";
      MESSAGE "Cancel: Esc";
      VALID LEN( TRIM( gc_seek)) > 0;
      ERROR "No search condition entered"
    READ
    IF READKEY() <> 12
       gc_seek = LTRIM( TRIM(gc_seek))
       mrec = RECNO()
       SEEK gc_seek
       IF .NOT. FOUND()
          GO mrec
       ENDIF
    ENDIF
    DEACTIVATE WINDOW seek
    ACTIVATE SCREEN
CASE gn_pick = 7
    *-- Forward search
    ACTIVATE WINDOW search
    @ 0,1 SAY "Enter search string:" GET gc_search PICT "@S21";
      MESSAGE "Cancel: Esc";
      VALID LEN( TRIM( gc_search)) > 0;
      ERROR "No search condition entered"
    READ
    DEACTIVATE WINDOW search
    ACTIVATE SCREEN
    IF READKEY() <> 12
       gc_search = LTRIM( RTRIM( gc_search))
       mrec = RECNO()
       LOCATE REST FOR &gc_search.
       IF .NOT. FOUND()
          GO mrec
       ENDIF
    ENDIF
CASE gn_pick = 8
    *-- Backward search
    ACTIVATE WINDOW bsearch
    @ 0,1 SAY "Enter search string:" GET gc_search PICT "@S21";
      MESSAGE "Cancel: Esc";
      VALID len(trim(gc_search)) > 0;
      ERROR "No search condition entered"
    READ
    DEACTIVATE WINDOW bsearch
    ACTIVATE SCREEN
    IF READKEY() <> 12
```

7

continues

Continued

```
                gc_search = LTRIM( RTRIM( gc_search))
                mrec = RECNO()
                DO WHILE .NOT. (BOF() .OR. &gc_search.)
                   SKIP -1
                ENDDO
                IF BOF()
                   GO mrec
                ENDIF
            ENDIF
      ENDCASE
      DEACTIVATE MENU
RETURN


PROCEDURE Get_exit
     CLEAR GETS
     *-- Prepare variable to exit loop
     gl_extloop = .T.
     DEACTIVATE MENU
RETURN


PROCEDURE Pause
PARAMETER lc_msg
*-- Parameters : lc_msg = message line
IF TYPE("lc_message")="U"
     gn_error=ERROR()
ENDIF
lc_msg = lc_msg
lc_option='0'
ACTIVATE WINDOW Pause
IF gn_error > 0
     IF TYPE("lc_message")="U"
        @ 0,1 SAY [An error has occurred !! - Error message: ]+MESSAGE()
     ELSE
        @ 0,1 SAY [Error # ]+lc_message
     ENDIF
ENDIF
@ 1,1 SAY lc_msg
WAIT " Press any key to continue..."
DEACTIVATE WINDOW Pause
RETURN
```

```
*-- UDF library ------------------------------------------------------------------
FUNCTION Center
*-- UDF to center a string.
*-- lc_string = String to center
*-- ln_width = Width of screen to center in
*--
*-- Ex. @ 15,center(string,80) say string
*-- Will center the <string> within 80 columns
PARAMETER lc_string, ln_width
RETURN ((ln_width/2)-(LEN(lc_string)/2))
*-- End UDF library --------------------------------------------------------------


PROCEDURE Cont_hlp
gc_readvar = VARREAD()                          && Could do context sensitive help
ACTIVATE WINDOW Cont_hlp
CLEAR
TEXT
    Navigation HELP:
    ----------------
    F1: Displays this message
    F9: Takes you from the top of your invoice to the line items
    F10: Takes you to the menu system at the top of the invoice

    PgDn: Takes you to the next invoice
    PgUp: Takes you to the previous invoice
    Ctrl-PgDn: Takes you to the last invoice in your database
    Ctrl-PgUp: Takes you to the first invoice in your database
    Esc: Exits the invoice
ENDTEXT
@ 16,5 say "Press any key..."
x = INKEY(0)
CLEAR
TEXT
    Line item HELP:
    ---------------
    F1: Displays this message

    PgDn: Displays next screen of line items
    PgUp: Displays previous screen of line items
    Ctrl-PgDn: Takes you to the last screen of line items
    Ctrl-PgUp: Takes you to the first screen of line items
    Esc: Returns to header information part of invoice
ENDTEXT
```

continues

7

Continued

```
@ 16,5 say "Press any key..."
x = INKEY(0)
DEACTIVATE WINDOW Cont_hlp
ACTIVATE SCREEN
RETURN

PROCEDURE Defnmenu
   *-- This menu simulates the F10 menu for edit for this edit program
   *-- Not all of the actions will be able to be duplicated though.

   SET BORDER TO DOUBLE

   DEFINE MENU editmenu
     DEFINE PAD records OF editmenu PROMPT "Records" AT 0,2
       ON PAD records OF editmenu ACTIVATE POPUP records
     DEFINE PAD go_to OF editmenu PROMPT "Go To" AT 0,14
        ON PAD go_to OF editmenu ACTIVATE POPUP go_to
     DEFINE PAD exit OF editmenu PROMPT "Exit" AT 0,24
       ON PAD exit OF editmenu ACTIVATE POPUP exit

   * -- Define popup menu
   DEFINE POPUP records FROM 1,0
     DEFINE BAR 1 OF records PROMPT "   Undo change to record";
     MESSAGE "Undo Change to current record"
     DEFINE BAR 2 OF records PROMPT "-------------------------------------" SKIP
     DEFINE BAR 3 OF records PROMPT "   Add new records";
     MESSAGE "Add records to the end of the database file"
     *-- Bar 4 is determined on the record being deleted or not
     DO Chkdele  && Define bar 4 done in procedure
     DEFINE BAR 5 OF records PROMPT "   Blank record" SKIP ;
     MESSAGE "Erase the contents of all the fields in this record"
     DEFINE BAR 6 OF records PROMPT "   Lock record";
     MESSAGE " " SKIP
     DEFINE BAR 7 OF records PROMPT "   Follow record to new position  YES" SKIP
     DEFINE POPUP go_to FROM 1,12
     DEFINE BAR 1 OF go_to PROMPT "   Top record";
     MESSAGE "Move to the first record in this database file"
     DEFINE BAR 2 OF go_to PROMPT "   Last record";
     MESSAGE "Move to the last record in this database file"
     DEFINE BAR 3 OF go_to PROMPT "   Record number";
     MESSAGE "Move to the specified record number"
     DEFINE BAR 4 OF go_to PROMPT "    Skip";
     MESSAGE "Move by skipping the specified number of records (minus for backwards)"
```

```
    DEFINE BAR 5 OF go_to PROMPT "---------------------------------" SKIP
    DEFINE BAR 6 OF go_to PROMPT "   Index key search"  SKIP FOR "" = gc_mdx;
    MESSAGE "Use the index file to search for the specfied string"
    DEFINE BAR 7 OF go_to PROMPT "   Forward search        ";
    MESSAGE "Search a field for the specified string from the current record forward"
    DEFINE BAR 8 OF go_to PROMPT "   Backward search       ";
    MESSAGE "Search a field for the specified string from the current record backward"
    DEFINE BAR 9 OF go_to PROMPT "   Match capitalization  NO" SKIP

 DEFINE POPUP exit FROM 1,22
    DEFINE BAR 1 OF exit PROMPT "   Exit";
    MESSAGE "Save changes to current record and exit"
    DEFINE BAR 2 OF exit PROMPT "   Transfer to Query Design  " SKIP

 ON SELECTION POPUP records DO Get_recs
 ON SELECTION POPUP go_to DO Get_goto
 ON SELECTION POPUP exit DO Get_exit

 DEFINE WINDOW seek FROM 8,15 TO 11,44
 DEFINE WINDOW search FROM 9,15 TO 11,60
 DEFINE WINDOW bsearch FROM 10,15 TO 12,60

    SHOW MENU Editmenu
 RETURN
 *----------------------------------------------------------------------
 *-- EOP: CONTACTQ.PRG
```

Creating Multiforms in DataEase

Not every database management system uses the dBASE approach to defining views. DataEase, for instance, offers a more visual approach to
forms design, including multitable forms that DataEase calls *multiforms*.
DataEase, unlike dBASE, stores the relationship definitions and does not
require the programmer to redefine relationships each time they are
needed.

DataEase offers simple commands to create multiforms. To create a multiform in DataEase, follow these steps:

   1. From the DataEase Main menu, choose Form Definition (choice
      number one). Select View or Modify Form, and choose the main
      form to which you will add a subform; for example, in the DataEase
      Form Definition screen, start with the main form (Clients) and
      place the cursor where you want the subform (Contacts) to appear
      (see fig. 7.9).

```
Form: Clients              R 19 C   3

  ┌Clients─────────────────────────────────────ID:──────┐
  │      Name:                    ,                      │
  │              Last              First        Title    │
  │   Company:                                           │
  │  Position:                                           │
  │   Address:                                           │
  │                              ,                        │
  │ Salutation:                                          │
  │      Phone:          FAX:              Last Contacted:│
  │    Entered:        Updated:        by                │
  └──────────────────────────────────────────────────────┘



  F4CMDHELP ESCEXIT F2SAVE F3CUT F5COPY F6PASTE F7DELLN F8INSLN F9SUBFRM F10FIELD
```

Fig. 7.9. *DataEase Clients form.*

2. Press the Subform key, F9. A list of related files appears at the top of the screen.

3. Choose Contacts and then enter the number of records to be displayed at one time (see fig. 7.10).

4. Press F2 to save your choices. The subform appears at the bottom of the screen (see fig. 7.11).

You can edit the background text (including the box) and rearrange the fields within the subform as you desire. Figure 7.12 shows how the resulting subform appears to the user.

Like the preceding dBASE program (but unlike the dBASE Query), the DataEase subform may be used for viewing and also for record entry and editing. Although you specify the number of records shown in the subform, the window scrolls through any number of records when the records exceed the size of the box.

```
Form: Clients

  ┌─Clients────────────────────────────────────ID:─────────┐
  │     Name:                                        Title   │
  │          ┌──────────────────────────────────────┐       │
  │  Company:│         Subform Definition            │       │
  │ Position:│                                       │       │
  │  Address:│  Relationship Name    Contacts        │       │
  │          │                                       │       │
  │          │  No. of Rows Minimum   5  Maximum  5   │       │
  │Salutation│                                       │       │
  │    Phone:│  Define Subform as    Automatic Table  │       │
  │  Entered:│                                       │       │
  │          └──────────────────────────────────────┘       │
  │                                                          │
  └──────────────────────────────────────────────────────────┘


AltF1HELP ESCEXIT F2SAVE F6FIELD CLR F7DELETE
```

Fig. 7.10. *The F9 Subform Definition menu.*

```
Form: Clients              (INSERT)

  ┌─Clients────────────────────────────────────ID:─────────┐
  │     Name:                    ,                           │
  │               Last                  First      Title     │
  │  Company:                                                │
  │ Position:                                                │
  │  Address:                                                │
  │                                                          │
  │                                     ,                    │
  │Salutation:                                               │
  │    Phone:            FAX:           Last Contacted:       │
  │  Entered:            Updated:        by                   │
  └──────────────────────────────────────────────────────────┘
  ┌────────────────────────────────────────────────────────┐
  │Date    │ Time  │ Type │ By │ Staff Name                 │
  │                                                         │
  └──────────────────────────────────────────────────────────┘
                                        «END»

F4CMDHELP ESCEXIT F2SAVE F3CUT F5COPY F6PASTE F7DELLN F8INSLN F9SUBFRM F10FIELD
```

Fig. 7.11. *The Contacts subform.*

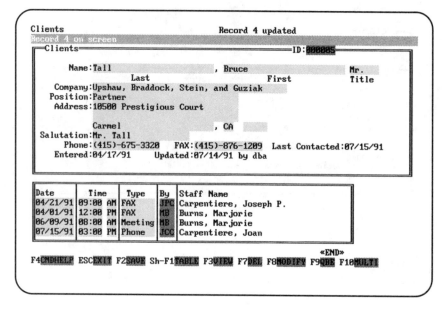

Fig. 7.12. A subform in record entry.

Creating Views in Paradox

Creating views in Paradox requires no programming, but creating a multiform view requires a few more steps in Paradox than in DataEase. (Exact steps vary from version to version. If you need more information about any specific step, refer to your program documentation.) To create a multiform view in Paradox, follow these basic steps:

1. Create the tables to be used for the form, as shown in figure 7.13. Note that the CLIENT CODE is the common field in both tables.

2. Define a multirecord form for the table containing the detail (child) records (see fig. 7.14).

   A *multirecord form* repeats the fields for each record so that you can view more than one record at a time. Make the form show as many rows as you need in the finished view. The form shown in figure 7.14 has a multirecord area of six lines, showing fields from the Contacts table.

3. Press F7 to define a default form for the parent table.

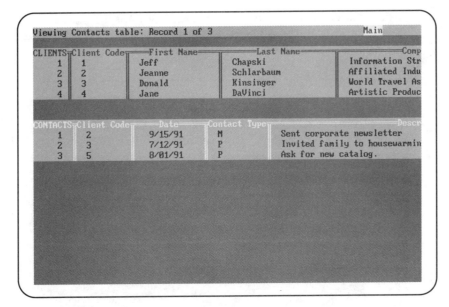

Fig. 7.13. *Tables for a subform.*

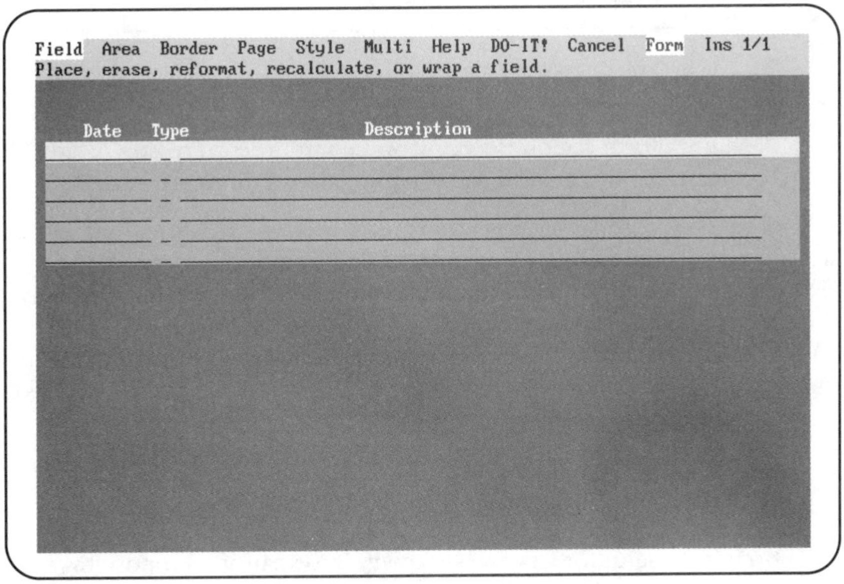

```
Field  Area  Border  Page  Style  Multi  Help  DO-IT!  Cancel  Form  Ins 1/1
Place, erase, reformat, recalculate, or wrap a field.

    Date   Type           Description
```

Fig. 7.14. *A Paradox multirecord form.*

7

4. Add a multitable region to the data-entry form for the master (parent) table. Position this region so that it does not overlap with fields or background text from the main table (see fig. 7.15).

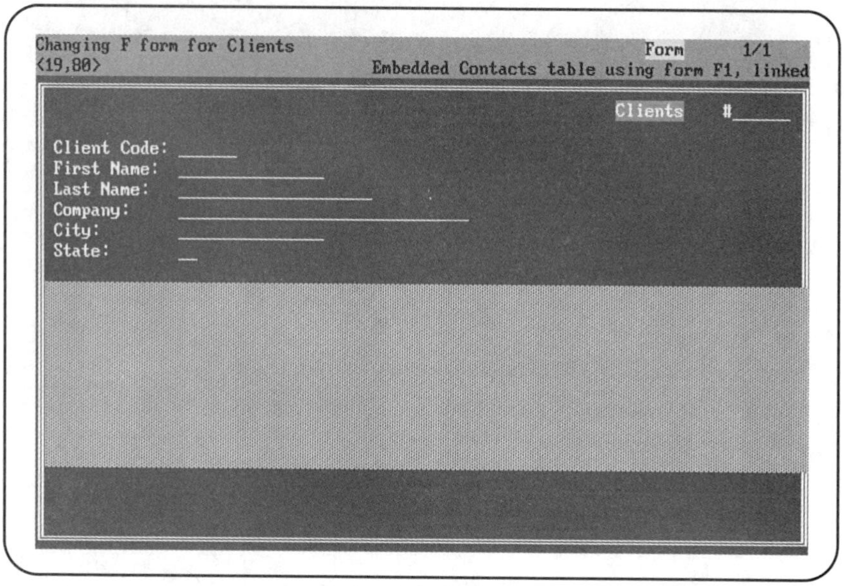

Fig. 7.15. A Paradox multitable region.

The multiform region is a copy of the multirecord region in the Contacts form. The multiform region shows up to six related records for each Client record.

Paradox offers the additional feature of side-by-side subforms. You can edit these subforms with the standard Paradox editing commands, moving from the master to the detail tables with the Up Image (F3) and Down Image (F4) keys. Figure 7.16 shows the finished form in data-entry mode.

Substituting Views for Printed Reports

Subforms are useful for viewing summary information. Suppose that you want to view the names of all clients who come from the same state. You would create a subform in the STATES file to show the names of all clients whose addresses include the same state (see fig. 7.17).

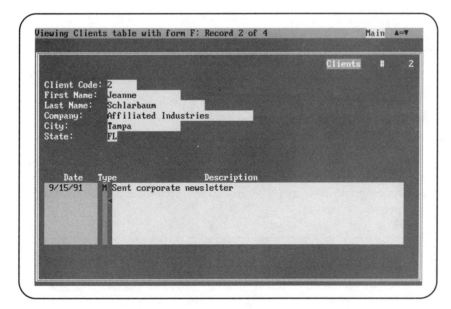

Fig. 7.16. *The finished form in data-entry mode.*

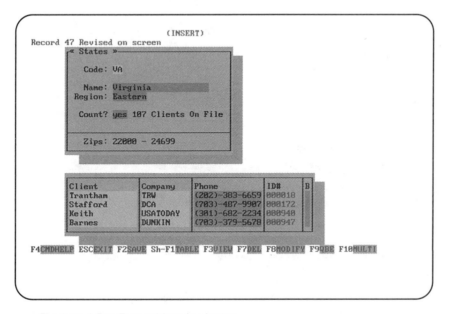

Fig. 7.17. *A DataEase subform for viewing.*

You can retrieve the same information in a report, but the subform is quicker and also provides for additions, updates, and deletions. Users often do not need a report but instead want to find records quickly by state (or other criteria).

Using Views for Security

You can use views to enforce data security. When you do not want to give users access to all the fields in a table, views can control which fields users can see or modify. Figure 7.18, for example, shows the data-entry form for a high-level user. You then can use a view for users who have fewer privileges (see fig. 7.19).

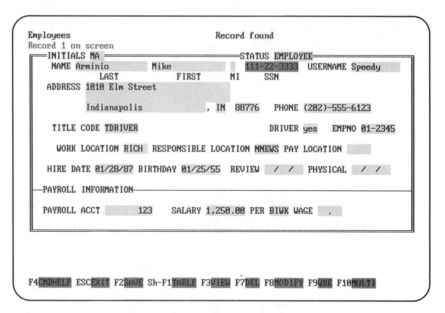

Fig. 7.18. *A DataEase data-entry form for high-level users.*

Maintaining Referential Integrity

The ability to enter data into more than one table from a single view raises important issues for data integrity. The most important issue is that of *referential integrity,* which refers to the way changes in one table are reflected in other, related tables.

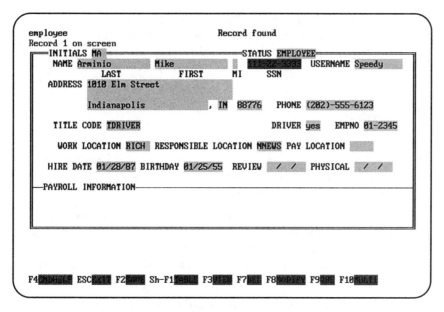

Fig. 7.19. *A restrictive view in DataEase for lower-level users.*

Invoices, for instance, may be stored in two tables, Invoice Header and Line Items. If an invoice is deleted, however, what should happen to the line items? One possibility is that all the line items are deleted along with the invoice header. Another is that the line items remain, but with no related header. Similarly, if the invoice number is changed in the header, should that change also apply to the line items?

The options you choose for referential integrity depend on your business rules. Although a deleted invoice header probably should cause the line items to be deleted, deleting a customer should not delete that customer's invoices. Indeed, you may want to create a rule that no customers may be deleted if they have any invoices.

Some DBMS enforce referential integrity automatically after you declare the rules. No matter how a record is changed—through a table, form, or view—changes are made to the related records by the DBMS. This kind of feature is desirable because it protects the accuracy of your database.

Other DBMS require programmers to take care of referential integrity by making explicit changes to related files for all the different scenarios that affect referential integrity. This approach assumes that users can access data only through the program. This approach is much more complicated to maintain than DBMS-enforced referential integrity, because every procedure that can affect a record must be programmed systematically to include all the implications for referential integrity.

Summary

Database views provide alternative ways to look at your data. A view can display fields from more than one table so that users do not have to switch from one form to another to enter data. You also can use views to prevent users from accessing sensitive information.

Each DBMS has its own approach to creating and using views. Some packages require extensive programming for multitable views. Others can create such views with a few simple commands. You should consult your software documentation to see whether and how views are supported.

When defining views, use the same principles as in form design. Show only the necessary fields and make views easily understandable to users. After you create tables, forms, and views, the data-entry portion of your application is complete.

Generating Reports

Get your facts first, then you can distort 'em as you please.

Mark Twain

Entering information into a database is of little use unless you have a way to retrieve that information. Reports enable you to retrieve the information in the database, searching for any combination of fields you need. Reports may draw on information from one or several tables. In many cases, reports mimic the paper forms used to produce the database structure.

You can generate several types of reports. Some reports, such as personalized form letters and mailing labels, are for group mailings. Others (such as invoices, packing lists, and bills of lading) are commonly used in processing orders. Summary reports calculate totals and averages from large numbers of records, such as monthly or quarterly financial reports, or the expense summary you receive from your credit card company.

Graphs are another form of report. Capabilities for business graphics are increasingly popular in database software. Paradox and FoxPro, for example, boast built-in graphics; add-in graphics packages are available for dBASE and Clipper.

Reports are usually printed, but you also can display them on-screen or save them as a disk file. This chapter deals with all types of reports regardless of where or how they are displayed.

This chapter discusses the major steps in report writing, followed by some examples and broad guidelines for developing report formats. Like data-entry forms, reports are highly visible to database users and are governed by the same rules of graphic design.

Designing Reports

Before creating a report, consider its purpose. Each report has a specific audience—a shipping list might be created for forklift drivers, for example. Keep the purpose of the report in mind throughout the design process. Starting with a worksheet that shows how the finished report should look can be a helpful practice (see fig. 8.1; this worksheet was also discussed in Chapter 2).

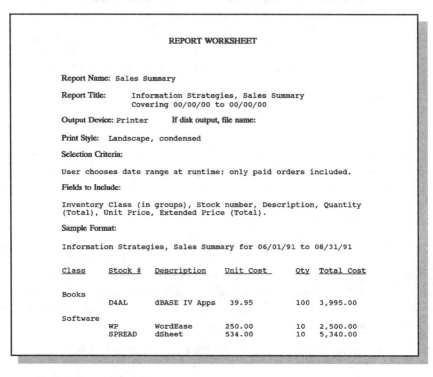

REPORT WORKSHEET

Report Name: Sales Summary

Report Title: Information Strategies, Sales Summary
                     Covering 00/00/00 to 00/00/00

Output Device: Printer   **If disk output, file name:**

Print Style: Landscape, condensed

Selection Criteria:

User chooses date range at runtime; only paid orders included.

Fields to Include:

Inventory Class (in groups), Stock number, Description, Quantity
(Total), Unit Price, Extended Price (Total).

Sample Format:

Information Strategies, Sales Summary for 06/01/91 to 08/31/91

Class	Stock #	Description	Unit Cost	Qty	Total Cost
Books					
	D4AL	dBASE IV Apps	39.95	100	3,995.00
Software					
	WP	WordEase	250.00	10	2,500.00
	SPREAD	dSheet	534.00	10	5,340.00

Fig. 8.1. A report worksheet.

This worksheet is a starting point; you may come up with enhancements to make the report more useful. You can add subtotals by product category, for example, or monthly subtotals for periods that span more than one month. The report worksheet might not give you all the information you need to create the report. If the purpose of the report is ambiguous, go back to the person who needs the report and ask for clarification.

Several characteristics separate good reports from inferior ones. Good reports help the reader reach the point with a minimum of distraction.

They are pleasant to look at and easy to read. Good reports are understandable immediately, even to a person who is not familiar with your database.

You can borrow from many good report formats. For financial reporting, check the tables in the back of corporate annual reports. Use preprinted business forms (invoices, shipping lists, form letters) as models for your database reports. Look at other printed tables, such as baseball box scores, for inspiration. All these samples can help you learn the principles of sound report design.

Make sure that your reports make a good first impression by using good graphic design principles. Leave ample white space (blank spaces and lines) between the text to provide a place for the eye to rest.

For detailed reports, you can set up fields in columns, with each record printing a single line, as shown in figure 8.2. Note that the decimal places in the dollar fields are aligned for easier reading.

```
Service Call Summary from 01/01/91 to 03/31/91                          November 2, 1991
Acme Appliance Service
Cleveland, OH
Page:   1

=================================================================================================================
Location   Call Date   Serial      Type      Labor Mileage Labor    Travel   Total   Part   Qty  Description        TOTAL
           Number      Number                 Hours        Price     Price    Parts   Number                        PRICE
-----------------------------------------------------------------------------------------------------------------
Washington (DC)
           000003  02/18/91 JUSTATEST   System Unit  2.5  122 132.50   28.06   82.00 547W00130 1 camshaft           242.56
           000005  02/22/91 721123769   System Unit  1.0   34  53.00    7.82    0.00                                 60.82
           000006  02/22/91 6146930     Display      1.0   34  53.00    7.82  297.00 2134      1 main knob          357.82

Office Total        Service Calls =  3                 238.50   43.70  379.00                                       661.20

St. Louis (STL)
           000001  01/18/91 121012802   Printer      2.5   76 132.50   17.48  106.75 130N124  1 bolt               256.73
           000001  01/18/91 121012802   Printer      2.5   76 132.50   17.48  106.75 5N21     1 paint              256.73
           000002  02/22/91 J34383794   System Unit  0.7   40  37.10    9.20  100.00 5N21     1 motor              146.30

Office Total        Service Calls =  2                 169.60   26.68  206.75                                       403.03

Albuquerque (ALB)
           000004  01/18/91 1501234     System Unit  1.5   36  79.50    8.28  106.75 5N21     1 IC                 194.53
           000004  01/18/91 1501234     System Unit  1.5   36  79.50    8.28  106.75 130N124  1 retaining screw    194.53

Office Total        Service Calls =  1                  79.50    8.28  106.75                                       194.53
```

Fig. 8.2. *Service Call Summary report.*

Use the appropriate paper size to accommodate your information, taking advantage of features such as boldface, underscore, and special typefaces (fonts) to set off important information. The report in figure 8.2 is too wide to fit on standard paper (8 1/2 by 11 inches, or *portrait* orientation), even using fine print, so it has been switched to *landscape* (11 inches by 8 1/2 inches) orientation.

Some reports include only summary information, without detail from the records. Figure 8.3 shows counts of referrals for a month, grouped by the type of referral. New columns have been added to the report to show

8

the percentage of referrals and total count for the year to date. These counts are not stored in the database; they are calculated when the report is run.

```
                                                            p. 1
Inquiry and Referrals -  Mode of Response
11/01/91 - 11/31/91

 ┌─────────────────────────────────────────────────────────────┐
 │ Code    Response Description        # Responses   %     YTD   │
 └─────────────────────────────────────────────────────────────┘

   01  Publication Distribution           200      32.35   1250

   02  Custom Letter                       88      14.29    399

   03  Form Letter                        122      19.77    751

   04  HOLD Request (pending)               5       0.14     13

   05  Referral to other Resource          75      12.19    142

   06  Direct (Phone or In-Person)         34       5.58     98

   07  Clearinghouse Response              40       6.55     79

   08  Database Search                     56       9.13    140
                                         ─────────────────────────
                         Total Responses:  620     100.00   2872
```

Fig. 8.3. *A referrals summary report.*

Other summary reports contain information from the records but omit long descriptions and comments. The activity summary report shown in figure 8.4 has only one line for each contact made. It provides a concise, readable picture of contacts. The report in figure 8.4 is not a summary report in the strictest sense because it contains some detail from each record. This report is much more concise than a report listing all fields from each record, however, and is therefore more useful to the reader.

In reports, as in many areas, less can be more. A concise report is easier to read and understand than a cluttered report with needless detail. Be sure to include only the fields necessary to understand the report.

Do not repeat fields for repeating groups of records. Figure 8.5 unnecessarily repeats the field labels. Although these field labels (NAME, ADDRESS, CITY, and so on) are an important part of the database, they are superfluous and distracting on a report. A report needs labels only when the meaning of a field may be unclear, as with the credit limit and year-to-date purchases of each customer. Figure 8.6 shows a revised version of the same report. Note that a blank line has been inserted between each record to improve readability.

```
Activity Summary                                              Page 1

November 2, 1991

Company    ID#     Name              Date              Purpose           Status     Type    Time

MOBILITE   003137 Grason, Mike       05/24/91 Friday   Schedule lunch.   Completed Letter  0.0
AHC        003067 Kole, Sharon       05/16/91 Thursday Customer support. Completed Letter  0.0
MILLST     003208 Michaels, Jon      05/16/91 Thursday Plan seminar.     Completed Letter  0.0
ATNT       004698 Balboa, Tim        05/16/91 Thursday Status check.     Completed Letter  0.0
DIXON      000007 Williams, Joseph   05/03/91 Friday   Probe for data.   Completed Meeting 1.0
HERSHIRE   003274 McCrea, Bill       05/02/91 Thursday Identify needs.   Completed Phone   0.1
LBIASSOC   003241 DeLillo, Mark      04/30/91 Tuesday  Customer support. Completed Phone   0.1
MHT        003186 Lindsey, John      04/29/91 Monday   Qualification.    Completed Letter  0.0
UMD        000124 Drew, Bob          04/23/91 Tuesday  Customer support. Completed Letter  0.0
CITIBANQUE 003260 Verity, Noelle     04/23/91 Tuesday  Customer support. Completed Letter  0.0
HENLE      004694 Wrobleski, Walt    04/19/91 Friday   Identify needs.   Completed Letter  0.0
TRENST     003258 Grant, JoAnn       05/10/91 Friday   Identify needs.   Completed Letter  0.0
DZSYST     003259 Benshetler, Chele  04/11/91 Thursday Probe for data.   Completed Letter  0.0
WB         003290 Weiss, John        04/11/91 Thursday Close sale.       Completed Letter  0.0
GT         004711 McHenry, Bill      04/06/91 Saturday Close sale.       Completed Letter  0.0
```

Fig. 8.4. An activity summary report.

```
CLIENT LISTING
DATE: 11/02/91
PAGE:    1

NAME: Mr. Paul Clay
COMP: President
ADDR: Acme Industrials
      1 Corporate Way
      Suite 550
CITY: Anytown, ME  12334
      CREDIT LIMIT: $ 1,000    PURCHASES YTD: $ 22,233.30
NAME: Ms. Eva Goodman
COMP: Chief Bureaucratic Officer
ADDR: National Assn. For Assn. Of Assn.
      1015 Delaware Ave.
CITY: Washington, DC  20007
      CREDIT LIMIT: $ 1,000    PURCHASES YTD: $ 43,299.10
NAME: Dr. John Hook
COMP: Human Resources Specialist
ADDR: National Baseball Association
      1575 5th Avenue
CITY: New York, NY  10007
      CREDIT LIMIT: $ 1,000    PURCHASES YTD: $ 43,345.10
NAME: Mr. Shelby Smith
COMP:
ADDR: Surfers R Us Unlimited
      10 Seaside Drive
CITY: Santa Monica, CA  98877
      CREDIT LIMIT: $ 1,000    PURCHASES YTD: $ 54,367.00
```

Fig. 8.5. A report with unnecessary field labels.

8

This report illustrates another standard of good reporting: it contains a header with the name of the report and the date produced. For columnar reports, the header identifies each column of data. Repeat the header on every page of the report.

If the report does not include all records in the database, the header should indicate the selection criteria. A sales report, for example, may read *From 01/01/91 through 06/30/91* to indicate the transactions that are included.

```
CLIENT LISTING
11/02/91
PAGE:   1

Mr. Paul Clay
President
Acme Industrials
1 Corporate Way
Suite 550
Anytown, ME  12334
CREDIT LIMIT: $ 1,000     PURCHASES YTD: $ 22,233.30

Ms. Eva Goodman
Chief Bureaucratic Officer
National Assn. For Assn. Of Assn.
1015 Delaware Ave.
Washington, DC  20007
CREDIT LIMIT: $ 1,000     PURCHASES YTD: $ 43,299.10

Dr. John Hook
Human Resources Specialist
National Baseball Association
1575 5th Avenue
New York, NY  10007
CREDIT LIMIT: $ 1,000     PURCHASES YTD: $ 43,345.10

Mr. Shelby Smith
Surfers R Us Unlimited
10 Seaside Drive
Santa Monica, CA  98877
CREDIT LIMIT: $ 1,000     PURCHASES YTD: $ 54,367.00
```

Fig. 8.6. *An improved report format.*

When you create a report, keep the purpose of the report in mind. Does the report need to convey detailed information on each item or summary information for the big picture? Can the reader quickly recognize the data in the report? How does the reader expect the information to be sorted?

Do not take shortcuts that reduce the clarity of the report. Avoid abbreviations not universally understood; use fields that the reader does not have to struggle to translate. A marketing report grouped by region, for example, may list customers by ZIP code, but it also should show their state.

Be sure to indicate units of measure (dollars, gallons, and so on) for numeric fields. Some reports do not differentiate millions of dollars from dollars, or units from dollars. Be sure to repeat headings on each page for columns of numbers.

Writing Reports

Like most aspects of database design, reports demand a certain amount of planning. To write a report, you must follow three basic steps:

1. Select the records for the report. When you select records, you specify search criteria to determine which records to include in the report. In this step, you are choosing the rows to appear in the report.

2. Determine the fields to list in the report (and the way data is to be sorted and grouped). When you choose the list fields, you are selecting the columns to be displayed in the report.

3. Design the report format. In this step, you specify the way that the report will look, by positioning fields, text, and other graphic elements in a pleasing, organized fashion. Designing the report format also involves choosing the destination for the report—whether it will go to the screen, the printer, or to a disk file.

The mechanics of creating a report are different for each DBMS. In some database software, you can combine two of these steps into one operation. Most database software provide defaults for the steps left undefined. The default for record selection, for example, is all records, and the default for field listings is all fields. In many packages, you use a query form to enter record selection criteria, so that you fill in the fields you want to match. In other DBMS, you write your record selection in a programming language.

Figure 8.7 shows a table from which records have been selected based on the instrument played. The record appears in the report only if the instrument played is the trumpet. The shaded area shows the selected records.

Artist	Instrument
Holiday, B	Voice
Davis, Miles	Trumpet
Marsalis, Wynton	Trumpet
Fitzgerald, Ella	Voice
Baker, Chet	Trumpet
Young, Lester	Saxophone
Armstrong, Louis	Trumpet
Bowie, Lester	Trumpet
Gordon, Dexter	Saxophone
Ellington, Duke	Piano
Kelly, Wynton	Piano

Fig. 8.7. *Selected records (Instrument = Trumpet).*

Selecting Records

The first step in report writing is to determine which records to list in the report. You can select records based on any number of criteria, using fields in the target table or any related table.

Imagine that each record in your database is on a file card. You have a fat stack of cards in your hand, each card representing a client, student, inventory item, and so on. During record selection, you decide which cards you need to pull out of the stack for the report.

Record selection is often simple, and you may need to search on only one field. To send fliers to all your new customers, for example, select the records for the new customers by searching on the date entered for records entered in the past month.

The record selection criteria may involve several fields. To obtain a list of all female students between the ages of 30 and 50 who have declared majors in the humanities, you select from the fields indicating sex, date of birth, and major subject.

You also can perform database searches by using wild cards to find matches based on incomplete information. *Wild cards* are special characters used in queries to represent one or more missing characters. Many database packages use the DOS wild cards ? (for one unknown character) and * (for one or more unknown characters). A search for J?N, for example, finds Jan and Jon but not John or Jean because the search retrieves only three-letter words. A search for CITY=NEW* yields records from New Haven, New York, Newark, and New Orleans. Not all databases use the standard wild card characters, however. Paradox and Q&A use .. instead of * for wild-card searches, and Microsoft SQL Server uses % for a string of zero or more characters and _ for any single character.

You can use another popular feature on database software for searches on inexact matches, including searches that are spelled incorrectly. Sounds-like (sometimes called Soundex) searches look for records that are phonetically close to the entered word. A sounds-like search on SHKSPR finds Shakespeare, Shakespere, Shakzpear, or even Sheikspear. Because of the many variant spellings in English, sounds-like searches can yield strange results. Paring down a search to the essential consonant sounds often achieves a better success rate.

To perform inexact searches in Paradox, simply type *LIKE* followed by the search pattern. In DataEase, precede the search pattern with the tilde (~) character. Note that different DBMS may achieve different results from searches for inexact matches. In Paradox, for example, a LIKE search must begin with the exact letter to match a value; in DataEase, however, you can use phonetically interchangeable letters (such as C and K).

Record selection also can employ fields stored in other, related tables. You can, for example, retrieve a list of all students from the eastern

United States who have earned at least six A's and no failing grades. To select Easterners, compare the ZIP code field to a certain range of ZIP codes. To select grades, look at the enrollment file for classes completed and check the grades received field.

Record selection uses commands to create and manipulate sets of data. A *set*, for the purposes of this book, is a group of zero or more items that share a common characteristic. Each table is itself a set consisting of all the records in the table. If you use no record selection criteria, the entire table is printed in the report.

The following examples use *pseudocode* (English words rather than an actual programming language) to express the search criteria. You use slightly different commands in different database products to achieve the same results. Some programs offer a feature called *query by example* or *query by form*, which you can use to select records without writing code.

Some database software is sensitive to capitalization when searching for records. If you search for Seattle but the database contains SEATTLE, the report will not find a match. To safeguard against this problem, many programmers routinely convert all search criteria and database values to uppercase before comparing them. If the user enters the desired city in a field called SCITY, for example, the search criteria may read UPPER(CITY) = UPPER(SCITY), where CITY is the field in the desired database table. Because the data and the search criteria are both converted, a match will be found if the entries are spelled identically.

Using the AND, OR, and NOT Operators

Although you can create convoluted record selections using a number of criteria joined together, the language for retrieving records is simple. The most basic operators for joining parts of a search are ordinary words—AND, OR, and NOT, along with the grouping symbols (usually parentheses). These short words, called *Boolean operators* in database jargon, are powerful and potentially dangerous.

The following examples use *Venn diagrams* of sets to show which records are being selected. The operator AND specifies the intersection of two sets. AND makes a search more restrictive because the records have to meet more than one criterion. (The search operators are capitalized in these examples for readability; your database software may not require that you capitalize these words in your queries.)

You can represent all students (the *universal set*) as in figure 8.8.

8

Fig. 8.8. *The universal set.*

From this set of all students, figure 8.9 marks students from California, and figure 8.10 shows students who are seniors.

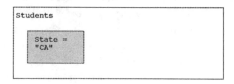

Fig. 8.9. *Students from California.*

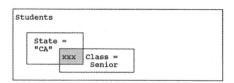

Fig. 8.10. *Students who are seniors.*

Figure 8.11 shows the next step—combining the search criteria with the AND operator.

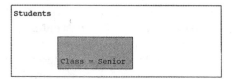

Fig. 8.11. *The result of searching with AND.*

The search for California students AND seniors yields only seniors from California. This result is the *intersection* of the subsets of California students and seniors. Using AND to link parts of a query often results in a smaller number of records.

What if you want to broaden the search to include students from Colorado and Arizona? If you use AND to link the searches for students from California, Colorado, and Arizona, you end up with no records because the intersection of these three subsets is *null* (see fig. 8.12). A *null set* is an empty set, with no records. This query always results in a null set because the students can have an address from only one state. No record in the database includes all the states of CA, CO, and AZ.

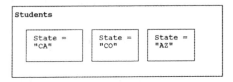

Fig. 8.12. *The result of searching with AND.*

You must use the OR operator to widen the search. The same search using OR in place of AND yields the result shown in figure 8.13.

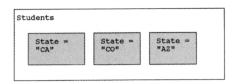

Fig. 8.13. *The result of searching with OR.*

The OR operator yields the *union* of the subsets, that is, all the records in one or the other of the subsets. OR is less restrictive than the AND operator. If your criteria include `State = "CA" OR State = "MD" OR State = "CO" OR State = "AZ"`, the record has to match only one of the four criteria to be included in the selection set.

When you use both AND and OR, the order in which you enter and group the operators affects the results of the query.

The following queries are not identical:

```
State = "AZ" AND Class = "Senior" OR State = "CA"
```

This query yields all seniors from Arizona and all students from California.

```
State = "AZ" OR State = "CA" AND Class = "Senior"
```

This query yields seniors from Arizona or California.

```
State = "CA" AND Class = "Senior" OR State = "AZ"
```

This query yields all seniors from California and all students from Arizona.

To eliminate this possible ambiguity, you can use parentheses to group search criteria together. For the preceding example, a less ambiguous query may read: (State = "CA" OR State = "AZ") AND Class = "Senior". This query produces the same result as the second example. For even more complex queries, parentheses are indispensable. To find all juniors and seniors from several states, for example, you can use the following query:

```
(State = "CA" OR State = "AZ") AND (Class = "Junior" OR Class =
"Senior")
```

The parentheses group all the state selection criteria and the class selection criteria.

You can use a third powerful relational operator, NOT, to retrieve everything that falls outside a subset. Figure 8.14 shows the results of the query State NOT = "CA". (**Note:** dBASE and some of its dialects use < > for NOT EQUAL TO.)

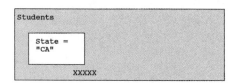

Fig. 8.14. *The result of searching with NOT.*

You can use multiple NOTs to exclude more records. You may, for example, want to run a variant of the preceding search, excluding students from California, Colorado, and Arizona. The criteria for this search are State NOT = "CA" AND State NOT = "CO" AND State NOT = "AZ". This query yields the result shown in figure 8.15.

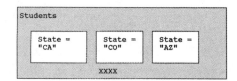

Fig. 8.15. *The result of searching with NOT and AND.*

All student records except those for students from California, Colorado, and Arizona are retrieved.

If you use OR rather than AND to link the parts of this query, the set includes all the records in the database because no single record meets all three of the criteria designed to exclude it. In other words, all records are not from California, not from Colorado, or not from Arizona, including those in the three states specified in the query.

Using several NOT conditions can be confusing at first, but drawing out a diagram of the set can help make it clear. Remember that using NOT can switch the function of AND and OR, making the AND operator broader and the OR operator more restrictive.

If you run a query that yields no records, check the order and grouping of your record selection statement. A small error can make a big difference in a query. You may want to break a complex query into its constituent parts to ensure that they retrieve the records you want to find. You can break down a compound query such as `State = "AZ" AND Class = "Junior"` by running each part as a separate query, listing both fields, to determine which of the selection criteria are working. As a last resort, you can go back to the tables themselves to make sure that records meeting your search criteria actually exist.

Using Other Record Selection Operators

In addition to AND, OR, and NOT, some database query languages offer additional operators to express searches more succinctly. DataEase, for example, uses BETWEEN to restrict a search to values that fall between a particular range. `Student Lastname BETWEEN "A" to "N"`, for example, yields all students whose last names begin with the letters B through M. This query is identical in function to `Student Lastname > "A" and Student Lastname < "N"`. The advantage of the BETWEEN operator is that it is quicker to enter than separate greater than and less than expressions.

As you may expect by now, not all database vendors have adopted the same terminology for record selection. Some databases do not use the words AND and OR explicitly, but rely on other means to link multiple search criteria. Paradox, for example, uses Query by Example (QBE) to retrieve records based on multiple criteria. QBE presents you with a query form that resembles the table. You fill in your search criteria in one or more fields. With Paradox, you can specify several criteria joined with an AND by placing them on the same line in the query. To use an OR with multiple criteria, you write the search values on separate lines in the query table. To use OR within a field, simply type both criteria separated by OR.

Paradox offers more powerful set comparison functions than most PC databases. In addition to building sets from one table with standard operators, you can build multiple sets and compare them to one another. You can, for example, use one on-screen query to determine which students from California have completed all required English courses. Table 8.1 lists the operators Paradox uses in its Query function to supplement standard set operators.

Table 8.1. Paradox Set Comparison Operators

Operator	Meaning
ONLY	Values in the group contain only members of the defined set.
NO	No values in the group are in the defined set.
EVERY	Values in the group include all members of the defined set.
EXACTLY	Values in the group exactly match the members of the defined set (combines ONLY and EVERY).

FoxPro has several ways to perform record selection. Perhaps the simplest is the Filter command, which lists only those records that meet the specified conditions. After choosing a table (which FoxPro, like dBASE, calls a *database*), you can enter conditions for the records to be included in the report. Figure 8.16 shows the Clients table in FoxPro.

To enter record selection criteria, choose Database and then Setup. The screen shown in figure 8.17 appears. If you choose Filter, you can enter your search criteria in the filter screen, as figure 8.18 shows.

The result of this filter is that the browse list contains all prospects from the District of Columbia (that is, with the state abbreviation DC). You can use the Filter command with complex selection criteria.

You also can use Filter in dBASE. By using the Filter command, you can change the selection criteria without rewriting the rest of the report.

Another method of selecting records stems from the way dBASE uses index files to find records. dBASE relies heavily on indexes to perform searches and handle relationships between tables. If a record is not found in an index, dBASE ignores the record even though it actually exists in the table. To choose those records that meet your criteria, you therefore can build a special index that purposely ignores records, as in the example following figure 8.18.

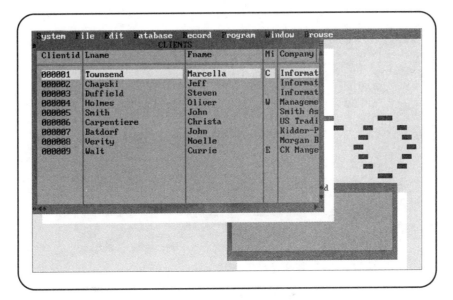

Fig. 8.16. The Clients table.

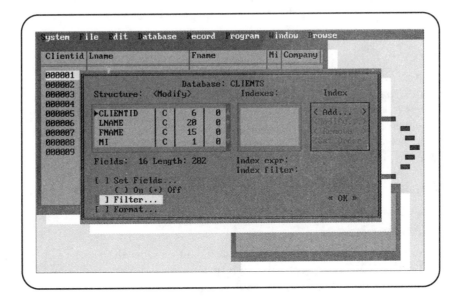

Fig. 8.17. The FoxPro database setup.

8

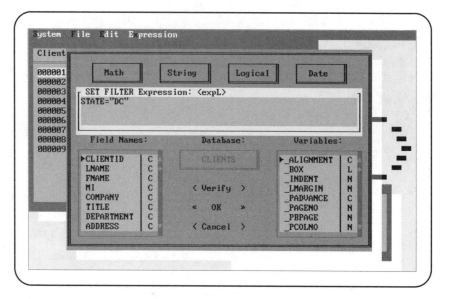

Fig. 8.18. *Search criteria in the filter screen.*

```
USE Students
INDEX ON State FOR State = "DC"
LIST
```

The result of this query is the same as for the Filter command: only students from DC are displayed. You can apply any criteria for building indexes (such as multiple fields) to record selection with this technique. A disadvantage of using these conditional indexes is that building the index takes time and space on the hard disk. For a large data file, the time needed could be prohibitive. Moreover, a new index has to be built for each set of search criteria, making it a cumbersome way to perform searches.

Listing Fields

After you choose the records to be listed, you need to choose the fields to list from each of the records. To return to the index card analogy, record selection has given you a subset of the stack that meets your search criteria. At this stage, you must decide which lines of information on the cards to include in the report. Sometimes you need only a few of the fields. Mailing labels, for example, do not include telephone or fax numbers.

In *structured query language (SQL)*, you use the Project command to choose the fields to list. SQL is the standard language for relational databases, and is available in many DBMS. Suppose that you want to print a list of alumni names and telephone numbers to conduct a survey. The Project command specifies the names of the fields to be included in the report.

Many fields to be listed are fields entered in the database forms themselves. In addition to these fields, you may want to create new fields by manipulating existing fields or performing calculations to show fields such as today's date, page number, totals, and counts.

Sorting Data

Sorting (also called *ordering*) determines the order in which records print. Most reports are more useful when the data is sorted rather than printed in random order. For mailing labels, for example, you may want to sort by ZIP code to make assembling a bulk mailing easier.

> **NOTE:** This section does not discuss physically sorting the order of records in a database table, but changing the order of the output.

You can sort in ascending or descending order. Ascending sorts are more common, especially for alphabetical listings. Descending sorts of date fields show most recent activities first.

Sorting on different field types yields different results. Text fields, for example, are sorted from left to right, whereas number fields are sorted by their numeric value. A sort of text fields that contain numbers places 1,000 before 50 because the initial character of the text value 1,000 (1) is lower than the initial character of 50 (5).

In some DBMS, such as dBASE, you can sort records in ASCII or in dictionary order. ASCII (the American Standard Code for Information Interchanges) uses a special code for each character, with different codes for upper- and lowercase letters. As a result, a file sorted in ASCII order separates *jones* and *Jones*. Dictionary order, on the other hand, sorts records in alphabetical order regardless of case. For most reports, dictionary order is preferable.

In a university, for example, class rosters might be sorted by last and first name. Semester grades for posting on the bulletin board are sorted by Social Security number (with the name fields not shown), as follows:

123-90-3323	A
176-63-0324	A
287-07-7632	D
342-09-6732	C
371-76-8762	B
572-82-7722	B
777-23-4822	B
787-23-9763	A

You can sort on more than one field. Starting with the unsorted class roster shown in table 8.2, a sort by last name yields the result shown in table 8.3. This listing does not alphabetize the first names, however. Adding a secondary sort to the first name field produces the desired list, shown in table 8.4. Records that deal with people are commonly sorted by last and first names.

Table 8.2. Unsorted Class Roster

Last Name	First Name
Hoopes	Java
Lynch	D. K.
Snyder	Joel
Greene	Greta
Greene	Arthur
Holley	Ivey A.
Ingres	Jean
Greene	Graham
Snyder	Jane M.
Birch	Lief
Bush	Ben T.
Twig	Ben T.

Table 8.3. Class Roster Sorted by Last Name

Last Name	First Name
Birch	Lief
Bush	Ben T.
Greene	Greta
Greene	Arthur
Greene	Graham
Holley	Ivey A.
Hoopes	Java
Ingres	Jean
Lynch	D. K.
Snyder	Joel
Snyder	Jane M.
Twig	Ben T.

Table 8.4. Class Roster Sorted by Last Name (Primary) and First Name (Secondary)

Last Name	First Name
Birch	Lief
Bush	Ben T.
Greene	Arthur
Greene	Graham
Greene	Greta
Holley	Ivey A.
Hoopes	Java
Ingres	Jean
Lynch	D. K.
Snyder	Jane M.
Snyder	Joel
Twig	Ben T.

8

When you sort on more than one field, the order in which you choose the fields to sort is important. In table 8.4, the names are sorted first by last name and then by first name. Switching the order of the sort fields results in a list of names in order by first name, as shown in table 8.5.

Table 8.5. Class Roster Sorted by First Name (Primary) and Last Name (Secondary)

Last Name	First Name
Greene	Arthur
Bush	Ben T.
Twig	Ben T.
Lynch	D. K.
Greene	Graham
Greene	Greta
Holley	Ivey A.
Snyder	Jane M.
Hoopes	Java
Ingres	Jean
Snyder	Joel
Birch	Lief

Some reports are more useful when sorted in reverse order. A report listing contacts with clients may show them from most recent to oldest by sorting in reverse on the date field.

Grouping Data

Grouping is functionally equivalent to sorting because it prints the records in order by the grouped field, but does not repeat the grouped field in every record. Instead, grouping displays the grouped field only at the beginning of each group.

A list of students sorted in order by state is shown in table 8.6.

Table 8.6. Students Sorted by State	
State	*Name*
AZ	Hoopes, Java
AZ	Lynch, D. K.
AZ	Snyder, Jane M.
CA	Greene, Greta
CA	Holley, Ivey A.
CA	Ingres, Jean
DC	Birch, Lief
DC	Bush, George
DC	Twig, Ben T.

This report is in order (a secondary sort) by last name. If the secondary sort were not specified, the names within a state would appear in no particular order.

Grouping by state, however, makes each state stand out more clearly from the rest. Table 8.7 shows the list of students grouped by state.

Table 8.7. Students Grouped by State	
State	*Name*
AZ	Hoopes, Java
	Lynch, D. K.
	Snyder, Jane M.
CA	Greene, Greta
	Holley, Ivey A.
	Ingres, Jean
DC	Birch, Lief
	Bush, George
	Twig, Ben T.

8

Grouping makes the report easier to read, by setting the states apart from one another. To make the report even more meaningful, you can add counts by state at the end of each group, although in this example the counts are clear.

You can use grouping and sorting in one report. A sales summary, for example, may group sales figures by state, county, and ZIP code, and then list each company in order. A university may list its students grouped by class, in alphabetical order.

Using Functions to Create Fields

Database software typically provides the report writer with a number of techniques for manipulating the fields displayed in a report. These *functions* are special commands to perform mathematical operations, modify text fields, and otherwise manipulate the data to produce the desired result. The specific commands vary by DBMS, but the following overview covers some commonly provided functions.

Suppose that you need to create a field value for a report that does not exist in the database tables. You may, for example, have a number of records in your client database with blanks in the SALESREP field. Rather than print the field label with a blank, you can use an IF statement to check the value in the field and print N/A if the field is blank. The derivation formula may look like the following:

```
IF (SALESREP = blank , "N/A" , SALESREP)
```

This formula prints N/A when the SALESREP field is blank; otherwise, it prints the value in the SALESREP field. Beware of the way in which the results are sorted. Unless you place a space before N/A, N/A appears between the names that start with M and the names that start with N.

Arithmetic Functions

Most DBMS contain functions for mathematically manipulating the data they store. Suppose that you want to add two or more numbers, calculate sales tax as a percentage of purchase price, or print running subtotals on a report. You usually can use standard mathematical symbols (+, −, *, /) for arithmetic functions. You can use these functions together to perform complex calculations such as determining loan interest or amortization.

In DataEase, you can use math functions in several ways. A simple formula suffices to add two fields: FIELD1 + FIELD2. To show the total amount for a sale, a report may specify total purchases + sales tax to add the two fields. You can combine multiple math functions in one equation and apply grouping using parentheses. You can, for example, calculate a balance due with the following formula: `total purchases + (total purchases * sales tax rate) + shipping - payment received`.

Relational Mathematical Functions

The math so far has added, subtracted, multiplied, or divided fields within one record. Databases also offer powerful capabilities to add several records together, calculating subtotals based on groupings of records.

Databases that use Structured Query Language (SQL) support such aggregate functions as SUM, AVG, COUNT, MAX, and MIN to show totals, averages, counts, and maximum and minimum values. A query in Microsoft SQL server might read as follows:

```
select stocknum, type, price from inventory
order by type, stocknum
computer sum (price) by type
```

The result of the query appears as follows:

type	stocknum	price	
hardware	C286	1000.00	
hardware	M100	149.00	
hardware	Z601	99.00	
		1248.00	sum
software	L123	500.00	
software	P35	750.00	
		1250.00	sum

The query retrieves the fields TYPE, STOCKNUM, and PRICE from the Inventory table (the list fields step), sorting them by TYPE (primary sort) and STOCKNUM (secondary sort) and calculating totals for each group (by TYPE).

In DataEase, the SUM OF function calculates the total of a field in all related records. You can calculate the total outstanding balance for a customer by adding the outstanding balances of each related invoice record using the following formula:

```
sum of invoices "outstanding amount"
```

8

The similar functions COUNT OF and MEAN OF produce a respective count of the number of related records and an average of the values in the related records.

Table 8.8 shows the mathematical and financial functions available in dBASE IV. Most DBMS offer similar capabilities.

Table 8.8. dBASE IV Mathematical and Financial Functions	
ABS	Absolute value
ACOS	Angle size in radians from the cosine
ASIN	Angle size in radians from the sine
ATAN	Angle size in radians from the tangent
ATN2	Angle size in radians from the sine and cosine
COS	Cosine value from angle in radians
DTOR	Degrees to radians conversion
EXP	Number from its natural log
FIXED	Converts long, real floating point numbers to binary coded decimal
FLOAT	Converts binary coded decimal numbers to long, real floating point
FLOOR	Largest integer less than or equal to the specified value
FV	Future value of investment at fixed interest for a given time
INT	Conversion to integer by truncating decimals
LOG	Natural logarithm to base e
LOG10	Logarithm to base 10
MAX	Greater of two values
MIN	Lesser of two values
PAYMENT	Periodic payment on a loan with fixed interest
PI	Mathematical constant for the ratio of circumference to diameter
PV	Present value of equal payments invested at fixed interest for a given time
RAND	Random number generator; seed number is optional
ROUND	Rounds the number to the number of decimal places specified
RTOD	Converts radians to degrees
SIGN	Mathematical sign of a number of expression
SIN	Sine from an angle in radians
SQRT	Square root of the specified number
TAN	Tangent from an angle in radians

String Functions

In addition to mathematical functions, most databases provide special functions for manipulating text. One useful function is the capability to *concatenate*, or combine, two or more fields into one field. Although names are commonly entered in several distinct fields (first name, middle initial, last name), you may want to present them in one field in a report.

In DataEase, the function jointext enables you to concatenate fields. The following formula

```
jointext ( lname , "' ", " , jointext ( fname,
jointext ( " " , middleinit )))
```

applied to the following data

FNAME	MIDDLEINIT	LNAME
Reginald	P.	Jones
Veronica	C.	Woods
Archie	D.	Anderson

results in the following output:

> Jones, Reginald P.
> Woods, Veronica C.
> Anderson, Archie D.

This function prints the last name first with a comma and space between the last and first names and a space between the first name and middle initial.

By using a string function to retrieve the first letter only of a last name, you can print a phone directory with each new letter of the alphabet starting on a different page. The following is a sample DataEase query:

```
for personnel ;
list records
firstc (lname , 1 ) in groups ;
jointext ( lname , "' " , jointext ( fname, jointext ( " " , middleinit ))).
```

The result of the query would look something like the following:

> A
>> Anderson, Jean
>> Atwell, Henry
> B
>> Barnes, Charlotte

C
Chatterley, Elaine

and so on for the rest of the alphabet.

String functions are also useful in data conversion. They can convert text from all caps to mixed case or split fields apart into two or more new fields. If a database is set up with only one field for the customer name, you can use the string functions to divide the field into first and last names by placing the last word in the last name field and all other text in the first name field. This kind of operation can be tricky, because names with suffixes or multiple word last names (such as de la Renta) pose challenges.

String manipulation functions offered by database software packages are often quite extensive. Table 8.9 shows the functions offered by Paradox.

Table 8.9. Paradox String Manipulation Functions

Function	Description
ASC	Converts a character to an ASCII value
CHR	Converts an ASCII value to a character
DATEVAL	Converts a string to a date
FILL	Returns a filled string
FORMAT	Formats an expression
LEN	Returns the length of a string
LOWER	Converts a string to lowercase
MATCH	Compares a string with a pattern
NUMVAL	Converts a string to a number
SEARCH	Searches for a substring in a string
SPACES	Returns a string of spaces
STRVAL	Converts an expression to a string
SUBSTR	Returns a substring of a string
UPPER	Converts a string to uppercase

Defining the Report Format

A report should show information from the database in the format most useful to its readers. To achieve this goal, you need a clear understanding of the business problem and a good eye for graphic design.

In addition to the database and derived fields, the report probably contains *background text* such as report headers, footers, boxes, and field labels.

Figure 8.19 shows a report from a fund-raising application. This report illustrates a number of useful standards for written output. A report title, *Pledges and Contributions by Campaign*, indicates the contents of the report. Report titles are invaluable in distinguishing one report from another. The header also shows the date the report was run, the range of dates covered, and the page number. Reports covering variable time periods should always include the date range in the format, and multiple-page report formats should include page numbers.

This report uses a blank line (white space) to separate one group from the next and a combination of single and double lines to show totals. This layout is easier to read than a single-spaced format because it highlights the key information.

Make a note of your personal style preferences. Do you prefer page numbers at the top or bottom of the page, centered, flush right, or flush left? Do you prefer to print the number alone or with *Page:* or # before it? These small touches affect the overall appearance of a report and can make more professional-looking output.

Designing the report format is not difficult. Most DBMS offer a special screen for *painting* the format of the report. One popular method for report writing is the *banded* report design screen. The format screen is divided into several regions with horizontal lines. Each region prints on a different part of the report. Alpha Four, dBASE, File Express, PC-File, R:BASE, Paradox, Reflex, and many other DBMS use banded format screens. Other DBMS (such as DataEase) use formatting commands that approximate these functions. A typical banded format contains the regions shown in table 8.10.

8

```
Pledges and Contributions by Campaign
July 17, 1991
From 01/01/90 to 07/17/91
Page:   1

===========================================================================
     Campaign          Type          Total       Average       Count
...........................................................................
Unrestricted

                    Pledge          9,500.00      2,375.00        4
                                    ===============================
Pledges and Contributions           9,500.00      2,375.00        4

Fall Campaign 1988

                    Donation        5,000.00      5,000.00        1
                                    ===============================
Pledges and Contributions           5,000.00      5,000.00        1

Fall Campaign 1989

                    Donation        6,125.00      1,531.25        4
                                    ===============================
Pledges and Contributions           6,125.00      1,531.25        4

Membership drive 1/91

                    Pledge         17,777.00     17,777.00        1
                                    ===============================
Pledges and Contributions          17,777.00     17,777.00        1

Office reparation

                    Donation        2,500.00      2,500.00        1

                    Pledge          1,000.00      1,000.00        1
                                    ===============================
Pledges and Contributions           3,500.00      1,750.00        2

Reserve Fund

                    Donation        2,500.00      1,250.00        2

                    Pledge          1,000.00      1,000.00        1
                                    ===============================
Pledges and Contributions           3,500.00      1,166.67        3

Spring Campaign 1990

                    Donation       34,250.00      2,140.62       16

                    Pledge         94,963.00      6,783.07       14
                                    ===============================
Pledges and Contributions         129,213.00      4,307.10       30
...........................................................................
GRAND TOTAL                       174,615.00      3,880.33       45
===========================================================================
```

Fig. 8.19. A report of contributions.

Table 8.10. Banded Report Writer

Band	Intended Use
Page Header	Prints at the top of each page; usually is the report header (including report title, date, and page number)
Group Header	Prints before the first item in a group
Report Intro	Prints on only the first page of the report
Detail	Prints once for each record retrieved; usually includes the data fields unless the report is for summaries only; sometimes called *items*
Group Trailer	Also called a *control break*, prints after the last item in a group; may be used to display group subtotals
Report Summary	Prints after the last detail item, at the end of the report; this section includes grand totals
Page Footer	Repeats at the bottom of each page of the report

Figure 8.20 shows an example of a simple dBASE IV report that uses grouping. To create the report, first USE the table from which you are reporting. Choose Reports from the Command Center main menu and select <create>. The report format screen appears. You can start with the default format (see fig. 8.20).

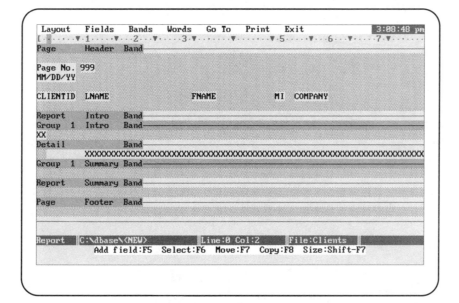

Fig. 8.20. The default format for Group by State.

To add a section in the format for group header and trailer, press F10; then choose Bands. Choose Add a group band (see fig. 8.21).

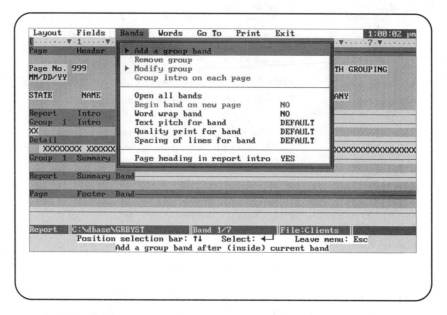

Fig. 8.21. *Adding a group band.*

For this report, the STATE field is selected for the group band, but you can create additional levels of grouping. You can save the report and run it to check the results.

Although the records are grouped by state, the field layout is less than optimal. You can edit the format to produce the format shown in figure 8.22, which deletes unnecessary fields and moves the headers to create a less cluttered format.

An excellent way to learn dBASE is to use the Command Center to generate forms, queries, and reports and then examine the report you have generated. The results can help you understand the proper flow of commands and the structures for defining procedures, IF statements, and other program elements. After you have learned these commands, you can write reports from scratch or use generated programs to create your own custom reports.

```
Page No.   1              PROSPECTS BY STATE -- SAMPLE REPORT WITH GROUPING
07/18/91

STATE     NAME                                      COMPANY

DC
    000001 Townsend Marcella                 Information Strategies
    000002 Chapski Jeff                      Information Strategies
    000003 Duffield Steven                   Information Strategies

MD
    000004 Holmes Oliver                     Management Systems, Inc.

PA
    000005 Smith John                        Smith Associates

DC
    000006 Carpentiere Christa               US Trading Company of Japan

NY
    000007 Batdorf John                      Kidder-Peabody
    000008 Verity Noelle                     Morgan Bros.
```

Fig. 8.22. *An improved format using grouping.*

Printing the Report

After you have created the layout of the report, you need to specify the destination for the report—the screen, a printer, or a disk file. You also need to specify fonts, paper size, and margins.

You can choose the report destination when you create the report, or the user can choose the destination at run time. If the same report needs to go to multiple destinations, you may want the user to determine the destination when running the report.

Each DBMS handles printer control differently. In most cases, printer defaults are available for typical printer settings. DataEase, for example, offers a Print Style screen, which accompanies each report (see fig. 8.23).

In Paradox, you choose the print style from a series of menus, much like Lotus 1-2-3. When you choose Report from the main menu, the menu bar shown in figure 8.24 appears.

From the Report menu, choose SetPrinter. To choose the standard printer configuration for a report, select Regular. To override the standard options, choose Override (see fig. 8.25). The Override menu is shown in figure 8.26. The Setup option enables the user to define the appropriate printer commands.

8

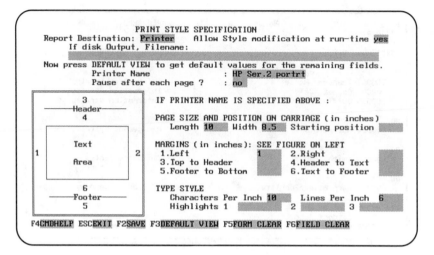

Fig. 8.23. The DataEase Print Style screen.

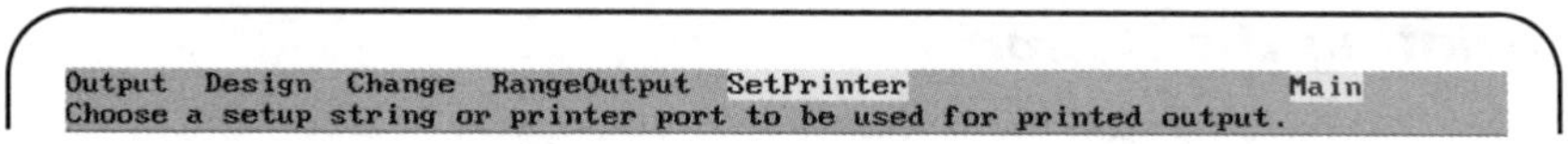

Fig. 8.24. The Paradox Report menu.

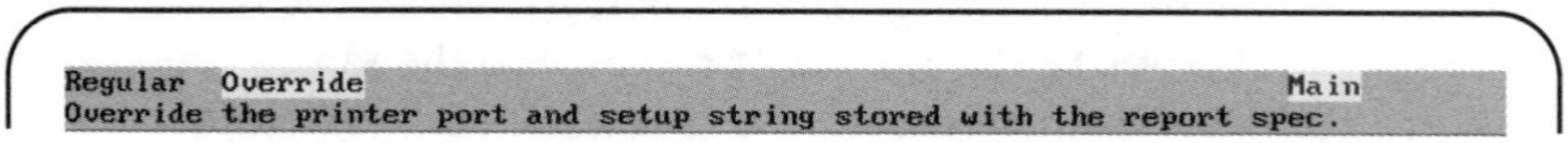

Fig. 8.25. The Paradox Printer menu.

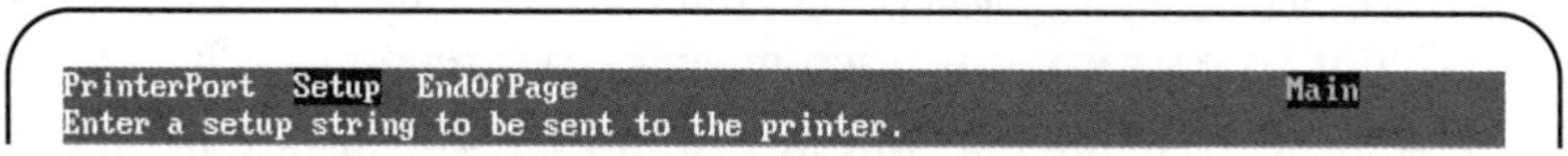

Fig. 8.26. The Paradox Printer Override menu.

This menu enables you to change the printer port, the setup string, and the end of page commands. The *printer port* is the communications port connected to your printer. The *setup string* is a special series of characters sent to the printer at the beginning of the report to start special printer options, such as font or orientation changes. The end of page command determines which characters are sent to the printer at the end of a print job. A form feed is often needed to eject the last page of the report.

Selecting Printer Orientation

Many printers, especially laser printers and inkjet printers, give you the option of printing vertically or horizontally on the page. These respective options are called *portrait* and *landscape orientation* (see fig. 8.27).

Fig. 8.27. *Portrait vs. landscape printer orientation.*

The printer must receive a special code at the beginning of a print job to switch to a different orientation. This code may be part of the report format. Refer to your printer manual for a list of printer control codes (sometimes called ESC sequences) for changing orientation, character sets, fonts, and other printer characteristics. If you include the code in the report format, you may want to send a code at the end of the report to switch back to the default settings. Otherwise, your office colleagues may be unpleasantly surprised at the results of later print jobs.

Another way to change printer orientation is to choose the appropriate printer driver software. Some packages have separate listings for portrait and landscape that automatically send initialization sequences.

Using Printer Fonts

Using different fonts, or *typefaces*, helps create polished, professional-looking reports. After you are accustomed to proportional fonts such as Times Roman and Helvetica, you will never want to return to typewriter fonts such as Courier.

The commands for controlling fonts depend on your printer and applications software. Generally, you need to send a special code to the printer to change the font. Fonts may be *soft fonts* downloaded to the printer random access memory (RAM), *resident fonts* included in standard

8

printer read-only memory (ROM), or *cartridge fonts* stored in removable ROM. You can enter the printer code directly in the report format or send it by the program that generates the report.

Be conservative with your use of fonts. One typeface in two or three sizes is usually sufficient. Using more than one typeface on a page can make your report look more like a ransom note than a business document. You may want to standardize your favorite fonts for all your reports. As with printer orientation, be sure to set the printer back to its default font when you are finished.

Remember that the availability of fonts depends on the printer, the software, and the font cartridges. Users with different printers may not be able to produce the same output that you can produce. You therefore may want to provide several formats to accommodate common printer types.

Looking at Sample Reports

The following sections show sample reports from several applications to illustrate some of the techniques used in report writing. Only one method for writing each report is given, although in some cases the DBMS offers several possible retrieval methods.

Mailing Labels

Mailing labels are easy to create, and they are among the most frequently requested type of report. Many DBMS have gone to extra lengths to automate the production of mailing labels. Symantec's Q&A, for example, contains predefined mailing label formats for dozens of different label stocks for laser and impact printers.

One way to create labels in dBASE IV is to use the Command Center labels facility. Follow these steps:

1. Open a database file by selecting <create> from the Labels column of the Main menu. The screen shown in figure 8.28 appears. This screen specifies the field layout for labels.

2. To place a field, position the cursor where you want the field to appear. Press Alt-F to access the Field menu and then select Add Field. Alternatively, press F10; then use the arrow keys to select Field. Press Enter. A list of fields similar to those shown in figure 8.29 appears.

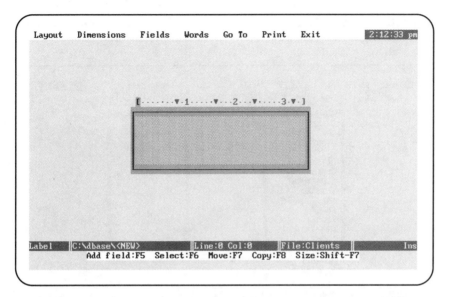

| Layout | Dimensions | Fields | Words | Go To | Print | Exit | 2:12:33 pm |

```
[······▼·1·····▼··2···▼·····3·▼·]
```

| Label | C:\dbase\<NEW> | Line:0 Col:0 | File:Clients | Ins |
| Add field:F5 Select:F6 Move:F7 Copy:F8 Size:Shift-F7 |

Fig. 8.28. *The dBASE IV Label Layout screen.*

3. Highlight the desired field, such as STATE in figure 8.29, and press Enter. The Display Attributes menu appears (see fig. 8.30). From this menu, you can use picture and template functions to control the appearance of the field.

4. Repeat steps 2 and 3 for all fields in the report, adding any additional background text that you desire, such as a comma between the city and state fields.

5. After you design the format of the labels, press Ctrl-End to save your work.

   dBASE generates a program based on your report design. You now may edit or run the program.

You can use more advanced features in your dBASE mailing labels. So far, all the fields chosen were entered in the Clients table. You also can use calculated fields in mailing labels (as in other reports).

When the addresses include nine-digit ZIP codes, the labels look better with a hyphen separating the five- and four-digit sections of the ZIP code. You can add a hyphen as background text in the label format, inserting it between the ZIP and ZIP_EXT fields. The hyphen, however, prints on all records, including records without extended ZIP codes. To solve this problem, you can create a calculated field to print a hyphen only for addresses that contain a value in ZIP_EXT. Press Alt-F to access the Field

8

menu; then choose Add Field. From the Field List screen, move the cursor to the right to create a calculated field and press Enter.

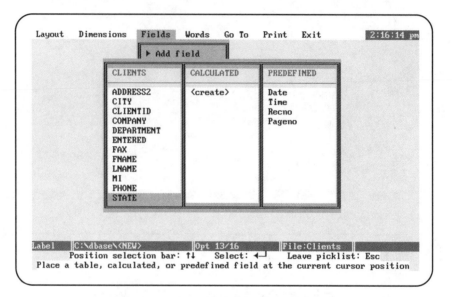

Fig. 8.29. *The dBASE IV Labels Choose Field menu.*

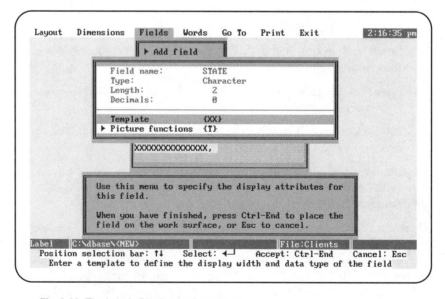

Fig. 8.30. *The Labels Display Attributes field.*

The derivation formula checks whether ZIP_EXT is blank (see fig. 8.31). If the field is blank, no character is sent to the printer; otherwise, a hyphen is sent. This task is accomplished with the use of the dBASE statement IIF entered in the expression area. You can use similar formulas to perform mathematical and other functions on fields. Figure 8.32 shows the finished labels.

The Labels program removes trailing spaces from fields that are not completely filled. If a field is left completely blank, such as the second address line in Joel Snyder's label in figure 8.32, the blank line is not printed, and the following lines are moved up. This feature is called *space suppression*.

In this example, the labels were formatted to print only one label across. You can modify the format to print any number of labels side-by-side.

To create mailing labels in Paradox, you choose from a series of bar menus at the top of the screen. When creating labels in Paradox, you must answer a number of menu prompts. The process has more steps than the process of creating dBASE mailing labels, but it takes no longer to produce the same results. After you learn the series of commands, you can move quickly through the menus by typing the first letter of your choice. To simplify the process further, you can write a script to play all these commands with one keystroke.

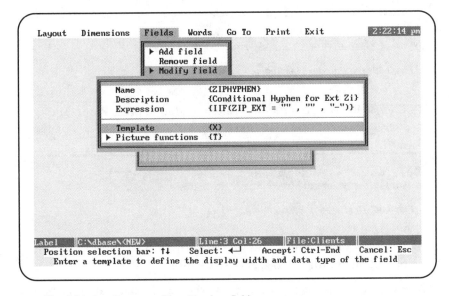

Fig. 8.31. Creating a conditional hyphen field.

```
John Smith
5500 Chestnut Street
Philadelphia, PA  12390



Christa Carpentiere
3000 Pennsylvania Avenue NW
Washington, DC  20006-1268



John Batdorf
1010 Avenue of the Americas
25th Floor
New York, NY  10005



Joel Snyder
1100 Wall Street
New York, NY  10012
```

Fig. 8.32. Mailing labels.

Figure 8.33 shows the Paradox main menu with the Clients table displayed. To create mailing labels, follow these steps:

```
View  Ask  Report  Create  Modify  Image  Forms  Tools  Scripts  Help  Exit
Output, design, or change a report specification.
```

Fig. 8.33. The Paradox Main menu.

1. Choose Report from the main menu and then press Enter. The Report menu appears (see fig. 8.34).

```
Output  Design  Change  RangeOutput  SetPrinter                    Main
Design a new report specification.
```

Fig. 8.34. The Paradox Report menu.

2. To create a new report, choose Design from the Report menu. To modify an existing report, choose Change.

3. A message appears prompting you to enter the name of the table. Type the name of the table or press Enter for a list of tables from which to select (see fig. 8.35).

```
Table:                                                      Main
Pclients  Contacts  Name  Unified  Removed  Deladdr  Clients  Lists  Listmemb ▶
```

Fig. 8.35. *A list of tables for a report*

4. A list of the reports prepared for this table appears, identified by a number (see fig. 8.36). When you place the cursor on the report number, the report name will be displayed on the message line (below the report number). For this example, choose 1 and press Enter.

```
R  1  2  3  4  5  6  7  8  9  10  11  12  13  14          Main
Mailing Labels
```

Fig. 8.36. *Paradox report numbers.*

5. Paradox prompts you to choose between tabular and free-form formats (see fig. 8.37). Choose Free-form. (The tabular format shows each record as a row and each field as a column, much as the data table itself appears. A mailing label report format, however, is not tabular.) The default format shown in figure 8.38 appears.

```
Tabular  Free-form                                         Main
Design a free-form layout for each record.
```

Fig. 8.37. *Paradox format choices.*

6. Paradox automatically creates a default header for the report that includes the report name and date the report is run. Delete the headers and margins by moving the cursor to those regions and pressing Ctrl-Y.

   This format contains all the fields in the table, but not in the desired arrangement. Note that all the fields that appear are needed for the mailing labels, although some (such as CITY, STATE, and ZIP) need to be consolidated on one line.

7. Press F10 to view the Edit menu. Use the editing commands to move and delete fields until they look like figure 8.39.

8

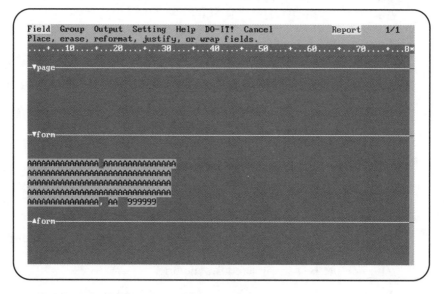

```
Designing report R1 for Clients table                    Report    1/1
Report Header
....+...10....+...20....+...30....+...40....+...50....+...60....+...70....+...8*
   ▼page

 mm/dd/yy                      Mailing Labels                  Page 999

   ▼form
Client Code: AAAAAA
First Name: AAAAAAAAAAAAAA
Last Name: AAAAAAAAAAAAAAA
Company: AAAAAAAAAAAAAAAAAAAAAAAAAAAAAA
City: AAAAAAAAAAAAAA
State: AA
Zip Code: 999999

   ▲form
```

Fig. 8.38. *The Paradox standard format.*

```
Field  Group  Output  Setting  Help  DO-IT!  Cancel        Report    1/1
Place, erase, reformat, justify, or wrap fields.
....+...10....+...20....+...30....+...40....+...50....+...60....+...70....+...8*
   ▼page




   ▼form

AAAAAAAAAAAAAAA AAAAAAAAAAAAAA
AAAAAAAAAAAAAAAAAAAAAAAAAAAAA
AAAAAAAAAAAAAAAAAAAAAAAAAAAAA
AAAAAAAAAAAAAAAAAAAAAAAAAAAAA
AAAAAAAAAAAAAA, AA  999999

   ▲form
```

Fig. 8.39. *Paradox field layout for mailing labels.*

8. To suppress the blank spaces in this report, press F10 to view the Edit menu. Select Setting.

9. From the Setting menu, select RemoveBlanks (see fig. 8.40). The menu shown in figure 8.41 appears.

10. Use LineSqueeze and FieldSqueeze to suppress blank spaces. If you choose LineSqueeze, Paradox will not print a blank line for lines with blank fields; for example, Paradox pulls up the third line of an address label if the fields in the second line are blank. If you choose FieldSqueeze, Paradox brings fields closer together by suppressing extra spaces at the beginning and end of a field; for example, Paradox prints first and last name fields together without leaving blanks between the end of the first name and the beginning of the last name. Choose LineSqueeze first (again see fig. 8.41). Choose Yes to confirm that you want to use LineSqueeze.

11. Repeat these steps to use FieldSqueeze.

```
RemoveBlanks  PageLayout  Margin  Setup  Wait  Labels            Report  Ins 1/1
Specify removing blank lines or field positions.
```

Fig. 8.40. *The Setting menu.*

```
LineSqueeze  FieldSqueeze                                        Report  Ins 1/1
Suppress printing of lines which have all fields blank.
```

Fig. 8.41. *The RemoveBlanks menu.*

The Paradox label report is now complete. To run the report, choose Report from the Paradox Main menu (see fig. 8.42). Select Output from the Report menu and choose 1 (or the number you used to designate the report), as shown in figure 8.43.

```
View  Ask  Report  Create  Modify  Image  Forms  Tools  Scripts  Help  Exit
Output, design, or change a report specification.
```

Fig 8.42. *The Paradox Main menu with Report selected.*

8

```
Output  Design  Change  RangeOutput  SetPrinter                Main
Send a report to the printer, the screen, or a file.
```

Fig. 8.43. The Paradox Report menu with Output selected.

With slight variations, the steps for creating mailing labels are the same as for generating form letters.

Form Letters

After mailing labels, the most commonly requested report is probably some sort of form letter. You can use databases to generate personalized letters to large numbers of people. Such letters are an essential part of marketing and customer relations.

With a few additional fields, form letters also can serve as the basis for related reports, such as invoices. Form letters contain some of the same fields needed for invoices, such as names and addresses. All you need to add is billing information.

Form letters include essentially the same fields as mailing labels, with extra fields for the salutation and the date of the letter. The body of the letter itself is simply background text for the report.

To simplify writing the form letter report, copy your mailing labels report (naming it Formlet or something more memorable), and then edit the format. Unlike labels, letters are usually printed only one across. You need to add a page break at the bottom of the format so that each letter starts on a new page.

If you change the text of your form letters frequently, the number of report formats will proliferate, and you might have difficulty finding the right one when you need it. Depending on the database software you use, you may not want to create a new report each time the text of the letter changes.

Some database software specializes in form letter generation. Q&A, for example, includes a database to manage your addresses and an integrated word processor to create form letters and other documents. Because the two pieces of software are compatible, users can be quickly trained to use Q&A for correspondence management.

You can take two approaches to creating form letters with a database. One approach is to export a data file with the names and addresses to disk and then use the merge capability of your word processing program to produce the letters. Using mail merge has several advantages. Mail merge provides more flexibility in formatting the letter. Users can enjoy word processing features such as word wrap, cut and paste, spelling checkers, and others not available in databases. Word processing programs usually have better printer support, especially for handling special effects and fonts. Users may be more comfortable creating a new merge letter in their word processing software than writing a new database report. This approach, however, requires an extra step and may force you to leave one application and start another.

Another approach is to store the text of the letter in a database table rather than enter it as background text in the report format. You can, for example, create a table to store the name of the letter along with several lines of text, as shown in figure 8.44.

```
Letter Code: BLITS

Text1: Enclosed please find a trial copy of our exciting new
Text2: software package, the Business Lead Information
Text3: Tracking System (BLITS).  This package can be
Text4: customized to meet your specific needs.
etc.
```

Fig. 8.44. *A table for storing form letter text.*

You can enter any number of form letters in your database. When generating the letter, you specify the letter code for the appropriate text, in this case BLITS. The report contains all the text lines as fields in the format.

This method has several significant advantages. You need only one report to generate many different form letters, and the database is therefore easier to maintain. Users can modify the text of the letter themselves, without programming or exiting to another program (such as the word processing program). Finally, you can run letters in batches simply by entering the letter code and the name (or some other identifier) for each recipient in a table, using that data to generate the letters at a later time. If form letters are a major part of your business, the extra effort required to create this kind of generic form letter generator is worthwhile. This type of planning and data-driven design can pay off in large dividends.

Summary

This chapter shows how to retrieve data from your database in the form of printed reports, and offers guidelines for report design. The most important goal is to make reports useful to the people who read them. To achieve this goal, keep reports concise, clear, and easy to read.

Writing a report involves three basic steps. The first step is record selection: choosing which records from the table should appear on the report. Databases provide several different ways to retrieve records, based on values in fields or other criteria.

The second step in report writing is to choose which fields to list from the records you have selected. In some cases, your reports may not contain any fields at all, but only calculated summary information based on fields, such as totals, counts, and averages. At this stage, you also may opt for special sorting or grouping of records.

The third and final step in writing a report is to design its format. The same rules of graphic design discussed in reference to form definition apply to reports. Designing the report format also implies choosing the destination device, such as the printer, screen, or disk file.

Honing Your Reporting Skills

Where we cannot invent, we may at least improve.

Charles Caleb Colton

As explained in the preceding chapter, creating reports takes a great deal of planning. To create useful, easy-to-read reports, you must determine what information you need to include and think about the layout of the report. You should consider whether the report includes all the necessary information in an easy-to-read format, whether the report will run quickly, and whether other reports that you design will be as easy to understand as the first report you designed. This chapter builds on the preceding chapter to help you write even more effective reports.

Standardizing Your Reports

After creating a few reports, you will notice that many reports are similar to each other. In an inventory system, for example, the report listing a *group* of items in inventory is similar to a report listing *all* items in inventory; to create the report listing the group of items, however, you use a query to select only certain records. If you design your reports with the future in mind, you can use the reports you create today as patterns for the reports you will create in the future.

The following sections offer suggestions for you to consider when creating reports. If you follow these suggestions, you will be more productive when you design and maintain a database system.

Documenting Queries

As some of the programs in this chapter and the preceding chapter illustrate, the code you write to generate a report can become complex. Including comments within the code to explain various sections of the procedure can help you maintain the code. The syntax for comments varies with each DBMS.

Although many procedures are largely self-documenting, additional comments can be helpful, especially when parts of a query may not be obvious to another user. In a DataEase query, all text to the right of a dash (--) is interpreted as a comment. In dBASE, an asterisk (*) introduces a comment. Comments may be on separate lines or mixed with query statements.

Don't be stingy with space in the query. For readability, queries should not extend beyond the width of the screen. Add comments in the query itself if the query is complicated. You may, for example, want to add the comment `-- The following example of a documented query posts all unpaid invoices to the receivables file` before the portion of the query that performs the posting.

```
* Program.............Sample of Documented dBASE Program
* Date................11/20/91
* Author..............Jim Townsend
* Software............dBASE IV, v. 1.1
*
* NOTE: This is not a complete procedure. It illustrates how comments
* may be used in a program.

*--Parameters -- Declare program parameters here
PARAMETERS gl_plain, gl_header

*-- Test for no records found
IF EOF() .OR. .NOT. FOUND()
 RETURN
ENDIF
```

Using indenting and comments to set off sections of the program also makes your code easier to read, especially when you are using long, nested IF clauses. Blank lines also can make a query easier to read.

Comments can help you test programs. When you mark part of a procedure as a comment (programmers call this *commenting out*), that part of the program is ignored when the program is run. By commenting out parts of a program, you can remove those parts without deleting them.

Using Data-Entry Forms to Generate Reports

Some reports ask the user for information when the report is run. A sales report, for example, may ask for a specific range of dates to be covered. Using data-entry forms with reports makes the report more flexible. The same report can provide information based on many search criteria, with no programming required.

All the guidelines pertaining to form design apply to data-entry forms for reports. Include a data-entry screen in every report a user runs, even if no data entry is required. The data-entry form shows what has been chosen and gives you an opportunity to exit from the report without running it. The data-entry screen should contain a brief description of what the report will list. Be sure to remind the user what to do after completing the fields. You may want to indicate which key to press to continue running the report and offer the option of cancelling the report. You do not need to provide a data-entry form for chained procedures—procedures used to link together several programs—or for utility programs that require no user intervention, such as index maintenance.

Special conventions are useful for data-entry forms. Using the same field names for data-entry forms can speed query writing. Use the generic labels START DATE and END DATE, for example, to name the fields for calculating a range of dates rather than change the names of these fields for each report to show the context of the query (PURCHASES SINCE DATE, for example). Another convention is to use single boxes for data-entry screens that do not require data-entry and double boxes for those requiring user input.

Achieving Data-Driven Reporting

The need for reports never seems to end. No matter how many reports you build into a database, new reporting needs always emerge. With some planning, you can anticipate future reporting needs and make a system that can respond easily to changes. Flexibility is one of the hallmarks of creating good reports. By using tables to store variables needed for reporting, you can make a system much simpler to create and maintain.

You can write database procedures in two basic ways. The first approach, the hard-coded method, relies on rigidly defining the selection criteria, sorting, and other report characteristics. The second approach, the one advocated in this book, is to make your database data-driven so that users can change parameters rather than rewrite programs. You can calculate sales tax for a report, for example, in two ways. You can write a program with the logic for calculating sales tax and include the program in the report. The pseudocode for this routine may look like the following:

```
If tax exempt = no then     if state = NY , price * 0.05
                            if state = CA , price * 0.07 ,etc.
```

As the report runs, the sales tax for each invoice is calculated.

The problem with this coded approach is that the program must be re-written, possibly in several parts of the database, if the tax rate changes. A better approach is to build a database table that contains sales tax rates (maintained by the system users) such as the following:

State	Sales Tax Rate
CA	0.07
DC	0.08
NY	0.05

The logic in the report looks up the tax rate from the sales tax table, based on the state name. If the tax rates change, you can easily modify the tax rate table without modifying any programs.

This technique is useful for many similar cases in which information may change during the life of an application. Although making your application "data-driven" may take a little extra time, your efforts will pay off in the long run.

Recycling Reports

You may find that during the development process, reports proliferate faster than rabbits. Reports often have variants to be run weekly, monthly, quarterly, and annually. You also may need reports that furnish the same information based on different sets of search criteria.

The best way to keep an application lean and elegant is to combine re-ports so that one report fulfills the functions of many. This process is similar to normalizing your data table structure (see Chapter 4).

First, do not duplicate reports to cover different periods of time. Instead of creating weekly and monthly reports, set up the data-entry form for the report so that you can specify the starting and ending dates to be covered by the report. If necessary, add monthly subtotals. In this way, you can generate the report for a day, a week, a month, a year, or a longer period.

If two reports have the same format but different search criteria, consider combining them into a single report into which the user can enter multiple criteria when the report is run. If, for example, your reports select students by state, by class, and by major, consider combining them into a single report that enables you to fill in one or more fields for record selection.

You also can build batch selection queries to flag records based on any number of search criteria and then print all the selected records. A batch processor enables you to add and remove records in the batch based on specified criteria, so that you can specify more complex record selection than in a single search. After you have built the batch to your satisfaction, you can print it or save it.

You also can borrow an old report and make a few changes to add new meaning. The report shown in figure 9.1, from the Service Call Tracking Database, is a variation on the Service Call Summary Report shown in figure 8.2. Note that some detail fields have been removed (such as the spare parts description) and that cost figures have been added. This report shows the costs and price for each service call during the specified period.

```
Service Call Cost and Price Summary from 01/01/91 to 03/31/91                        November 2, 1991
Acme Appliance Company
Cleveland, OH                          -- FOR INTERNAL USE ONLY --

=====================================================================================================
Location   SCR     Date      Serial      Type      Labor  Labor   Labor    Mileage   Travel   Parts   Parts    TOTAL
           Number            Number                 Hours  Price   Cost               Price    Price   Cost     PRICE
-----------------------------------------------------------------------------------------------------
Washington (DC)
           000003  02/18/91  JUSTATEST   System Unit  2.5  132.50  87.50    122       28.06    82.00   0.00     242.56
           000005  02/22/91  721123769   System Unit  1.0   53.00  35.00     34        7.82     0.00    0.00      60.82
           000006  02/22/91  6146930     Display      1.0   53.00  35.00     34        7.82   297.00  121.00    357.82

Office Total        Service Calls =   3                   238.50  35.00    190       43.70   379.00  121.00    661.20

St. Louis (STL)
           000001  01/18/91  121012802   Printer      2.5  132.50  87.50     76       17.48   106.75   55.00    256.73
           000002  02/22/91  J34383794   System Unit  0.7   37.10  24.50     40        9.20   100.00   50.00    146.30

Office Total        Service Calls =   2                   169.60  24.50    116       26.68   206.75  105.00    403.03

Albuquerque (ALB)
           000004  01/18/91  1501234     System Unit  1.5   79.50  52.50     36        8.28   106.75   50.00    194.53
Office Total        Service Calls =   1                    79.50  52.50     36        8.28   106.75   50.00    194.53


=====================================================================================================
=====================================================================================================
```

Fig. 9.1. *A modified report.*

9

You probably will find similar cases in which you can make small changes to an existing report without having to create a report from scratch. Often I start by designing the most detailed report and then simply remove the detail sections to leave the group summary statistics.

Retrieving Data through Alternate Methods

You can approach a report that contains data from more than one table from either file (in a relational database). An invoice report, for example, may start in the Invoice Header table, then go to the Line Items table to list the detailed information. You also can start in the Line Items table and then go to the Invoice Header table for header information. Which direction is preferable?

The performance of multiple-table reports varies from one database package to another and is influenced by the indexing scheme and the sizes of the two files. The following are some rules of thumb, but the only true guide is experimentation.

Another way to increase productivity is to build your report based on a view. As Chapter 7 discusses, views can consolidate fields from several tables. Using a view also protects your report from changes in the underlying table structure because the view can remain the same even when you modify the tables.

If your software has a query optimizer, have it make these decisions for you. A query optimizer evaluates the best method to perform your search by building indexes, changing the order of the searches for different criteria, and other means. If the current version of your software does not have a query optimizer, the next version probably will.

Optimizing Queries

As you have seen, some search methods are more efficient than others, even if they yield the same result. Many factors are at work behind the scenes, including the way the indexes are built and the performance of the DBMS itself.

Optimization is tricky business. Some software optimizes the query for you. Paradox, in many cases, obtains a result in the same amount of time for two different versions of the same query because it processes the query and optimizes it before running it. You must tune dBASE manually, however, for each report you create. Database software originally written for minicomputers or mainframes, such as Ingres, Oracle, and Sybase, usually comes with a query optimizer.

Optimization requires detailed knowledge of the storage structure of the data and the inner workings of the DBMS. The performance of a query may be affected by other software and by techniques such as *disk caching* (using memory to minimize disk access).

Although query optimization varies widely according to the DBMS, some broad principles apply:

- Seek the smallest file possible.
- Search on the most restrictive criteria first.
- Minimize the number of files needed to get the information.

Understanding Processing Procedures

In addition to reports that list information from the database, you may need procedures to import, export, or modify data. This section explains how to perform these and other types of data manipulation.

I have played down the importance of programming skills for the earlier stages of the development process. These skills become important when you create processing procedures, however. If you are not a skilled programmer, be sure to find someone to back you up when you encounter difficulty in writing procedures.

To write processing procedures, you probably need to learn a database programming language such as Xbase (dBASE) or SQL. Although you can design tables, forms, and reports by using more visual tools, processing procedures need a language to express their meaning exactly, often with a great deal of subtle detail. With a programming language, you can express your commands succinctly and unambiguously.

Using Data-Entry Routines

You can write procedures to take the user through a controlled series of repetitive actions. You may, for example, want to chain together several data-entry forms so that the user enters records in one or more tables and then runs a report. Using a procedure ensures that the user carries out these steps in the correct order and frees the user from memorizing a sequence of menu choices or commands. Pseudocode for a telephone order entry application, for example, may read like the following order entry procedure listing.

1. Enter Customer last name and ZIP code. The system displays the customer's order history, if available, with orders listed in reverse

9

chronological order. If the customer is new, a customer ID number is generated.

2. Verify customer address (or enter address for new customer).

3. Enter order items.

4. When order is complete, display a notice of special items on sale that correlate with the customer order, with a message such as
   `Would you care to order a matching camisole?`

5. Print shipping list.

6. Clear screen for next order. Go to step 1.

In real life, this procedure may be more complicated. It may branch out to other forms and procedures based on the circumstances and should provide for possible interruptions or cancellation of the process.

Maintaining Data Security

Procedures have security advantages over an application in which users can peruse forms at will. You can use a procedure to add new records to a table, for example, prompting the user to enter each field, but not giving access to browse through the records in the table. You also can have the procedure check for duplicates before saving the new record.

Procedures themselves may be associated with different security levels so that access is restricted to sensitive information. In this way, only users with the proper security level can run a procedure.

Importing and Exporting Files

Some of the most commonly used procedures are imports and exports, transferring data from one database to another. Your accounting software may have little flexibility for report writing, and you want to move data into your familiar DBMS. You can buy data, such as a mailing list, from someone else and include it in your database tables. Most DBMS provide a mechanism for performing these transfers, even for data created with otherwise incompatible software from their competitors.

You can move data in two directions. *Imports* bring external data into a database, and *exports* send data in the opposite direction, from inside the database to another "foreign" format. Many formats are available for exchanging data. The following sections describe the most popular formats.

ASCII Fixed-Length

ASCII fixed-length files, most commonly used by mainframe computers, consist of readable ASCII characters (letters, numbers, and punctuation marks). If a field is not full, spaces are added so that each field and record is exactly the same length. A name and address file in fixed-length format may appear as follows:

```
Jeanie M.      Townsend        100 Sunny Lane
                               Palm Beach       FL33456
Jeffrey Clay   Townsend        100 Sunny Lane
                               Palm Beach       FL33456
Scott          Montgomery      321 Bayshore Dr.
                               Tampa     FL33511
Jodie R.       Montgomery      321 Bayshore Dr.
                               Tampa     FL33511
```

Note that each field starts in the same column for each record. Blank fields (such as the middle name for Scott Montgomery) are represented with spaces. For a field that is completely filled, such as Jeffrey Clay, the field runs into the next one. If a fixed-length file is viewed by using a word processing program or other text editor, the fields line up in straight columns.

ASCII Delimited or Variable Length

Like ASCII fixed-length, delimited files contain only readable characters. The difference is that a special character (called a *delimiter*) separates one field from the next. A carriage return or some other character at the end of each record indicates a new record.

Do not use characters that appear in the data as delimiters. If you do, the import may cut off the field where that character occurs and ruin the following fields in the record. The best delimiters to use are characters that are unlikely to appear in the data. Exotic punctuation marks such as the vertical line (|) and the tilde (~) are popular delimiters. My personal favorite is the circumflex (^), as shown in the following:

```
Jeanie ^ M. ^ Townsend ^ 100 Sunny Lane ^ Palm
Beach ^ FL ^ 33456
Jeffrey ^ Clay ^ Townsend ^ 100 Sunny Lane ^ Palm
Beach ^ FL ^ 33456
Scott ^ ^ Montgomery ^ 321 Bayshore Dr. ^ Tampa ^ FL ^ 33511
Jodie ^ R. ^ Montgomery ^ 321 Bayshore Dr. ^ Tampa ^ FL ^ 33511
```

9

In variable length format, spaces are not needed to separate each field. The field and record lengths vary according to the number of spaces actually used, giving a jagged appearance to the data file.

dBASE Format (.DBF)

Because it is the most popular database file form, many DBMS enable you to import and export files to the dBASE standard .DBF format. The .DBF file contains the structure of the table and of the data and can be accessed by other programs that accept this format.

Lotus 1-2-3 Format (.WK1)

For exporting to or importing from spreadsheets, many DBMS support the Lotus .WK1 file format. You often must mark and save a range of cells under a range name before running the import.

Data Interchange Format (.DIF)

The data interchange format translates spreadsheets into specially coded text (ASCII) files. Many spreadsheets contain options to save .DIF files, which can be imported into popular database software.

Archiving

As a database grows, its performance may worsen. Reports have to process an increasing number of records, backups take longer, and overall operation may slow. You may run out of disk storage space and be unable to afford more.

For these reasons, you can transfer inactive records in a database to an archive file on- or off-line. To write an archiving procedure, determine when records should be moved to the archive and write a procedure to copy the records and then delete them from the main table.

Packing the Database

Another common database procedure is called *packing*, or reorganizing. To understand packing, you need to know how database records are deleted in many DBMS. When you press the appropriate key to delete a record (or enter a delete command in a procedure), the record is not immediately deleted from the disk file. Deleting the record requires adjusting the entire file to a new size and may take considerable time. Instead, a special field is marked that tags the record for future deletion. Deleted records therefore are recoverable for a certain period of time.

Packing a database file physically deletes all records tagged for deletion. In some packages, such as DataEase, packing also rebuilds the related index files. To clear the clutter of deleted records, you should perform packing periodically.

Debugging

Sooner or later you will run into procedures that do not do what they are supposed to do, and you must resort to the fine art of database troubleshooting, also known as *debugging*. Debugging is the process of finding and eliminating software flaws. These flaws may arise from a number of different sources. They may be caused by programming errors, glitches in the database management software itself, operating system problems, or even hardware incompatibility.

When debugging, you must find the source of the problem and eliminate the problem with extreme prejudice. Above all, debugging requires a systematic approach. I learned the following hints from a seasoned computer professional. The specific techniques you use will depend on the nature of the debugging problem and the hardware and software environment in which you are working.

- *Make only one change at a time.* You may break this rule of debugging only at great peril to yourself and your users. The cause of a problem can never be determined conclusively if you try more than one fix at a time. If your program works after you remove a certain device driver and switch from a color to monochrome monitor, you may think the application cannot run with a color monitor.

- *Eliminate potential causes one by one to isolate the problem.* If you suspect hardware, move the software to another machine and try it there. If you have extra peripherals, swap them and test again.

- *Write down the result of each test.* As you make changes, indicate what happened. Did new error messages appear? When did the problem go away? You often will find that you must go through several layers of a problem to arrive at a solution, so it is important to record your progress.

- *Use status messages within procedures to monitor their progress.* dBASE and FoxPro provide facilities for stepping through a query one command at a time to determine what is going astray.

  Many DBMS have special memory variables associated with the status of a process that can help you in debugging. You can, for

9

example, show a variable as each calculation is performed for complicated procedures such as account aging. This technique helps pinpoint where the error is occurring.

- *Urge your users to be cautious about making any changes that may affect the database,* including modifications to the operating system environment (the CONFIG.SYS file in DOS, for example), memory management programs, operating system upgrades, and even hardware upgrades. If several such changes are introduced before the problem is noticed, it may become much more difficult to trace.

Many DBMS contain their own program debuggers to help you find software errors. Debugging packages are available for other DBMS from third-party vendors. Take advantage of these packages if they can save you time in testing and fixing your applications.

Summary

This chapter offers suggestions for taking your reporting skills to a higher level. It discusses how to make your databases less rigid and more data-driven, so that they can respond to changing business needs with a minimum of programming. The following guidelines can help you achieve this goal:

- Create style standards for reports to include the following elements: header layout (report title, date, page number), standard abbreviations (such as *p.* for page), display of selection criteria on report, and format conventions (such as paper size).

- Make reports data-driven.

- Give reports meaningful names.

- Document all queries and program code.

- Document all processing procedures. Tell users what will happen, warn users about slow processes, and show progress when appropriate.

Advanced reporting requires mastery of your chosen database software. Depending on your DBMS, you may also need to learn about structured programming techniques.

Designing Menus

*A man is too apt to forget that in this world he cannot have everything.
A choice is all that is left to him.*

K. Mathews

Although you can write a database application without menus, most users want menus. Navigating your way through an application with menus is easier than learning the many commands necessary to perform all database functions. Almost every database management software includes a facility for creating user menus. Some DBMS packages (such as Alpha Four) are menu-driven for nearly every operation.

As in the world's finest restaurants, menus are included in database applications to make consumer choices easier. Menus help organize the cornucopia of choices so that users can perform the actions with the least amount of effort.

In most DBMS packages, making menus is one of the easiest steps in database development. The required programming is relatively simple; your real challenge is to understand how the user works and thinks. As usual, analysis counts more than programming. This chapter outlines the menu creation process from planning through implementation.

Why Use Menus?

A menu system makes the database easier to use and more productive. A menu frees users from memorizing commands and helps users move from place to place within the database. By offering a list of choices, a menu system also reminds users of all the functions they need to perform.

Menus can combine a number of choices and commands into a single keystroke. They make the application appear simple, even when complex work is being performed. One menu option, for example, can activate a procedure to run a report, export the results to a disk file, and then call up your word processing program so you can edit the report.

Menus also control access to sensitive database functions. They protect confidential information and shield the data from destructive actions (such as commands to purge all data or reformat the hard disk) that the system administrator should perform. Menus provide this control by giving users access only to the options they need.

You may not want all users to have access to the Control Center in dBASE, for instance, because through it they can create and modify tables without restriction. Most database users do not want or need access to the functions used for database programming and design.

A database application can have more than one set of menus. Some applications require a different list of functions for different categories of users. A publication sales system, for example, can include different menus for the order-entry personnel, the stockroom, the accounting department, and the marketing department. The stockroom staff must have access to shipping screens and reports, but they do not need to see accounts payable information. By tailoring the menus to the needs of each group of users, you provide options that reflect each group's special requirements.

Menus have the additional benefit of speeding the training of new users. Menus explain the functions of the database and illustrate the application's typical use. With a menu system, you can explore all the functions of a database with little fear of causing serious damage. The menus warn you about your actions and help you see everything the system has to offer. Menus make some applications so simple to understand that a printout of the menus can take the place of a user manual.

Finally, the menu interface can provide navigational clues to the user. The menu can show how to exit, how to make a choice, and how to get help. Have you ever had the frustrating experience of running a mysterious program on your computer and then finding that the only way to exit was to reboot? A good menu system does not leave you hanging. It explains how to cancel actions and how to exit from the application when you are finished.

The Myth of Intuition

In the pursuit of clarity, many software designers strive to build intuitive—easy to understand—interfaces to make the computer application understandable to someone with little or no training in its specifics. Unfortunately, the word *intuitive* can mean different things to different people, and is not necessarily a good measure for computer interfaces.

Some of the best interfaces are the least intuitive, depending on whose intuition you measure. What is intuitive for the database designer may not be intuitive for the user. Moreover, many things that are easy to use are not intuitive. Steering a sailboat with a rudder is counterintuitive, for instance, because you point the rudder in the opposite direction of the turn. Handling a mouse is not natural or intuitive (unless you are a cat), but many people love using a mouse with a graphical interface such as Windows or the Macintosh.

Visual interfaces are not necessarily more intuitive than those that depend on words (character-based interfaces, such as DOS). Some graphical icons make sense to almost anyone. Using a small image of a trash can on the screen is a good way to represent file deletion. Some operations, however, defy simple visualization. What icon could you use to signify index rebuilding? The symbol for a stop sign is widely understood, but designing a symbol to represent "no parking or standing from 4:00 through 6:30 p.m." would not be an easy task.

Perhaps truly intuitive interfaces someday will appear on computers. These interfaces might include speaking to the computer or pointing at the screen with your finger. Although a number of touch-screen applications (such as campus directory maps and library catalogs) are currently available, voice-activated interfaces are not common yet on business desktops.

In the absence of a perfectly intuitive interface, a reasonable goal is to create an interface that is easy to learn and easy to use. Menus can go a long way in aiding learning. A menu offers a list of possible actions, in an order that resembles a typical work flow. Menus can make an application easier to use because no commands need be memorized.

Sometimes ease of learning conflicts with ease of use. A long series of menu choices may simplify operations for a novice but frustrates a veteran user who wants to accomplish the job as quickly as possible. Similarly, complex systems may be harder to learn but much better to use. The powerful word processing software that I prefer has many features that might confuse beginning users. To accommodate both beginners and experts, you can set up your database so that the same tasks can be accomplished in more than one way.

Choosing Menu Options

Like the art of form design, menu building requires analysis. Your first step in designing a menu structure is to make a comprehensive list of the functions that users will perform. List all data-entry forms, reports, and other procedures (posting, data backups, and so on) the user will need. If your application requires menus for several groups of users, repeat the menu designing process with the needs of each group in mind.

The following is a list of functions for a client tracking database:

> Enter, edit, or delete client information
> Enter, edit or delete company information
> Print mailing labels
> Print envelopes
> Create form letters
> Print form letters
> Enter sales figures
> Search for duplicate entries
> Enter mailing lists
> Assign clients to mailing lists
> Print client phone directory
> Schedule appointments
> Print activity report
> Print calendar
> Back up database to diskette
> Restore database from diskette
> Export client file to word processing software
> Import mailing list from mainframe

This list of functions is in no particular order. You will group and order the functions in the next stages of menu design.

> **NOTE:** Each menu should have an option to exit to the preceding menu without performing any database actions. This option is inherent in the menu schemes of some DBMS products (DataEase menus use Esc or 0 to exit), but others require the programmer to add a special option. Always make Exit the last option, because this is the most common convention for commercial software packages. If possible in your database software, use the Esc key for this purpose.

Grouping Menu Options

If you have a very small application, you may be able to fit all your options on a single menu. The following menu has only seven options.

Murphy's Garage Main Menu

1. Auto Information
2. Repairs
3. Spare Parts Inventory
4. Print Invoices
5. Print Parts Used
6. Stock Level Report
7. Back Up Database
8. Exit Database

If all your choices fit on a single menu, your work is nearly finished. Most applications, however, have more user options than can be placed without crowding onto a single screen.

Do not make menus too long. I recommend no more than nine choices on a single menu. Working with short menus, the user can view all options at a glance and make a selection by pressing one key. If your menus hold only two or three options, they may be too short; consider consolidating some of the menus.

Unless all your options fit on one menu, you need to create a series of menus that enable the user to move from one menu to another. This collection of menus is called a *menu tree* (see fig. 10.1).

Fig. 10.1. *A sample menu tree.*

After you create the list of database functions, group them into menus. You can group functions in several ways, as explained in the following sections.

Grouping by Function

You might want to group similar functions, such as adding, viewing, printing, and exporting. You can, for example, place all printed reports on the same menu. The following menu tree is an example of this approach:

```
Main Menu
    Maintain Data
        Clients
        Companies
        Mailing Lists
        Appointments
    Print Reports
        Letters
            Thanks for your order
            New product announcement
            Change of address
            New employee introduction
        Mailing Labels and Envelopes
            2-across
            Cheshire
            Large single labels
            Envelopes
        Activity Report
        Monthly Calendar
    Database Maintenance
        Backup
        Restore
        Export Data
        Import Data
        Exit to DOS
```

The top-level menu, or *main menu*, controls access to the three sub-menus, but does not contain any database functions. Note that some menu choices branch to other menus, and some perform a database action.

Grouping by Work Flow

You can group menu choices in the order in which operators will use them. This approach is most effective when the flow of operations is rigid. A telemarketing company, for example, might use a menu tree like the following:

```
Main Menu
    Call Processing
        Search for New Prospect
        Qualify Lead
        Take Order
        Print Invoice
    Utilities
        Backup Database
        Other Functions
            Word Processing
            Electronic Mail
```

Throughout most of the work day, the telemarketer uses only the Call Processing menu. At the end of the day, the telemarketer uses the Utilities menu options to generate a report to summarize the day's activities, write memos, and send electronic mail to the sales supervisor.

Grouping by Other Methods

You can group menu options in other ways, though the methods are less popular than the two described in the preceding sections. You can group menu options alphabetically by the first letter of the functions. The Client Address List, Client File Editing, and Client Import options would appear together in such a grouping. I do not recommend alphabetical grouping for menu options, because related options can end up far from one another. Using alphabetical grouping also encourages you to use twisted phrasing to manipulate the menu order.

You can invent your own rationale for grouping and ordering menu choices, as long as your grouping is consistent and meaningful to the user. Different people respond differently to menus, so feel free to try several approaches until you find a good fit. Some users find a main menu without direct options to be bothersome; they prefer more actions on the main menu, even if the resulting menu looks busy.

Ordering Menu Options

You enhance menu effectiveness when you properly order all menu options. You can choose from several ordering approaches that apply to menus and to options that are presented when running reports.

Frequency of Use

The most common (and arguably the most productive) way to order menu options is by frequency of use, in which you place the most frequently used option first on the menu and the least frequently used option last. A menu ordered by frequency of use for the Acme Order Entry database might read as follows:

>Enter New Orders
>Delete Cancelled Orders
>Print Shipping Slips
>Edit Customer File
>Add Inventory Items
>Back Up Database
>Exit Program

Users at Acme spend most of the day entering orders and printing shipping slips. They occasionally correct addresses in the customer file and infrequently add inventory items. Once each day, they back up the database.

Alphabetical Order

You can arrange menu choices in alphabetical order. The advantage of alphabetical ordering is that you can find an option easily (if you know the option's title).

The drawbacks of using alphabetical order, however, usually outweigh the advantages. Many different words can describe any particular option, so the user may have to read the entire menu to find a desired choice. Another problem with alphabetical ordering is that frequently used operations can fall anywhere on the menu. The following menu is the Acme Order Entry database menu in alphabetical order:

>Add Inventory Items
>Back Up Database
>Delete Cancelled Orders
>Edit Customer File
>Enter New Orders
>Exit Program
>Print Shipping Slips

In the alphabetized menu, one of the least used options, Add Inventory Items, is in the top position. This menu separates the functions for entering and deleting orders, and reverses their logical order.

Alphabetical order can be effective if your menu is long and users know the precise names of options. A conference planning system, for example, could have a menu that displays all the locations for a company, as follows:

> View calendar by location: (choose a location)
> Boston
> Dallas
> Detroit
> Los Angeles
> New Orleans
> San Francisco
> Seattle
> Tucson

If your menu options, like those in the preceding example, have no particular order by frequency (or any other pattern), alphabetical order is better than no order at all.

Chronological Order

Chronological ordering is similar to alphabetical ordering. If menu choices have an inherent time element, and if ordering by frequency of use is impractical, chronological order may be your best choice. As a simple example, a scheduling menu for a haute couture show might look like this:

> Choose apparel line:
> Spring
> Summer
> Fall
> Winter

A chronological listing also can show the time of day or the date, as appropriate.

Numerical Order

You also can place menu options also in numerical order. This approach is the least common of those discussed in this book, but is useful for some applications. You might create the following menu for processing loan applications with choices based on the amount of the loan:

> Enter amount of loan:
> <1,000
> 1,000–5,000
> 5,000–50,000
> 50,000–100,000
> >100,000

The user might be prompted for different information depending on the size of the loan sought. Displaying the choices in ascending order makes the menu easier to use than displaying them randomly.

Choosing Menu Styles

After you have designed a menu tree, creating the menus is easy. Most DBMS provide facilities for quickly generating menus. In some, such as Paradox, you must write a program to create a menu, but most packages give you menus to create menus.

You can choose from a variety of menu styles. Each DBMS package has its own way of creating menus; no overall standards for database menus exist. dBASE IV, for example, supports four types of menus: *pop-up*, *horizontal bar*, *pull-down*, and *free form*. Looking at samples of these menu types may help you decide which to use.

Bar Menus

A *bar menu* (not the kind that contains potato skins and nachos) displays choices in a row across the top of the screen, as in a spreadsheet. Users select items by entering the first letter of a choice or by moving the highlight to a choice and pressing Enter. Bar menus are short and compact. Because bar menus resemble spreadsheet menus, they look familiar to many users. Figure 10.2 shows a screen with a typical bar menu across the top.

To create a bar menu in dBASE IV, follow these steps:

1. Select Applications Generator from the dBASE Control Center menu.

2. Press F10 and select Design, the first menu option.

3. Choose Horizontal Bar Menu. The screen shown in figure 10.3 appears.

4. Fill in the name of the menu and a description of what the menu does.

5. Press Ctrl-End to save and continue.

   You now can enter text and spaces on the menu bar, positioning the choices as you want them to appear to the user. After you complete the design of the bar, you can define each of the menu actions. Press F10 and select Item. The menu shown in figure 10.4 appears.

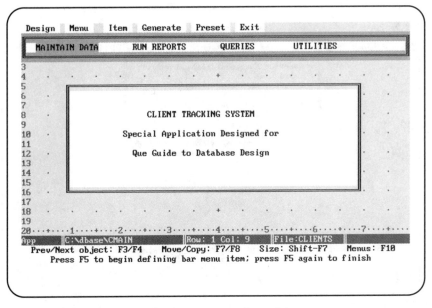

Fig. 10.2. *Client Tracking System main menu (bar style).*

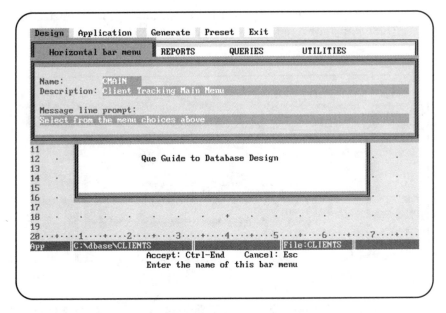

Fig. 10.3. *The dBASE Bar Menu menu.*

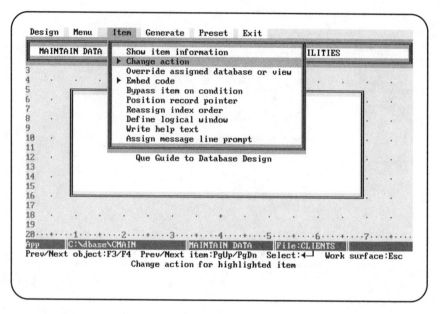

Fig. 10.4. *The dBASE Menu Item menu.*

6. Use the Change action option to select or modify the menu action. The menu shown in figure 10.5 appears when you select Change action.

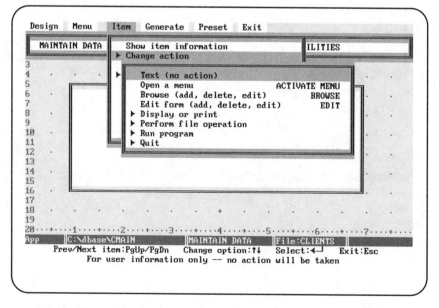

Fig. 10.5. *The dBASE Change action menu.*

In dBASE IV, the Applications Generator is an excellent way to create first drafts of your menu structure. Later, if necessary, you can edit any dBASE command for special functions not provided by the Applications Generator. The dBASE Applications Generator created the following program for the main menu of the Client Tracking system.

```
**********************************************************************
* Program......: CMAIN.PRG
* Description..: Client Tracking System Main Menu
* Description..: Menu actions
**********************************************************************
PROCEDURE CMAIN
PARAMETER entryflg
PRIVATE gc_prognum
gc_prognum="01"
SET COLOR OF NORMAL TO W+/B
CLEAR
PRIVATE lc_ApGen
lc_ApGen=LTRIM(STR(gn_ApGen))

DO SET01
IF gn_error > 0
   gn_error=0
   RETURN
ENDIF

*-- Before menu code


ACTIVATE MENU CMAIN

@ 0,0 CLEAR TO 2,79

*-- After menu

RETURN
*-- EOP CMAIN

PROCEDURE SET01
ON KEY LABEL F1 DO 1HELP1

DO DBF01 && open menu level database

IF gn_error = 0
```

continues

Continued

```
    IF gl_color .AND. .NOT. SET("ATTRIBUTE") = "W+/B,RG+/GB,N/N "+;
       CHR(38)+CHR(38)+" W+/N,W/B,RG+/GB,B/W,N/GB"
       SET COLOR OF NORMAL TO W+/B
       SET COLOR OF MESSAGES TO W+/N
       SET COLOR OF TITLES TO W/B
       SET COLOR OF HIGHLIGHT TO RG+/GB
       SET COLOR OF BOX TO RG+/GB
       SET COLOR OF INFORMATION TO B/W
       SET COLOR OF FIELDS TO N/GB
    ENDIF

    SET BORDER TO
    @ 0,0 TO 2,79 DOUBLE COLOR RG+/GB
    @ 1,1 CLEAR TO 1,78
    @ 1,1 FILL TO 1,78 COLOR W+/N
    @ 1,3 SAY "MAINTAIN DATA" COLOR W+/N
    @ 1,23 SAY "RUN REPORTS" COLOR W+/N
    @ 1,41 SAY "QUERIES" COLOR W+/N
    @ 1,56 SAY "UTILITIES" COLOR W+/N
ENDIF
RETURN

PROCEDURE DBF01
CLOSE DATABASES
*-- Open menu level view/database
lc_message="0"
ON ERROR lc_message=LTRIM(STR(ERROR()))+" "+MESSAGE()
USE CLIENTS
ON ERROR
gn_error=VAL(lc_message)
IF gn_error > 0
   DO Pause WITH ;
   "Error opening CLIENTS.DBF"
   lc_new='Y'
   RETURN
ENDIF
lc_new='Y'
RELEASE lc_message
RETURN

PROCEDURE ACT01
*-- Begin CMAIN: BAR Menu Actions.
*-- (before item, action, and after item)
```

```
*
PRIVATE lc_new, lc_dbf
lc_new=' '
lc_dbf=' '
DO CASE
CASE "PAD_1" = PAD()
   IF .NOT. gl_batch
      DO BefAct
   ENDIF
   SET SCOREBOARD ON
   SET MESSAGE TO
   APPEND

   SET SCOREBOARD OFF
   IF .NOT. gl_batch
      DO AftAct
   ENDIF
CASE "PAD_2" = PAD()
   lc_new='Y'
   DO CREPORTS WITH "B01"
CASE "PAD_4" = PAD()
   lc_new='Y'
   DO CUTIL WITH "B01"
OTHERWISE
   @ 24,00
   @ 24,21 SAY "This item has no action. Press a key."
   x=INKEY(0)
   @ 24,00
ENDCASE
SET MESSAGE TO
IF gc_quit='Q'
   IF LEFT(entryflg,1) = "B"
      DEACTIVATE MENU
   ELSE
      DEACTIVATE MENU && CMAIN
   ENDIF
ENDIF
IF lc_new='Y'
   lc_file="SET"+gc_prognum
   DO &lc_file.
ENDIF
RETURN
```

Pop-Up Menus

A *pop-up menu* is a box containing a list of menu options. Pop-up menus can appear anywhere on the screen, although they usually are centered. To select items from a pop-up menu, you type the first letter of the choice or move the highlight bar and press Enter.

The screen in figure 10.6 is a typical pop-up menu. To view additional options, the user presses F10 to return to the menu at the top of the Applications Generator screen. You can create help text to accompany this screen, as shown in figure 10.7. The user displays the help screen by pressing the help key (usually F1).

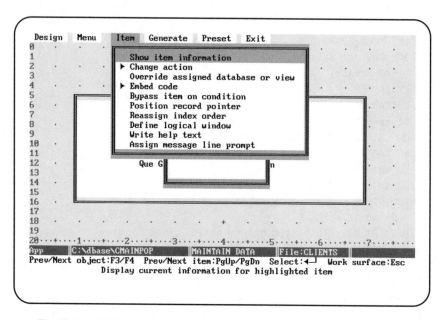

Fig. 10.6. *A dBASE IV pop-up menu.*

Notice that the help text for the Main menu contains the database name and a brief description. You can include additional help, such as a graphic schema of the database or a sketch of the menu structure. Use your imagination to make help screens answer questions users may have about a menu. Help screens are also a good place to document your system.

After you have created a help screen, assign a function to each of the menu options. Whether working with pop-up menus or bar menus, you use the same technique to assign functions to menu options. Press F10 and the menu shown in figure 10.6 appears again. Repeat this step to assign a function for each of your menu options. When you are finished, save the entire menu with Ctrl-End.

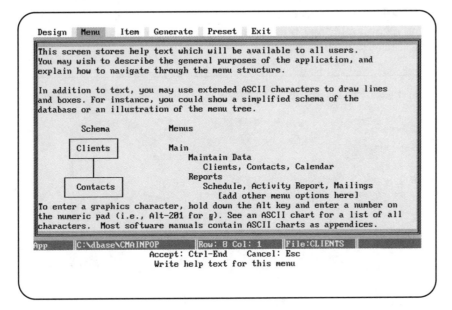

```
Design   Menu   Item   Generate   Preset   Exit
┌─────────────────────────────────────────────────────────────┐
│This screen stores help text which will be available to all users.│
│You may wish to describe the general purposes of the application, and│
│explain how to navigate through the menu structure.             │
│                                                                │
│In addition to text, you may use extended ASCII characters to draw lines│
│and boxes. For instance, you could show a simplified schema of the│
│database or an illustration of the menu tree.                   │
│                                                                │
│        Schema           Menus                                  │
│      ┌─────────┐                                               │
│      │ Clients │       Main                                    │
│      └─────────┘          Maintain Data                        │
│           │                  Clients, Contacts, Calendar       │
│           │               Reports                              │
│      ┌──────────┐             Schedule, Activity Report, Mailings│
│      │ Contacts │                 [add other menu options here]│
│      └──────────┘                                              │
│To enter a graphics character, hold down the Alt key and enter a number on│
│the numeric pad (i.e., Alt-201 for ╔). See an ASCII chart for a list of all│
│characters.  Most software manuals contain ASCII charts as appendices.│
└─────────────────────────────────────────────────────────────┘
App     ║C:\dbase\CMAINPOP     ║Row: 8 Col: 1   ║File:CLIENTS ║
                Accept: Ctrl-End    Cancel: Esc
                Write help text for this menu
```

Fig. 10.7. A dBASE IV pop-up menu help screen.

Pull-Down Menus

Like bar menus, pull-down menus contain a horizontal list of commands at the top of the screen. As you move from one option to another, however, submenus are displayed in a box below the Main menu option. Windows and Presentation Manager applications use pull-down menus, as do drawing packages such as Microsoft Paint and DrawPerfect. dBASE uses pull-down menus extensively, as in the Applications Generator Main menu.

Free-Form Menus

With most DBMS packages and a little extra programming time, you can construct more sophisticated menus than those discussed in the preceding sections. *Free-form menus* can show anything you want on the screen and can process input from the user as you desire. With dBASE, for example, you can write programs with nearly an infinite number of menu choices or even branch between free-form menus.

DataEase supplies the Menu Definition Facility to create standard menus; you also can use the DataEase Query Language (DQL) for more complex free-form menus. One advantage of these free-form menus is that you can make them look just about any way you choose. The menu shown in figure 10.8 was created with a DataEase DQL procedure. It is a procedural menu for a client tracking system, the Business Lead Information Tracking System (BLITS).

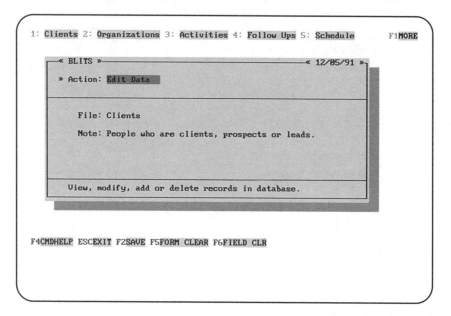

Fig. 10.8. *The BLITS main menu.*

Free-form menus have some serious drawbacks, however. They are not standard, so you must make sure that free-form menus are consistent with one another. Free-form menus are more difficult to create and maintain (adding and deleting menu choices). Finally, unlike standard menus, free-form menus allow for many abuses of good menu design. You could place all the actions for your application on one large free-form menu, for instance, but the menu will be difficult to read and will have essentially defeated the original purpose for its creation.

Context-Sensitive Menus

You can make your menus more context-sensitive by adding conditions to check the time of day or which user is using the database. You can have a maintenance menu, for example, show backup as an option in the afternoon but not in the morning, but be careful. Before you rely on the system clock to trigger routines, remember that many system clocks show the wrong date and time. If you use the system clock date and time, make sure that they are properly set on the computer.

Consistency and Clarity

Several kinds of consistency are needed in menu design. You should be consistent in grouping choices, and make the flow of the menus obvious to the user. Your menu language throughout the application should be consistent in words choice and in details such as capitalization and punctuation. Make your menu structure visually consistent by using as few different menu types as possible.

Being consistent helps the user understand what you mean when you use a term and makes the application easier to master. Consistent language also saves you time because you use standards rather than spend your time remaking routine choices.

Presenting Options

Use consistent language to describe menu choices. You can express a single function in many ways, but you should use the most natural terms possible in your descriptions. You can describe a menu option for modifying customer data, for example, in many ways, including the following:

> Edit Customer File
> Update Customers
> Append Customer Records
> Maintain Customer Information
> Add/Edit/Delete Customers
> Change Customers
> Modify Customer Data

Choose titles your users will understand and then use the same selections in all menus. Avoid computer jargon at all costs. Append Customer Records is probably the worst choice in the preceding list because it contains two words (*append* and *records*) that are computer jargon and may confuse the user. Use consistent phrasing and grammar in all application menus. If you use verb phrases in one menu option, such as Delete Inactive Customers, do not use Invoice Deletion as another option on that menu.

Keep your menu text concise. Do not say Print Out Student Class Roster when Print Class Roster will suffice. Short text makes a menu quick to read and pleasing to the eye. Long menu options are especially bad for bar menus and pull-down menus, because they leave little room for other choices. Do not use abbreviations to make options shorter, unless you are confident that all users will understand them.

Use consistent option names throughout all menus. The submenu name should be the same as the name used for the option that calls it up from the main menu. If, for example, the main menu contains an option called Print Reports, the reports menu should have the title Print Reports, too. This consistency helps the user navigate without getting lost in a menu labyrinth.

As in form design, use consistent capitalization and screen colors in all menus. Some programmers use uppercase letters to indicate options that call up other menus, and mix upper- and lowercase letters for options that call up functions.

Selecting Options

Within an application, be consistent about the ways users choose options from menus. Do not let users choose by number on one menu and by letter on another. If the mouse can be used to select from one menu, let it be an option for all menus.

Avoiding Redundant Menus

In most applications, have users call each function from only one menu. This arrangement makes menu maintenance simpler and can be easier to learn than a system with multiple paths to the same destination. You can have good reasons, however, to break this rule. Functions grouped by work flow, for example, may appear on more than one menu.

Recycling Menus

As in other aspects of database design, a good practice is to establish your own standard menus and use them in all your applications when appropriate. Nearly every database, for example, needs a utilities menu. To save time and promote consistency, you can create your own utilities menu, such as the one shown in figure 10.9.

Make all menus as close to the same length as possible, and remember that short menus are quick to use because they can be read at a glance. Make your menu names easy to understand, but not unnecessarily long.

Consistency with Other Applications

You may want to create menus that resemble those in other applications to simplify training and support. Users of WordPerfect, for example, may be more comfortable using F7 rather than the Esc key to exit their database application.

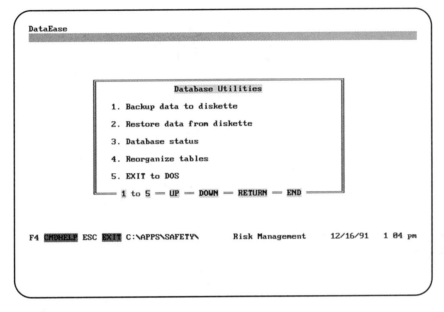

```
DataEase

                    Database Utilities

            1. Backup data to diskette

            2. Restore data from diskette

            3. Database status

            4. Reorganize tables

            5. EXIT to DOS
          1 to 5 == UP == DOWN == RETURN == END

  F4 CMDHELP ESC EXIT C:\APPS\SAFETY\      Risk Management    12/16/91   1 04 pm
```

Fig. 10.9. *A sample utilities menu.*

Summary

Menus provide users with a convenient way to navigate through all the possible actions in a database application without learning a command language. Except for forms, users spend more time looking at menus than at other parts of the database. Consequently, your application will be judged on the appearance and convenience of your menu system.

Consistency is as important for menus as in all the other aspects of database design. Choose a menu style and use it throughout your application. Use a consistent approach for ordering and grouping menu choices. Above all, be careful about the words you use to describe menu choices. Make your menus as consistent and unambiguous as possible.

As indicated by its treatment at this stage of the book, save menu creation until after you have built all the parts of the application. Remember to update menus when you add, delete or rename database functions.

Testing Your Database

From principles is derived probability, but truth or certainty is obtained only from facts.

Nathaniel Hawthorne

Good testing an important part of your database project. You must put even the best design and programming through its paces before you release the package to waiting users. Development is not truly complete until you test your system. You test to verify the correctness of all data structures and application functions.

Like documentation, testing is not glamorous, but it is necessary. Testing requires concentration and an eye for detail; a zest for finding flaws also helps.

The more complex the system, the more difficult the testing process. Complex systems have more potential failure points, and as the number of database actions grows, so does the number of interactions among the processes.

Tests can reveal problems in design and implementation. If data fields are the wrong type or length, testing shows which fields you need to add or modify. Testing discloses hardware or software incompatibilities, besides application problems. Your program may run out of memory when running a report or suddenly be jettisoned from a menu or data-entry screen to the operating system. Testing can uncover software flaws in the DBMS.

Choose hardware that you know to be trouble-free before you begin testing so that you can narrow the sources of problems quickly. Be certain, however, to test with the same type of hardware that the application's users will have. Testing an application on a stand-alone 486 computer running UNIX does little good if the application will be used on a Novell local area network with 286 PCs running DOS.

Do not refer to problems in the application as software *bugs*; call them *defects* instead. Calling these problems bugs makes them seem like cute, innocuous things that spring up on their own, when they really are flaws in programming. Users cannot and should not tolerate software defects. (Of course, a special name exists for defects that cannot be fixed—"features.")

Fig. 11.1. *After testing, you know how this feels.*

Making a Checklist

Your first step in testing is to make a checklist of all the application's functions. Making lists is an essential part of good database design, and lists are as important in testing as they are in analysis or implementation. Testing an application is much easier, more thorough, and more systematic if you have a list of application requirements to check.

Develop a test plan early in the analysis phase of your database design. Include tests for all functions of the database, along with the expected level of system performance. The testing stage is too late in the process to develop a test plan. Users' expectations are no longer fresh in your mind, and the way you wrote the application can influence your test plan design, prejudicing the outcome of testing.

Make the test plan as specific as possible. Include at least the following items:

- User actions or tasks to test

- The order and schedule for tests

- The number of times to perform each test

- Who will perform each test

- The data to use for the test

- The test environment (hardware and software)

Testing is the perfect time to dust off the requirements document you created during the analysis phase. Go through the document one item at a time to make sure that the system performs as specified. You may have a requirement, for example, that the system must find customer records in five seconds or less. Now is the time to test this type of requirement.

Testing Menus

I find that testing works best from the top of the application down— from the sign-on screen to the farthest branches of the menu tree. I therefore suggest that you begin by testing the user menus.

Test every menu option to verify that the option points to the proper function. Check menu responses to invalid choices. Confirm that menu titles make sense and that functions are grouped logically. Make sure that options that must be performed in a certain sequence are listed that way in the menus. Look for unclear or ambiguous menu option names.

Have each tester write suggestions for a new menu structure. Menu preferences depend on individual approaches to using a database and can be quite personal. Patterns emerge, however, when you compare the suggestions of a number of testers.

When you discover a menu option that does not work, print the screen and highlight the failed menu selection with a marker. Screen printouts are invaluable in all phases of testing. As you correct problems, check them off the list and print the revised screens to show that repairs were made.

Testing Data Entry

For the next stage in testing, enter some records into the database. Select a data-entry option from the menu. If several forms are available, choose the one that users probably will fill out first. You ultimately must enter records in every table accessible to users.

Data-entry testing requires special techniques. Good data-testing techniques are the opposite of good data-entry practices. Enter sloppy, incomplete, and impossible data to find out how the system responds. See what happens when you try to enter invalid values (such as February 30 as a date or ZA as a state). Try to enter alphabetic characters in numeric fields. Test negative and positive numbers where appropriate. (An order entry system, for example, might accept negative entries for refunds.)

Where do you get sample data? Although inventing records is not an easy task, sample data is all around you. When testing records about people, I have entered everything from U.S. presidents to my jazz idols. You even can enter names and addresses straight from the telephone directory.

The best test data uses real records. Real data is more likely to present the data-entry problems that users will face when using your application. Be sure to test records for the high and low ends of the data range. For text fields, use the longest legitimate entries to check field length. Enter big and small orders, complex and simple addresses, and so on.

While you enter data, make notes on the way the system handles errors when data is missing. Intentionally enter duplicates to assess how your system deals with duplicate records. If yours is a multiuser system, be sure to test an attempt at simultaneous entry into a table from two or more terminals.

Many data-entry errors are obvious, but some are subtle. I received a call because a meeting planning database had slowed to a snail's pace. The system stored hotel information for thousands of meeting attendees, including records for each night of their stay. I discovered that a user had entered 06/15/19 rather than 06/15/91 for the arrival date and 06/21/91 for the departure date. The database recorded room assignments for the more than 26,000 nights between the arrival and departure dates. June 15, 1919, was a valid date, and the database was set to ensure only that the arrival date was before the departure date. We solved the problem by setting a range for the starting night, to fall within a week of the starting date of the meeting.

If the system enables users to enter data in multiple tables using views, check that the data is properly saved, modified, or deleted. In particular, beware of referential integrity problems. *Referential integrity* refers to the way that changes in one table may affect related records in other tables. One clue of referential integrity problems is the existence of "orphan" detail records that remain after the main record is deleted or modified. If you delete an invoice, for instance, the corresponding line items automatically should be deleted also.

You also can create your own special database administrator reports to look for potential problems. Make a report to detect duplicate records, for example.

Generating Reports

The next step in testing your application is to generate all the database reports. Test the appearance and accuracy of the reports and the performance of the system (how long each report takes to run).

Check the output format. Ensure that the finished report resembles the user's original specifications. Make sure that the system sends reports to the correct device (screen, printer, or disk) and formats reports with the correct margins and fonts.

Check the accuracy of all reports. Compare the report data to the tables, beginning with the most detailed records. Check all calculated figures, such as subtotals, percentages, and averages. I have known people to trust their reports without checking them, only to discover later that the reports contain large errors.

To test report performance adequately, you must build the tables up to a size comparable to the production database. If the tables have few records, you can enter test data by hand. If you need a large number of test records, you should write a procedure to enter random, meaningless records. Reports will be run against the test data specially entered for this purpose.

Identify which reports take longest to run. If waiting for these reports delays the work of users, try to optimize the reports for speedier performance. *Optimizing* the report may mean changing your indexing scheme, or the way that records are selected. The specifics of performance tuning are different for each DBMS.

Processing Procedures

After testing the reports, try out all procedures in the application, such as imports, exports, and posting. You may have to simulate record entry to test posting.

If your database uses posting procedures such as account aging, check to see whether the totals match your manual calculations. Posting procedures can create insidious data errors, because an incorrect posting routine often compounds its mistakes each time it runs.

Be sure to complete the system's entire posting cycle. If some procedures are conducted on an annual basis, you must simulate an entire year's entries, completing monthly, quarterly, and annual closing procedures.

Next, test to see how the system deals with procedural errors. If a monthly account aging procedure moves balances from current to 30 days, 30 days to 60 days, and 60 days to 90 days, what happens if a user tries to post twice in the same month? Do archiving procedures prevent active information from being removed? What does the archiving program do if it encounters a bad disk?

Be assured that users eventually will put all your worst nightmares to the test. I once left a powerful procedure in a database prototype but did not include the procedure on user menus. A few weeks later, I got a call from a distressed user who had lost several weeks' entries. She had gained access as a high-level user and used the Delete All Data procedure (although she wasn't sure what the procedure was meant to do). Unfortunately, she had not backed up the system in several weeks, so keyboard overtime was the only remedy.

Finding Testers

A key challenge of testing is to find people who want to take the time to work their way through an application and patiently point out its flaws and inconsistencies. Testing requires a rare combination of patience, technical skills, and innocence.

Many sources for testing personnel are available. You can call upon friends, relatives, or colleagues to review your work. The most obvious options, in most situations, are to do the testing yourself or to draft future database users as "guinea pigs."

Developers as Testers

Doing your own testing can be risky. A test pilot friend of mine once told me a story that may even be true. He pointed out that the tenure of aircraft test pilots is inevitably short—not because the risk of death is high (although it is), but because test pilots become too good at their job to do it well.

After hundreds of hours at the controls of a variety of aircraft, test pilots know too much. They instantly compensate for shortcomings in the instruments or controls. If the aircraft pulls to the left, the test pilot instinctively brings the jet back to a straight course. Test pilots no longer can identify flaws in the aircraft controls because they are too good at correcting them.

The same syndrome affects software testers. After running a few dozen applications, the developer intuitively knows which keys to use, even without documentation. The developer does not fall into the same traps as a beginner and will not even attempt error-prone operations. A system's developer, therefore, is often the worst person to test the system.

Another problem with testing your software yourself is author's pride—a blindness to the flaws in your creation. You may be reluctant to reveal problems that necessitate extensive revisions to the application. Moreover, by the testing stage, you have spent so much time staring at the application that you may not want to see it again for a long time.

Try to find someone more objective than the developer, someone who can assess the application with an unprejudiced eye. You may find this person among the potential users of the system.

Users as Testers

At some stage in testing, bring in the users to assist. No substitute exists for user perceptions of the system, and you may be surprised at how many errors and inconsistencies users detect. Of all potential software evaluators, actual users provide the most accurate and relevant testing feedback.

Be sure to give users enough time to test properly, and conduct testing in an unhurried atmosphere. If rushed, testers are tempted to overlook flaws and offer minimal input to the design. Show users that you value their assistance. Listen to all their suggestions and explain how you can address their concerns.

Using Feedback

You have little reason to test your application if you do nothing with the results. Write down all your findings and follow up on all reported problems. You may want to group the problems by menu, by type (table, form, or report), or in some other manner that makes them easy to address. For a large project, you can create a database to store test results and record all changes made to the application. Such a database should have a table resembling table 11.1.

Table 11.1. Database Changes

Date	Initials	Type	Description
02/12/92	JJT	Report	Add page number to Invoice Summary
02/12/92	MAT	Table	Delete weight field in Inventory
02/15/92	JJT	Menu	Add Backup Database to Main Menu

If you are billing for your work, you can add a field for the number of hours required for modifications.

Some reported defects may be caused by operator error rather than a software flaw. If the same problem occurs frequently, build in extra safeguards such as prompts, help screens, or validity checks to prevent data-entry errors. Some problems may require changes to the documentation and not to the application itself.

Summary

No database application is really complete until it has been tested. Testing helps reveal misunderstandings in requirements analysis and design as well as flaws in programming.

Start the testing process by writing a test plan. The test plan spells out the way that the database should perform. Next, enter a realistic number of sample records to simulate daily use of the application. Make sure that not only is the database accurate, but that it meets your performance requirements.

Although you can test the database yourself, finding someone else for this task is usually better. As the database designer, you may be too close to the project to evaluate it objectively. Moreover, your proficiency with the database may cause you to overlook potential problems. Ideally, the users of the database should be drafted for testing. If this method is not possible, try to find people with similar knowledge and computer skills.

Finally, be sure to write down all test results. Use change orders to record the areas to be fixed or enhanced. A written record helps you keep track of your progress.

Creating System Documentation

That is a good book which is opened with expectation and closed in profit.

Amos Bronson Alcott

When building a database, you spend hours interviewing users, designing forms, defining relationships, writing queries, and testing the application. After you complete these initial steps of database design, you feel an enormous sense of accomplishment. You may wonder, what's next? The answer to this question is *documentation*.

Why Write Documentation?

Writing documentation is often a thankless task. Database designers have their applications radiating from every monitor in the room. Customers, vendors, business associates, and managers are impressed with the screen layout, color, reporting capabilities, and processing speed. Documentation, however, rarely receives the attention it deserves.

Documentation is an integral part of an application. Without good documentation, it is difficult to get the most out of a database application. Imagine if your DBMS arrived as a box of disks without a manual to guide you.

Computer manuals have a reputation for being difficult to understand, so many users avoid reading them. The importance of writing documentation has been stressed only recently, and volumes are being written on the subject of application documentation. The key to writing good documentation is to write it as if you had to read it yourself. Well-written documentation is an asset to any application and ultimately enhances the system's performance.

Document your application even if you designed it for only yourself. You may discover shortcomings of the system when you write documentation. If your business grows suddenly, an application you use single-handedly today may have a dozen users in the next year. Consider these points before you postpone the task and convince yourself that you will write the documentation later.

Maintaining the Application

Maintaining the application—keeping track of changes and enhancements—is crucial for the designer and users. To maintain the database properly, you need to refer to something other than the database to check its integrity. Maintaining your application without documentation is like assembling a jigsaw puzzle without a picture of the finished puzzle. Application documentation gives you a hard copy against which to measure your application.

Even as the designer of the database, you may not remember what fields you included in a particular form. All the details of each field, calculation, and variable may be fresh in your mind now, but you may forget them after working on a new project for a few months. Written documentation can preserve this information forever. Suppose that your system crashes because of a power outage, and your backup disks are corrupted. You need printed documentation of your application to reconstruct your system. This example is an extreme case but illustrates why having a hard copy of your application is important. If you have a fully documented application, you take comfort in knowing that you can reconstruct your system after a disaster.

Training Users

User documentation is an invaluable tool for teaching users how to operate your application. Screen captures help users learn the "road" through the system (especially on menu-driven applications). Trying to learn how one menu leads to the next can be difficult from a dynamic medium such as a PC. With the static medium of print, users can map out the menus and study flow of the system. A screen capture program (such as Collage or Pizazz Plus) converts screens to files to include in documentation.

Revealing Shortcomings of the Application

Writing documentation is as good for the developer as for the user. Writing documentation helps you distance yourself from the application and approach it as a user.

Many chances for oversights occur during the development process. An oversight as simple as not including access to other software such as a word processing program, spreadsheets, and so on, may become obvious when you write about your application's impressive features. You may have forgotten to include a feature or you may think of one that will make your application better. You also may discover during the documentation process that you can modify a particular menu to make the sequence of the choices more logical.

Types of Documentation

You can choose from several types of documentation formats. Use the format that best fits the user's needs and the application. If all the users are programming wizards, they may need only a menu tree and an explanation of key features. A beginner, however, may need both these elements and introductory material (how to turn the computer on, how to log in, and so on). If the users have computer experience but no database experience, include in your documentation an explanation of database fundamentals so that readers can understand how a database works. Even if they do not comprehend fully all aspects of relational databases, users who are exposed to these concepts are better off than users who are not.

Always create two types of documentation for each application: user documentation and system documentation. The following sections explain the two types in detail.

User Documentation

User documentation is designed to meet the needs of the people who enter data and run reports from your application. The documentation is the primary resource for learning the application and for solving problems. User documentation falls into two categories: long and short.

Long User Documentation

You may need to create exhaustive, detailed documentation to describe every field, screen, report, and menu in the application. Even if written for small applications, such documentation quickly jumps to one hundred (or several hundred) pages.

Writing long documentation is a serious undertaking. You can build many applications more quickly than you can document them. Comprehensive documentation may be necessary, however, for users who have no one to provide technical support. If you are sending a database to branch offices around the world, long documentation can save money on your telephone bill. Similarly, if you sell an application, the extra work of writing a long manual can reduce support costs later.

Short User Documentation

Short documentation formats stress conciseness over thoroughness. These formats include quick-reference manuals, keyboard templates, and menu listings.

From my experience, short documentation is used far more than long documentation. People often keep a copy next to their computer, within easy reach. Even for systems with long documentation, quick-reference guides are useful.

Although they take less time (and paper) to write than long documentation, short manuals deserve at least as much attention as their longer counterparts. The writer must be careful to include the right elements. Special techniques for outlining complex topics and depicting menu and command structures are useful.

Short manuals call for a special style of writing. Keep chapters short (no more than three to five pages per chapter), summarize the procedural details, and offer hints so that users can figure out the system themselves. In short manuals, you cannot afford to repeat lengthy instructions in several places; you must assume that the user has some previous knowledge. When possible, use cross-references to direct the reader to other relevant sections.

A crucial element in a short manual is a reference of where to look for additional information. Include names and locations of other computer documentation and names and telephone numbers for technical support personnel. Users must feel that they can ask for additional assistance if they cannot solve problems from the manual alone.

System Documentation

Another type of documentation is system documentation. The intended audience for system documentation is not the user, but another programmer. The system documentation should contain all programming details needed to understand, maintain, and modify an application. System documentation does not need to define basic terms or introduce database functions.

System documentation can be a lifesaver if you inadvertently erase an important file on your computer. The system documentation can help you reassemble a broken query or restore a form that has been modified.

Keep system documentation up-to-date. Each time the application is modified, change the documentation to reflect these changes. For extra security, you can keep an archive of old system manuals in case you have to revert to an earlier design.

Include the following items in database system documentation:

- A statement of the purpose of the application
- A brief history of the project and any revisions
- A discussion of computer environment (what computer the system runs on)
- The system requirements
- Installation procedures
- A list of tables
- A list of reports
- A list of menus
- A list of data dictionary items
- Data-entry forms layout
- Report layout
- Procedure/program listings, where applicable

System documentation can be lengthy. Luckily, you can use add-on software packages to generate system documentation. Such software combines the layout of your tables, forms, reports, and menus with standard boilerplate text to make a comprehensive guide. Some packages create more than 200 pages of system documentation for even relatively simple applications. The result of a documentation generator is not necessarily enchanting reading, but it contains many details needed to maintain the application. Contact your database software vendor for a list of documentation add-in programs.

Packaging Options

At the outset, consider the format and packaging for the finished documentation. A number of attractive options are available, even for manuals produced in small quantities.

The simplest and least expensive option is to use binders (loose-leaf or report covers). Special covers can be printed to improve the appearance of the manual; clear sleeves can show off a cover you print from your word processing software or graphics program. If you use loose-leaf binders, you can update the manual by sending new or updated pages to users instead of reproducing the entire volume. For small print runs, you can use photocopying rather than traditional printing.

For heavily used documentation, use perfect (soft-cover) binding with professional printing. The softbound format accommodates lengthier documentation. This format is durable and portable, and all the pages usually stay in place.

Another appealing format is easel binding. The easel binds the pages at the top and provides a stand so that the user can place the manual next to the computer and read easily. This format is particularly good for tutorials because the user can follow along without fumbling to turn pages.

A quick-reference card is a useful addition to any documentation. The card should contain a list of frequently used commands and instructions for navigating the system. Some quick-reference cards contain a list of the menu tree. If your application uses special function keys, as do most databases, be sure to include a keyboard template to list these commands. The template should fit on the user's keyboard so that the explanations are next to the appropriate function keys. You can use the most popular PC packages, which come with quick-reference cards and keyboard templates, as models. Be sure to use heavy, coated stock for quick-reference cards and keyboard templates, because they will be handled more frequently than user manuals.

Goals of Documentation

As you stare at the blank screen of your favorite word processing program and ponder the task at hand, you may think that writing documentation is easy; all you need to do is to write down what you did to build the database. The process is more involved, however, and you as the author of the database must play dumb or relinquish the task to someone who can.

When writing documentation, do not make *any* assumptions about the users' knowledge. Put yourself in the users' place and write *for* them—not *at* them. To ensure that you are writing at the users' level, have a user—or better yet, several users—proofread a first draft. Ask the users to write down any questions that arise when they proofread the text.

One way to gather user comments is to let users type questions directly into the text in a word processing program. One set of questions evokes another set and so on. You then can address the issues and insert responses into the text. Have users earmark their comments in the text by a particular character and their initials.

You sometimes need help preparing documentation. The more difficult the subject matter, the better your writing skills must be to communicate effectively. If you cannot document your system to the satisfaction of your users, consider hiring a technical writer. The technical writer has the advantage of being removed from the design process. The technical writer may be seeing the database for the first time and will write from the uninformed perspective of a new user.

A disadvantage of hiring a technical writer is that you have to explain the system to him or her. You make a trade-off that depends on the nature of the application, the users, the software, the hardware, and the project budget.

What To Avoid

Make all documentation as short as possible. Use the following guidelines, which are by no means exhaustive, to decide what to avoid in your documentation:

- *Use humor sparingly*. Many "homegrown" computer manuals cross the fine line between cuteness and schmaltz. Humor can be distracting to the reader interested in facts.

- *Avoid excessive adjectives*. Keep your sentences short and direct.

- *Keep the manual objective*. In most cases, personal anecdotes and views distract the reader and add little to the value of the documentation.

What To Include

Which major topics you should include in your documentation depends on the application and the needs of potential readers. You (and perhaps a technical writer) must decide what to cover and what to exclude.

You must establish boundaries for the range of information your system documentation will cover. If you mention DOS, you don't have to cover all DOS functions in detail. Cover the most important functions and provide the reader with a source to consult for more information. You can explain, for example, how to create a subdirectory and move to that directory as part of the installation instructions. If you do not limit your range, you can find yourself covering every topic related to computers back to the times of punch cards.

Several ingredients should appear in all user documentation. Use screen captures liberally to show the application as it appears to the user. Nothing conveys the feel of an application more clearly than documentation that shows a succession of screens. I know users who have written their own documentation by pressing Print Screen for each action they perform, highlighting the characters they entered with a yellow marker, and storing all the pages in a binder in the order that the steps were performed. Such a manual is surprisingly easy to follow, even for a first-time user.

Be generous with white space when you design the layout of the manuals. Do not crowd your text and graphics; a pleasing visual appearance makes a manual more approachable. Use proportional fonts, if you have them, and the best quality printer at your disposal.

Refer to the following guidelines when you write your documentation. These guidelines are not laws carved in stone, however. If, for example, you think that a glossary is inappropriate for your user manual, do not include one.

- *Introduction*. The introduction includes the scope and purpose of the application. The introduction also can include background information on the history of the application and how it relates to the organization.

- *System operations*. Include step-by-step coverage of all menus, forms, and reports. Include screen captures in any discussion of system operations.

- *How to get help*. Tell users where to turn for additional information, including other documentation, in-house staff, and technical support telephone numbers.

- *Error messages*. Include a list of all error messages that users are likely to encounter and advice on how to recover from each error.

- *Glossary*. The glossary defines key terms used in the database and in the documentation, including basic database terms such as *table*, *record*, and *field*.

- *Index*. The index is a detailed cross-referencing of all topics. Most users do not read the manual straight through but resort to the documentation only when they are in trouble (and in a hurry to find an answer). The index points to the section where users can look for help. An index is crucial to any computer documentation.

- *Installation instructions.* Applications that will be distributed to users need step-by-step installation instructions so that users can load the database on their computer system. Be sure to reproduce the screens used by the installation program so that users can monitor their progress. Include a list of likely error messages and solutions.

- *File listing.* For backup purposes, include a list of all files (program, data, indexes, and other types of files) used by the system. Write a list of all the DOS file extensions (such as DBF, NDX, DB, and so on) with their meanings.

- *Quick start.* Some users are computer experts and don't want to wade through long introductory sections. For their benefit, be sure to provide a quick start section that summarizes the installation commands and tells them how to get into the application without delay. In the quick start section, unlike other parts of the manual, you can minimize explanations and assume that the reader knows the basics of the computer hardware and operating system. Be sure to include references to the more detailed sections of the documentation for inexperienced users who try to use the quick start.

The following table of contents is from a user manual for a client tracking system.

The body of a short user manual should contain enough information, including step-by-step instructions, to guide a user through major database functions. Keep background material in appendixes.

Try to locate related information on the same page so that readers do not need to hold their place in the index while scanning several pages for detail about a particular topic. Everything you need to know about a particular topic should be grouped together.

Don't feel compelled to write your entire user manual in complete sentences. Checklists and numbered steps for procedures can convey more information than lengthy paragraphs. Use eye-catching headers or icons to break up text and to make sections easier to find.

When users refer to a set of documentation, they usually are not interested in literary style, colorful images, metaphors, and other literary devices. Most people do not read documentation for pleasure. Readers want answers, not adjectives. Because readers expect to find clear solutions to their problems, documentation writers should produce a no-nonsense set of instructions for operating the application.

Reviewers

After you finish a draft of the documentation, submit it to readers for testing. Your readers should be no more familiar with the application than your prospective users. Do not submit your documentation to programmers who have been working on the project or to others with strong technical training.

If you have the time and resources, send the draft for field testing by users. You will be surprised at the feedback you receive on the manual. Review by users is the best way to identify the shortcomings of documentation.

Summary

Writing good documentation takes more time than you may realize. Writing documentation often takes as long as writing the application. The shortest time I have needed to write a brief user's manual was two days, and I borrowed quite a bit from earlier documentation I had written.

Documentation is an essential part of a professional database application. Good system and user manuals can pay for themselves many times over by making your application easier to learn, use, and maintain.

Database Administration

Nothing endures but change.

Heraclitus

Database applications rarely remain static. As business practices change, databases must grow and adapt. *Data administration* is the process of overseeing the daily management of a database and its long-term evolution. The person charged with this responsibility is the *database administrator*, or *DBA*. This chapter outlines some of the responsibilities of the DBA.

Typical DBA functions include the following:

- Backing up and recovering data
- Maintaining data security
- Performance tuning
- Archiving
- Handling user problems
- Troubleshooting (hardware and software)
- Maintaining the data dictionary
- Planning strategically for the application

If you are building a small database for personal use, you probably can perform these activities without any formal structure or plan. The more complicated the application, however, the more you need to define the database administration function, and the more people involved with the database, the more you need data administration. Large organizations must clearly define responsibility for database maintenance.

Many companies have no full-time DBA, and several people often share database administration duties. Many database administrators have no formal computer training, but are "super-users," who show a high degree of interest in the database and learn DBA duties on the job. No matter how the work is distributed, the tasks of data administration, when performed properly, keep your database in top shape.

Backing Up the Database

The DBA's most important duty is to make frequent backups of the database. The horror stories of failing to back up are legion. One such blood-curdling tale concerns a user making a backup of a database for the first time in three months. During the backup, an error message warned that the computer was unable to read the backup disk. The user stopped the backup and, worried that the error had damaged the database, restored data from the preceding (three-month old) backup. This restoration deleted all new data, and the new backup was useless because of the disk error.

The mechanics of performing a backup vary according to your hardware and software. Many popular database programs, such as dBASE and Paradox, lack an option to back up an application. Instead, you must rely on other backup software. BACKUP and RESTORE programs come with DOS, but some versions of these programs are unreliable, and you cannot use them to transfer data between two computers that run different versions of DOS. For these reasons, third-party backup programs such as Norton Backup, Fastback, and PC Tools commonly are used to back up all computer files, including database applications.

You need not make daily backups of the DBMS program itself, only the data files. This type of selective backup is quicker and uses fewer disks than a full backup. Most backup software offers an option for incremental backups, which back up only files created or modified since the last backup. If you choose this approach, be aware that to restore the database fully, you may need every backup since the last full backup was made.

The DBA may want to write batch files or macros to perform the database backup so the user doesn't have to decide what files to back up or to choose from several backup options. This backup routine would be included on one of the user menus.

For speed and high volume, backup tapes are more efficient than disks. Tape drives can be internal or external and can hold from 10 or 20 megabytes to over a gigabyte (1,000 megabytes). Tapes also are more convenient to use than disks because you do not have to swap them during a backup operation. Because nearly every database is too large to back up to one disk, unattended backups to disks are not usually practical. Most tape backup software provides for automatic, timed backups, even while unattended.

How often you back up your database depends on how often the data changes and the cost of restoring lost data if a system failure occurs. For maximum security, you should back up the database with every change, but this practice is not always practical.

Databases typically are backed up every day, but some systems call for hourly or even continuous backups. Less frequently used systems may be backed up only on a weekly basis. The DBA restores previous backups when necessary and checks on such integrity features as the *transaction log* (when available). Some DBMS create transaction logs, which record every change made to database tables.

For additional security, use different tapes or disks for each day of the week's backup. You can start with seven (or five) backup sets, labeled Monday through Sunday (or Friday). Once a month, send another backup set off-site for storage in case of fire, theft, or other disaster.

Keep a record of every backup. Your backup logs should be paper records rather than computerized records. You will need the backup log when the computer fails, precisely when you do not have access to on-line information. You can create a backup log like the one shown in figure 13.1 to record what you backed up and the backup media you used (disks or tapes).

```
Backup Log
Your Company Name Here

Date      Time     Backup Type       By        Disk/Tape #
_____

12/25/91  10:00    Full             JJT        541
```

Fig. 13.1. *A sample backup log.*

The DBA periodically should practice restoring the database from backup versions to ensure that the backup system works properly and that he or she properly understands the techniques for restoring data. Failing to test your backup system can lead to a false sense of security. I once worked with a database on a network with elaborate backup procedures. The data was stored on three separate file server computers, and each night the files from server one were copied to server two, from server two to server three, and from server three to server one so that, in the event of a server failure, a backup of the data from the day before always would be available. Unfortunately, as the databases grew, the servers could no longer hold the backup copies. Even worse, the automatic backup procedure didn't warn that the servers had run out of space and that the backups were no longer being made. The problem was discovered only after a power failure destroyed key files (which fortunately had been backed up to a tape drive).

Maintaining Data Security

The DBA controls and monitors data security, keeping passwords and access control lists (a security measure available on larger computers) and checking for security violations. The means for enforcing security vary with the operating system and database software you are using. Most PC DBMS offer few security options and do not keep logs of user activity.

A DBMS should provide several kinds of data security. A DBMS should write records to disk when you issue a save command. It should maintain indexes as needed for queries and reports to perform well, and to maintain relationships among tables. Older PC DBMS, such as dBASE III, require the user or programmer to maintain indexes. Newer packages automatically perform this task.

Password protection provides another level of security. Depending on the DBMS, passwords may be used to control access to the entire application, menus, forms, reports, tables, and even individual fields. In dBASE, you can enforce password protection through programs. You must be sure to prevent users from accessing the data files directly from the dBASE command line, however, because users who circumvent your menus and programs have full access to modify the table. Password protection also risks being too restrictive. The DBA should keep a list of passwords so that users and developers will not be "locked out" permanently if they forget a password.

In a network environment, special security precautions protect tables from inconsistencies created through simultaneous access by multiple users. The most common ways of controlling access in a LAN database are through locking files, pages, and records. File locking controls access to the entire file. Page locking limits access to a group of contiguous records. Record locking, the least restrictive of the three types, locks one record at a time. Each type of locking has several levels; users may be denied access altogether, allowed limited access (for example, read only), or given full access. Many DBMS take care of LAN locking without special programming. In this case, the DBA may tune the locking settings for best performance. Other DBMS, including dBASE, require additional programming to account for possible multiple-user conflicts.

When new software upgrades become available, the DBA tests them and installs them as needed, reporting DBMS software errors to the vendor and working with technical support to resolve problems as they arise. New software versions sometimes can hurt existing data or programs, so the DBA should protect the database from untested upgrades.

The cautious way to install an upgrade to your DBMS is to create two parallel databases, one running the old version and one running the new version. You then can test all the functions of the new version by performing data entry, running reports, and processing procedures. If the results from the new version are the same as the results from the old version, you can proceed safely with the upgrade. You can keep the old version available on disk or on a backup so that you may revert to it if you have problems with the upgrade.

Be sure to read the installation instructions and quality assurance notes that accompany your upgrade. Conscientious software vendors include lists of known bugs and fixes to bugs in the earlier release. Beware of incompatibility created by new features of the release.

Be sure to perform a full backup of the DBMS and the database before you start the upgrade. The backup is the best insurance against a catastrophe.

Performance Tuning

As the database grows, some operations, such as reports, can take longer to perform. The DBA monitors the performance of database functions and makes adjustments to achieve optimum performance.

The amount of tuning available (and necessary) depends on the hardware, operating system, and DBMS you are using. Simpler database software programs generally offer few tuning options, whereas more powerful DBMS boast a bewildering variety of parameters.

Nearly every database uses indexes to boost performance. To speed up processing, the DBA can change the indexing methods or the fields or combinations of fields that are indexed. As Chapter 5, "Building Tables," explains, building indexes results in a trade-off in performance. Although an index may speed searching and sorting for a report, its maintenance takes time and disk space.

The DBA monitors free disk space and disk fragmentation. Fragmentation occurs when large files are spread across noncontiguous disk sectors, leading to longer read times. PC users monitor disk usage by running diagnostic programs (such as those programs included in Norton Utilities, PC Tools, and Spinrite) to check the hard disk; periodically defragmenting the disk results in better performance.

To free up disk space, the DBA also periodically deletes error and log files created by the database and reorganizes tables to remove deleted records and rebuild indexes. If the database nears the capacity of the disk drives, the DBA requests more disk storage.

Despite all your tuning efforts, a database can grow too big for its hardware or software. When this situation occurs, the DBA will research options for new hardware and software. New options may mean migration to a faster PC (from 286 to 386 or 286 to 486 processor, for instance) or a faster DBMS (from dBASE to FoxPro). If your database has grown in size or number of users, you may have to move from stand-alone to a network, or from a microcomputer to a minicomputer or mainframe.

Like software upgrades, hardware upgrades can bring a host of problems to the database administrator. New equipment, even equipment from a single vendor, may be incompatible with old hardware or software. You may need a new operating system to take advantage of new hardware. Your database may conflict with other programs—from communications to mouse drivers to task switching programs. The DBA must sort out these incompatibilities and ensure that the functions of the database are not impaired.

If possible, the DBA should perform hardware upgrades in the same way as software upgrades—by running parallel systems. Install each new component separately and test as you go, to isolate problems.

Archiving

Archiving is closely related to performance tuning. A business may not need to store its most detailed transaction information on-line forever. To conserve disk space and promote faster searches, old data can be moved periodically to off-line storage on disks or magnetic tape.

I once worked on a database that tracked truck shipments for a beverage bottling company. A table called Trip Logs contained a record for every segment of every trip for each vehicle over a three-state area. Before long, thousands of records accumulated in the table. When performance started to suffer from the size of the table, users decided that they needed to keep only one year's worth of trip detail on-line and instantly accessible. They copied older information to disks or to a tape drive and deleted it from the hard disk. If needed, the archived files could be restored.

Detailed transaction data is the most likely candidate for archiving. Detail records can grow quickly to astonishing size. A video rental store, for example, tracks hundreds of transactions each day, as each tape is rented. Eventually, because the detailed records are not as important as summary information such as the popularity of a title or the number of rentals for a customer, the detail may be archived.

Archiving can speed up dramatically the processing time for active records by cutting the size of the table. Reports print more quickly, searches are faster, and even saving a record takes less time (because the system has fewer records to check for uniqueness). If the archived records are removed to off-line storage, the time required to back up the database will be reduced also.

The DBA helps to establish archiving criteria and performs the archiving operation. If necessary, the DBA restores off-line information to the database as needed.

Providing User Support

The DBA is often the first person users contact with questions or problems. The DBA can refer calls to vendors or to programmers for additional technical support as necessary.

The DBA may assist in training users and preparing user documentation. Training and documentation help reduce the amount of support users need, making the users more productive in their database work. You can view documentation, therefore, as part of user support. The DBA may write on-line help for the database as part of the documentation.

The DBA must make every effort to document the database application and the computing environment. Relying on a system that only one individual can maintain is dangerous. The DBA should train other staff members to serve as alternates, if only to avoid being interrupted by user problems while on vacation.

Hardware and Software Troubleshooting

The DBA must be able to uncover the nature of database problems as they arise and call in assistance to fix the problems, when necessary. The DBA, therefore, must be able to distinguish hardware problems from software problems, operating system failures from network failures, and DBMS flaws from poor application programming.

The best teacher for computer troubleshooting is experience. Only by encountering a wide range of problems can a DBA become proficient at troubleshooting. Documentation may be helpful, however, especially when an error message is displayed, and some computerized diagnostics are available, such as debuggers and hardware diagnostics.

Many PCs come with diagnostic software that isolates hardware failures. Packages such as Spinrite, Norton Utilities, and PC Tools also can help you recover and preserve data.

The most important rule of troubleshooting is to try only one change at a time. A call to technical support may result in several possible techniques to solve your problem. If you try them all at once, however, you will never know which one solved the problem and which ones had no effect. Some changes may even make the problem worse, so implementing changes one at a time limits your risk. Upgrading a PC's memory, for example, along with a new version of DOS, Windows, and a network card makes pinpointing problems relating to any of these improvements a difficult task. Testing each change takes time but is worth the effort.

The second rule of troubleshooting is to write down everything. Record the version numbers, settings, and exact circumstances that created an error. If possible, use the PrintScreen key to show the state of the computer and the error message. If the computer is frozen, write down the error message before you reboot. Detailed information is essential for technical support to provide meaningful responses.

If you have access to another computer, try to duplicate the problem there. Note any differences in the configuration of the machines to help narrow the possible problems.

Finally, do not be afraid to ask for help. You probably are not the first person to encounter your computer problem. Seek advice from technical support, a bulletin board, a user group, or your local computer store. A good list of phone numbers can be the DBA's best ally for troubleshooting.

Maintaining the Data Dictionary

Data administration means keeping track of the way your organization stores and manipulates data. The DBA should identify changes to the corporate data dictionary, define the data elements, and maintain the data dictionary for each database. (For a detailed discussion of the data dictionary, see Chapter 5.)

Ideally, the data dictionary should be computerized, although you can record it on paper. The dictionary should contain the name of each data element, field type and length, domain (range of valid entries), the source of the data, and a list of all places (tables, reports) in the database where the data is located. Dictionary maintenance includes enforcing naming conventions and coordinating all modifications to the database structure. The following is a typical data dictionary entry:

> Field Name: INVDATE
> Data Element: Invoice Date
> Table Name: Invoices
> Domain: Date
> Description: Date when invoice was created at distribution center

Many data dictionary programs are available. Some are included along with the DBMS; others are stand-alone products. Most computer-aided software engineering (CASE) software contains a data dictionary, such as IEW (Knowledge Ware), Analyst/Designer (Yourdon, Inc.), Canonizer (Six Sigma CASE), and EasyCASE Plus (Everygreen CASE Tools). If you do not have access to a data dictionary, you can record this information in your database or your word processing program.

The data dictionary can be a valuable tool for business analysis. Like other database tables, the data dictionary and system catalog can help generate reports. This external information about data is called *metadata* to distinguish it from data in the application itself. Because a database is a reflection of an organization's operations and rules, it can reveal hidden assumptions made by management and show how reality is modeled within a business entity. Does an organization, for example, consider its current customers as sales prospects for its new products? If these records are segregated in different tables or databases, business opportunities may be lost.

Strategic Planning

The DBA plays a crucial role in determining the future of the database application. When involved in all planning activities that affect the application, the DBA can contribute valuable insights into an organization's business practices as well as the strengths and limitations of the application. Strategic planning can cover a wide range of activities, including the following:

- Creating a new applications wish list

- Reviewing business rules

- Forecasting database growth

- Listing security considerations

- Planning for disaster recovery

- Measuring productivity

Data is a corporate resource and should be treated as such. Data is a repository of experience and a means of maintaining consistency despite personnel changes in an organization. The DBA, as guardian of this resource, must protect the data from damage without denying access to qualified users.

Summary

No matter how skilled the work of the database designer, the success of the system rests with the quality of the database administration.

The database administrator (DBA) is the last line of defense for your valuable corporate information. Database administration tasks depend on the hardware and software used for your application. At a minimum, the DBA should make frequent backups of the system and record all modifications to tables, forms, reports, and menus. Other DBA functions may include data security, performance testing, archiving, user support, and troubleshooting.

Choosing Database Software

Between two evils, choose neither; between two goods, choose both.

Tryon Edwards

Unless you already have chosen your database management system, or unless someone has chosen it for you, you must choose which database software to use from the bewildering array of offerings. Selecting software is not a task for the lighthearted. The selection process can be tedious and confusing even in the best of circumstances because so many factors need to be considered (see fig. 14.1).

If you approach the task systematically, however, you can see beyond the marketing claims to find the best software for your application. No single database is right for everyone in all situations.

This chapter helps you decide whether you need a flat-file or relational database management system. It offers a methodology for rating specific products and helps you express your requirements in terms of database features. Finally, this chapter compares three approaches to the database interface.

Understanding the DBMS Marketing Environment

Stark differences exist between different database products. With everything that database management systems (DBMS) have in common, why are the hundreds of software packages on the market so different? Are they really different, or is the proliferation of products just marketing and packaging, like shampoo or shaving cream?

Fig. 14.1. *The database software dilemma.*

The answer is both. Many DBMS have important differences, but some systems so closely resemble one another that their programs are interchangeable. Although they perform essentially the same tasks, different DBMS can force users to go through quite different steps to build an application.

One reason for these quirks is product differentiation, the desire to make a product stand out from the crowd. This competition drives continual software upgrades and the obsolescence they create. DBMS vendors put their development efforts toward different priorities. Some DBMS are optimized for easy access by end users. Others stress a rich list of programming options for the database developer. Still others focus on transaction processing speed. No single DBMS is best for all needs.

Some differences in software, particularly in the user interface, may be inspired by fear of litigation. Intellectual property laws are still a murky area in American jurisprudence, and software companies have been sued for using the same words or pictures in their menus. To protect themselves, companies do not slavishly copy another product's interface; rather, they modify it slightly to stay out of court.

DBMS vendors also want to give their products a personal touch, a special feeling that will endear their product to database users. Whatever the motivation, the result is that each DBMS uses slightly different menus and commands to accomplish the same result. Paradox, for example, substitutes the California-style DO-IT! for the more common DO or EXECUTE.

Marketing and legal issues do not explain the fundamental differences between packages, however. The underlying cause for differences in database software is the paradigm, or picture of reality, that they embody. DBMS come from disparate roots. Some products have been developed as a result of academic research. A relational DBMS may have evolved from a traditional programming language.

The hardware for which a DBMS was developed also exerts an influence. Packages converted from mainframe to PC use (such as Ingres, Oracle, and SQL Server) have different features than those developed on the IBM-PC or Macintosh. Because of their historical development and the orientation of their programmers, database packages end up with quite different approaches to common programming problems.

Determining Your Needs

I often read requests on the CompuServe network for help with choosing database software. The question is usually phrased as follows: "I'm about to build a database. I have little experience with database software, so please tell me which product I should buy. I have heard that Oracle (or dBASE or Paradox) is really great, but wanted to get a second opinion."

My response is invariably that you should look at your own needs before you start shopping for software. You can find a good fit more easily if you take your measurements before trying on anything. Choosing the wrong database software, like buying the wrong size bicycle, can hurt you in the long run.

What makes a software package good for you has more to do with your needs than with the strengths and weaknesses of the software. What is good for an expert programer is not necessarily the tool for you. Moreover, different applications demand different programs for the best results. Transaction processing may use different software than a full text retrieval system or a video image library.

You may want to write down the requirements for your application, as described in Chapter 2. If not, be sure to answer the following basic questions about your application:

- How big is your application? How many classes are you tracking? How many individual items will be included? Dozens, hundreds, thousands, or millions?

- How many people need access to the database? Will they be sharing a single computer, using a PC network, or working on a mainframe or minicomputer?

- What are the main items you will track? Are they related to one another?

- Do you need any special data types beyond standard text, numbers, dates, and times? Do you need to store and search complete documents? What about graphics, such as photos, engineering drawings, or other images?

- How much computer experience do you have at your disposal? How much time do you have to learn new software? When do you need to finish the application?

- How much money do you have to spend on hardware and software?

- What are your long-term plans for the application? Will the scope or the number of users grow?

Choosing between a Flat-File and Relational Database

The first hurdle in choosing PC database software is to decide how powerful a package you need. At the lower end of the cost and complexity spectrum are simple file management packages, often called *flat-file databases* because they manage one list at a time. These systems are usually for single users, although some multiple-user versions are available for networks and minicomputers.

Many database users start with flat-file programs. A simple file manager is adequate for storing names, addresses, and phone numbers. In fact, some simple databases are built without database software at all. I once visited a professor of management information systems who had built a huge database, using Ingres on VAX minicomputers. When I asked him for a telephone number of a colleague, he typed in a few commands and pulled up an address entry. I was a little surprised to learn that his electronic address file was in a single large document entered with EDT, the standard VAX text editor, not in his database.

A number of inexpensive, easy-to-learn, easy-to-use database packages, such as Reflex, Q+A, PGFile, and Professional File, are available on the market. These products generally lack features found in relational DBMS but may approximate some relational functions (such as multiple files and lookups). Table 14.1 summarizes the characteristics of flat-file vs. relational database programs.

Table 14.1. Flat-File vs. Relational Databases

Characteristic	Flat-File	Relational
Cost	Low	Medium—High
Ease of use	High	Low—High
Programming skills needed	None	Moderate—High
Report flexibility	Low—Medium	High
Referential integrity	Not available	Available
Set operations	Moderate	Excellent
Suitable for commercial applications	No	Yes
Multiple-user	Sometimes	Yes
Complex applications	Not well supported	Supported

Another selling point of simple file managers is their use of English-like queries to retrieve information. Users can work in most of these packages with little or no programming. The line between simple databases and full-blown "relational" databases is blurring, however, as multitable features are added to the simpler programs and more powerful systems are made easier. Many packages are difficult to categorize and may lie on the border between file managers and DBMS.

Some relational databases, however, are nearly as easy to use as a flat-file package. An easy-to-use relational database is a wise investment if you think that your information needs might grow beyond the capacity of a flat-file system.

Understanding Relational Databases

If you are choosing a relational database, you should determine how well it measures up to the standards for relational databases. Although no product may meet all the criteria, you can judge how close a database is to the most fundamental tenets of the relational model.

Many database products use Structured Query Language (SQL), the standard for relational database management. Many of these DBMS were developed originally for mainframe or minicomputers (Ingres, Oracle, and SQL Server, for example) and have been transferred (ported) to microcomputers.

Table 14.2 characterizes the features of DBMS built on the relational model. For a clear, thorough discussion of the relational data model as it relates to DBMS, see Fabian Pascal, *SQL and Relational Basics* (Redwood City, California: M&T Books, 1990).

Table 14.2. Key Relational Database Characteristics

Feature	Explanation
No duplicate records	After the key field has been declared for a table, prevents duplicates from being entered
Null values	Distinguishes empty fields from spaces
Referential integrity	Protects the integrity of related records when records are added, modified, or deleted
Set operations	Supports a full range of set operations
Data dictionary	Maintains a list of tables, fields, and other database objects as relational tables
Domain support	Supports a range of permissible values for database fields
Physical data independence	Accesses data by table name, column name, and value, not by physical storage location

A relational DBMS must embody the concept of a database—a number of data files related to one another in some way. The system catalog keeps track of the names of the files and the fields in each file, so that the relationships among the files can be stored for future reference.

Many PC database products do not contain a system catalog or data dictionary and thus do not fit the concept of a database in the relational sense. dBASE, for instance, is a loose collection of tables (each called a *database* in dBASE jargon) connected only by the application programs. No central repository of data about the database (such as a system catalog) exists within dBASE. Paradox works in a similar fashion to dBASE (or Lotus), showing data files within a single directory at a time. Simply copying a database file into the same directory with other dBASE or Paradox files makes the file accessible to the database.

With relational databases, the user can create relationships among tables to perform queries and other operations. Although dBASE enables multiple files to be related to one another, this relationship depends on the existence of properly maintained indexes on the linking field, an implementation detail not called for in the relational model. Users cannot relate tables by unindexed fields, and failing to specify the proper index creates unpredictable results with the relationship.

In the relational model, the order of rows in the table is irrelevant. Although dBASE files superficially resemble the tables found in relational databases, dBASE permits navigation through the records by the record number, a violation of one of the tenets of relational database theory. Unlike SQL and its relatives, the dBASE language is record-oriented and not truly set-oriented. Consequently, dBASE does not translate easily into SQL commands; it can take many dBASE commands to fulfill the same task as one SQL command.

Relational DBMS can perform *set operations* (such as union, intersection, difference) to manipulate tables, but many PC database products fail to provide full support for these operations. Record-oriented DBMS such as dBASE lack the set operations that are part of the relational model. Some PC packages, however, such as Paradox, do a good job of providing set functions.

Relational database theory also demands that the database permit a distinction between *null* (empty) fields and fields filled with zeros or blanks. DBMS built on the relational model have such support; dBASE does not.

Finally, relational DBMS have built-in controls to prevent duplicate records and to protect referential integrity. To enforce similar controls, extensive code must be written in a dBASE application. The lack of relational data integrity features is a serious drawback in a database. A "relational" DBMS without relational integrity is like a car advertised to have antilock brakes with the specification that the driver must skillfully pump the brake pedal to avoid skidding.

Understanding Database Interfaces

The most popular PC database programs fall into three groups based on the interfaces that the programs follow. The different concepts on which these database programs are based lead to quite distinct styles of software that impose different demands on the database designer.

The three common database paradigms are the programming interface, the spreadsheet interface, and the form-oriented interface. The following sections give some background on each interface and compare them to each other. These comments are not software reviews; this chapter does not attempt to delve into the details of any packages, much less offer comparisons of competing software. Instead, the three interfaces are models to help understand the fundamental orientation of a package.

Some database products contain the elements of more than one interface. Competitive pressures force vendors to incorporate features found in other products, making them more similar than in their original conception.

The Programming Interface

The first PC database packages to appear were based on the programming interface—their basis was a programming language especially suited to database operations. One reason for this interface is that the packages were designed for computers with limited memory and storage and no graphics support. Their makers intended to create a database equivalent of BASIC, which at the time was the ubiquitous programming language of the personal computer.

By the early 1980s, Ashton-Tate's dBASE II emerged as the leading PC database. Since then, dBASE has dominated the PC DBMS marketplace and continues to enjoy more than half the market, despite sales gains by its competitors. dBASE is the most widely used database software and has set standards for other PC DBMS with its file format and programming language.

Like BASIC, dBASE is a procedural, interpreted language. It executes one command at a time, converting the English-like commands to machine language at run time. A dBASE user can enter each command one at a time and watch the results as the command is executed.

Like BASIC, dBASE contains a large and growing number of commands and functions. dBASE programs can be simple or complex. With enough programming, dBASE can do just about anything you want a database to do. You even can write programs that are not databases.

Programmers have discovered that they can achieve significant performance improvements (and profits from selling applications) by compiling their dBASE code before run time. Compiling translates the English-like commands of the programming language into a machine language for faster execution. An additional benefit of compiled programs is that their source code cannot be viewed or modified, so compiled programs can be distributed with less fear of losing proprietary programming secrets.

The need for a dBASE compiler helped Ashton-Tate's competitors gain a foothold in the PC database market. Several companies have produced compiler software (such as Nantucket's Clipper, Wordtech's Quicksilver, and Sophco's Force) to perform this function. Ashton-Tate promised to deliver its own compiler, but delays of months have turned into years and its grip on the market has loosened.

In addition to the lack of a compiler, competitors identified missing commands and functions in dBASE and seized this opportunity to compete. Taking advantage of dBASE's shortcomings, several companies created dBASE clones, enhanced database programming languages that shared the dBASE DBF file format. These companies introduced their own features, many of which Ashton-Tate emulated in subsequent releases of their products.

The popularity of dBASE clones has created a new word—*Xbase*—to describe dBASE-compatible databases. Programmers adept at several dialects of dBASE often call themselves Xbase programmers. Some dBASE-oriented magazines (such as *DBMS*) use capitalization to distinguish *dBASE*—the Ashton-Tate product—from *Dbase* programming languages in general. Of course, these semantic developments do not help to clarify the uses of these products.

Over the years, the dBASE language has grown richer, accommodating an ever widening range of tasks. It provides for extensive add-ons to handle exotic data types (images or voice files, for example) or to run other computer functions. Both Clipper and FoxPro have added enhancements to the latest versions of their products that make them incompatible with dBASE.

Like all programming languages, dBASE presents the programmer with a "blank canvas," so that the programmer can perform nearly every conceivable database action. The programmer has complete control over the look and feel of the application, from screen layout and color to function keys to the flow of the application. Security may be imposed loosely or strictly. Network file and record locking may be managed at the program level, controlling each database file separately.

Advantages of the Programming Interface

The greatest advantages of the programming interface are its power and flexibility. The programming interface gives the programmer control of high-level and low-level functions. You can strip the application to its bare essentials or customize it by adding special features and enhancements. Low-level programming enables you to communicate directly with other programs and integrate subroutines written in languages such as Fortran, BASIC, or C.

14

After you become familiar with it, a programming interface can be quick to use. You can type commands directly without navigating through complex menu structures. Unlike other macro-oriented products, a programming interface has no modes (data-entry mode, edit mode, and so on).

Programs with a programming orientation may present a highly productive environment for programmers who take the time to master it. A database programming language is much more productive than a general purpose programming language. Because it is designed expressly for building database applications, a database programming language contains commands that accomplish in one line what requires dozens or hundreds of lines in a programming language such as BASIC or COBOL.

Still, learning to program in any language is no small feat. Few business users are experienced programmers, and even those who are may look for a quicker way to build an application. The daunting prospect of writing hundreds or thousands of lines of code has spawned an industry of dBASE code generators, report writers, and other programs. dBASE IV itself contains a greatly enhanced code generator to relieve the programmer of the tedium of generating routine code for screens, reports, and menus (see fig. 14.2). After it is generated, the code can be modified (*tweaked* in programmer terminology) for special requirements.

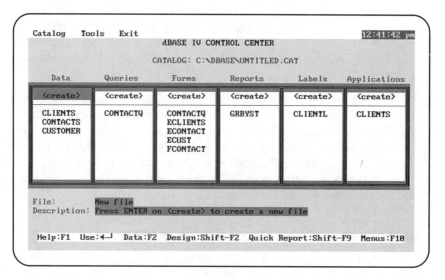

Fig. 14.2. *The dBASE Control Center screen.*

Drawbacks of the Programming Interface

The biggest advantage of the programmer model is also its weakness. The control that Xbase languages give the programmer is virtually unlimited. These languages do little, however, to prevent a programmer from creating a bad application, breaking standard rules for data integrity, and presenting the user with cryptic or untidy entry screens and prompts.

Moreover, the complexity of even a small application programmed in an Xbase language makes the application difficult to test and debug. Many problems can and do go undetected until after the system is in operation. dBASE, for example, relies on the application to enforce *referential integrity* (the effect of a change in one file on related files). Deleting a customer record may leave uncollected accounts or payment information floating in limbo; the dBASE programmer must explicitly account for possible threats to data integrity in all entry and editing programs.

A DBMS with poor data independence and lack of relational capabilities forces users and developers to remember many trivial details concerned with data storage rather than with the content of the data itself. Nothing can be taken for granted in any part of the program. To perform a search in a single table, for example, you must know which indexes are available for the table and activate them by name. For some routine features required by a relational database (referential integrity, for example), serious programming time must be invested. Even when a program enforces data integrity, integrity can be easily circumvented if a user gains direct access to a table.

Programming languages may become rooted in obsolescence as they struggle to maintain compatibility with previous versions while incorporating new features. A similar problem is created by clinging to a standard such as the dBASE DBF data file for backward compatibility rather than taking advantage of new structures.

A programming language provides many tools for tuning database performance. The burden of knowing how to tune a particular database operation is placed squarely on the user, however. This is a mixed blessing, because a database may be badly tuned as easily as it may be well tuned. As the database grows and the needs of its users change, the database may deviate from the assumptions initially used to tune the system, resulting in a need for modifications.

Although code generators can help, they have their limitations. Programmers do not have to labor long to discover that they need the full language to build a workable application. This need to master a verbose language imposes a steep learning curve. The increasing complexity of Xbase languages has led some programmers to stop trying to keep up with all the dialects (dBASE, FoxPro, Clipper, and so on) because they cannot afford to master them all. Nantucket is developing new products that may lead programmers to forsake some of their dBASE code in favor of Structured Query Language (SQL).

The Spreadsheet Interface

A second paradigm for database design takes advantage of one of the world's most popular user interfaces—the spreadsheet. By co-opting an existing interface, spreadsheet-inspired programs such as Borland's Paradox give the user a familiar work area (see fig. 14.3). Like a spreadsheet, Paradox uses a series of menus at the top of each screen. Paradox has different modes of operation for adding, viewing, and querying the database, and even enables you to view several tables at the same time.

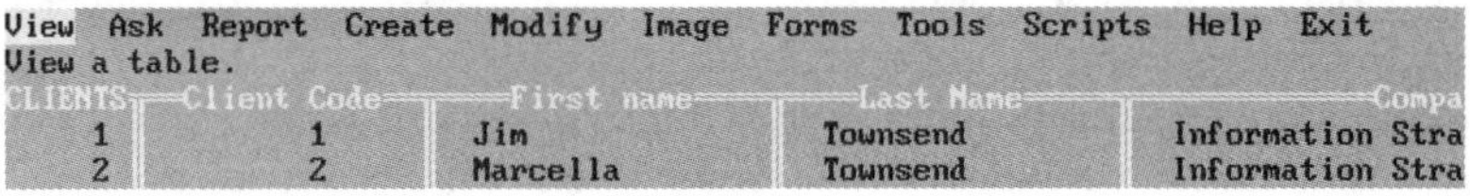

```
View  Ask  Report  Create  Modify  Image  Forms  Tools  Scripts  Help  Exit
View a table.
CLIENTS   Client Code      First name        Last Name           Compa
   1          1            Jim               Townsend            Information Stra
   2          2            Marcella          Townsend            Information Stra
```

Fig. 14.3. The Paradox Main menu.

Paradox emphasizes a *table-view* of its database files—a display of several records in tabular fashion on the same screen. Paradox contains integrated business graphics so that you can display database values as graphs by using only a few keystrokes.

Paradox does not embody the concept of an application consisting of a number of interrelated tables. Instead, like Lotus 1-2-3, Paradox simply recognizes all the data tables stored in the current default directory.

Paradox has its own programming language: PAL. PAL is a script language, which the developer can use to string together a series of commands so that the application behaves as though the user is selecting options from menus.

PAL resembles the macro programming capability currently available in word processing software, and has a full list of commands to create self-contained applications. You can use the script language to automate repetitive tasks and to control what the user sees from the database.

Advantages of the Spreadsheet Interface

The spreadsheet interface saves time for users and developers by adopting a time-honored interface and enabling the creation of powerful macros to perform repetitive functions. This form of programming is similar to writing keyboard macros in WordPerfect or macros in Lotus 1-2-3.

Using the spreadsheet interface saves time in training users and presents them with a familiar command interface.

Drawbacks of the Spreadsheet Interface

The spreadsheet interface has its disadvantages, however. Dealing with databases as spreadsheets is expedient, but may blind users to some of the possibilities available with a database. The modal nature of the program forces users who are writing applications to be conscious of the current state of the program and does not resemble traditional structured programming as much as does a DBMS that uses the programmer interface.

The Form-Oriented Interface

A third approach to database design uses the paper form as the model for building tables. These packages, such as the relational DataEase and flat-file DataPerfect and Q&A, omit the step of building tables altogether. The user simply creates a data-entry form, and the program automatically creates the table for storing the data.

These packages typically keep programming to a minimum. In addition, the form-oriented interface usually contains an interface for record entry, so that you do not have to invent your own interface. DataEase, for instance, uses function keys in record entry for commands such as SAVE, MODIFY, DELETE, and SEARCH. Users familiar with one DataEase application easily can learn another.

Advantages of the Form-Oriented Interface

The chief advantage of the form-oriented interface is that it cuts out a step in database design and begins with the most prominent part of the application—the data-entry form. Such an interface makes prototyping quick and painless. Field names and lengths can be changed directly on the form and easily moved.

Compared to a programming interface, a form-oriented interface saves a great deal of time because it provides its own record-entry facilities for end users. This approach promotes consistent standards for all applications developed with the package.

Many programmers find the form-oriented interface simple and natural because it resembles paper forms in an office. This interface is a good choice for graphical user interfaces such as Microsoft Windows.

Drawbacks of the Form-Oriented Interface

Like all software options, the form-oriented interface has drawbacks. Because the table is intimately connected to a single form, the form-oriented interface does not fully support multiple views for the same table.

The interface is usually far less flexible than that offered by a programming interface. If you don't like the record-entry interface provided by the software vendor and want to create your own interface, you must do a great deal of work.

Choosing a DBMS

The database packages on the market have something for nearly everyone. Packages vary widely in their power, flexibility, ease of programming, and ease of use.

To select a database program, first determine whether you need a relational database. Second, decide with which programming model you prefer to work. Although nearly all products contain elements of two or more paradigms, table 14.3 identifies some of the features of each paradigm and how the major products fit in.

> **NOTE:** Table 14.3 is accurate as of this writing. If you are in the process of purchasing a DBMS, make a thorough investigation of all current versions.

After you have chosen a database product, try to follow its fundamental orientation. Changing the paradigm of the product to suit your personal style leads to frustration and low productivity. If you want your final applications to look like spreadsheets, purchase a spreadsheet-style DBMS rather than try to invent your own interface from scratch. Similarly, nonprocedural, graphically oriented systems do not work as well when choked with procedural, step-by-step code.

Table 14.3. Paradigms for Popular Packages

	dBASE IV	FoxPro	Clipper	Paradox	DataEase
Interpreted language	X	X			
Language compiler			X		
Record oriented	X	X	X		
Macro language	X	X	X	X	
Integrated business graphics				X	
Mode oriented				X	
Set operations				X	X
Domain support				X	X
Enforces unique rows				X	X
Referential integrity	None	None	None	Limited	Limited
Update within views	X	X	X	X	X
Data dictionary					X
Query optimization		X		X	

Considering Your Hardware

You can run database software on many different classes of computers, from calculator-size pocket organizers to huge corporate mainframes. Because many DBMS are written for a specific type of hardware, knowing which computers will be used to run the application will eliminate some DBMS packages from consideration.

If you are buying hardware as well as software, you need to determine the best match between your needs (and budget) and the cornucopia of hardware offerings. Establishing criteria for sizing applications is beyond the scope of this book, but the following are some basic questions you can answer to narrow down your hardware choices.

- *How many people need simultaneous access to the database?*

    If the answer is one, a microcomputer (PC) is your best choice, unless your data is prohibitively large. A single-user system rarely has a large volume of data when the only source of data is data entry.

- *How big will your database be? Will you store hundreds, thousands, or millions of records? How detailed is each record?*

If you plan to store a high volume of data, you have many options at your disposal, including networks, minicomputers, and mainframes. You may want to consider client-server architecture. The range of these hardware platforms also may widen your software choices.

- *Do you expect your database to grow significantly?*

  As your database grows, you may need to move it to another computer. If you can foresee this eventuality, be sure to consider how your software will run on other (probably larger) machines.

If you think that database migration (moving your database to a different class of hardware) is in your future, you can save time and money by looking at migration options for the software you choose now. Many packages have versions that run on several classes of hardware, simplifying the move to a new computer.

Applying Evaluation Criteria

You may want to adopt some of the evaluation criteria used in the computer press. The following list of evaluation criteria consolidates many of the criteria used in computer periodicals such as *DBMS*, *Data-based Advisor*, *PC Week*, *InfoWorld*, *Database Programming and Design*, and *PC Magazine*.

Functions and Features

Sizes:
Field size
Fields per record
Fields per database
Record size
Records per data file
Indexes per file
Data files per database
Records per database

Field types supported:
Text
Numeric string
Number
Date
Logical
Time
Graphic

Binary
Choice

Tests valid data ranges
Provides default values
Permits lookup tables
Uses forced upper- or lowercase
Converts date formats
Supports sequenced fields
Supports carryover from previous record
Contains a data dictionary
Automatic
User-defined

Set operations:
Product
Union
Difference
Intersect
Divide
Outer extensions

Data Manipulation:
Maximum number of join tables
Maximum number of project tables
Maximum number of union tables
Maximum number of intersect tables
Maximum number of append tables
Maximum number of open data files

Sorting:
Permanent
Temporary
Sorts on any field
Sorts on indexed field only
Maximum number of simultaneous fields sorted

Search parameters:
First occurrences
All occurrences
Index field only
Multiple fields
Case-sensitive
Whole word
Value or character range
Soundex searches

14

Wild cards
Boolean
Compound Boolean

Query Language:
Proprietary
SQL
Query by example
Query by forms
Multiple file access
Query editor support
Stored queries

Mathematical functions:
Date arithmetic
Time arithmetic
Arithmetic functions
Exponential functions
Trigonometric functions
Financial functions
Totals
Subtotals
Average
Count
Maximum
Minimum

Statistics:
Standard deviation
Variance

Command strategy:
Static menus
Dynamic menus
Typed commands
Mouse support

Macros:
Automatic recording
Keystroke macro
Macro language

Input Facilities:
Maximum screens per file
Maximum number of files per screen

Screen definition
    Painting
    Coordinates specification
    Automatic field name placement

Output facilities:
    Multiple file reports
    Page breaks
    Breaks when fields change
    Report definition method
        Painting
        Forms duplication
        Automatic
        Predefined mailing labels
        Programmable
        Stored report definitions
        Line-based
        Form-based
    Destinations
        Screen
        Printer
        Disk

Backup/restore
    Two-phase commit
    Backup/Restore facility

Security
    Database passwords
    File passwords
    Menu passwords
    Report passwords
    Read, write, delete control

Performance

Import
Sort
Extract
Search
Delete
Index
Multitable reporting

Other

> Ease of development
> Ease of maintenance
> Technical support
>> Cost of telephone support
>> Automatic on-line help
>> Tutorial
>> Prompt messages

Price

> Licensing price
> Support price

Many of these criteria require little more than a cursory look. Most relational database products share a list of base features. Unless your application has unusual requirements, record and file sizes are usually adequate.

Not all evaluation criteria are equal. Comparing the number of check marks in each column of a features list is a poor way to compare products. Features such as reliability and speed may overshadow lesser capabilities (such as the capability to generate mailing labels).

If performance is a critical consideration, you may have to test the DBMS yourself. Published software benchmarks are often optimistic and may not reflect the particular requirements of your application. If you are not expert in programming the DBMS that you are testing, poor test results may reflect programming ignorance more than the innate characteristics of the software. Such errors of oversight can occur also in magazine software reviews. One DBMS, for example, came up with a slow performance for importing data. This poor showing, however, was because no fields had been indexed on the destination form and the database had been set to check for duplicates. An experienced developer would not commit this type of error.

The most important characteristics of a DBMS are often subjective; they include ease of use, consistency of the user interface, and expressiveness of a programming language. Selecting a package from a list of features is like buying a high-fidelity sound system based on its technical specifications; nothing can substitute for experiencing a system up close.

Application designers and end users taint the results of the evaluation criteria with personal and professional biases, knowledge, and experience. Unless you will be the sole user of the DBMS, you must account for the skills of all users when you judge the criteria.

Consulting the Experts

Fortunately for the evaluator, outside expertise is available in many places. A good place to start is with computer magazines. Read advertisements as well as the software reviews and articles. Ads reveal quite a bit about a product and even more about its competitors. You also can learn about the depth of market penetration and acceptance of a product based on the amount of compatible and add-in software available.

Watch out for a comparison trick that many software vendors employ. From the hundreds of measurable characteristics of a DBMS, they choose only those in which their package scores well and then rank their competitors on the same scale. The competitors, of course, are not as highly rated in some categories. The way to overcome this bias is to look at several such comparisons, ignoring the product promoted in the advertisement.

You may want to take software reviews with a grain of salt. Software reviewers sometimes have connections with vendors whose products are under review. In other cases, specialists in one package have applied their biases in writing reviews of competitive database products, resulting in assessments that differ dramatically from more objective reviews. If you rely on published reviews, you temper the prejudices of any one reviewer by using several sources.

Computer bulletin boards are another source of expert advice. The DBMS vendors themselves maintain bulletin boards. Through meeting places such as CompuServe Forums, you can find colleagues who are happy to assist you in your quest. You also can learn quite a bit from eavesdropping on the debates over the merits of competing software packages. Some computer programmers rely on bulletin boards rather than the DBMS vendor for technical support.

Evaluating the Choices

You must address the issue of DBMS acquisition methodically if you expect to find the best system for your needs. When evaluating any package, you should weigh it on several scales:

- ❑ *Paradigm*. Is the paradigm consistent with my programming skills and orientation? Will it address my business needs?

- ❑ *Software*. Is the software consistent with my business and/or computing environment? Does it have the speed, flexibility, and reporting features required? Will it continue to meet my needs in the future?

❑ *Application requirements*. Does the package fit the special requirements of the application? Does it support special field types that
you need, such as time fields or graphics? Will the package enable
you to share data with other programs you use?

A candidate package must succeed on all these scales.

To take a more mathematical approach for ranking software packages,
build a matrix showing the features you seek and the packages under
evaluation. In the intersecting cells, rank the feature for that package on
a numeric scale. You can set up a spreadsheet to tally your results automatically.

The mathematical approach takes largely subjective criteria and makes
them seem more objective. The danger is that the numbers you assign to
the products may hide more important qualitative criteria. Despite this
risk, the technique is useful.

An evaluation may result in the comparison shown in table 14.4.

Table 14.4. Database Evaluation

Package/Feature	YourBASE	MyBASE	HisBASE	HerBASE
Reporting speed	4	2	3	6
Large capacity	4	5	1	8
Easy to maintain	10	2	4	7
Uses mouse	0	3	9	0
TOTAL SCORE	18	12	17	21

By adding up the columns, you can calculate a cumulative score for each
package. The imaginary product HerBASE comes out on top with 21
points.

To make the evaluation more sophisticated, you can assign weights to
each score so that the most important evaluation criteria are taken into
greater consideration than less important criteria. After adding the
weights, multiply the scores by the weight to come up with a weighted
score.

Table 14.5 applies weights to the preceding evaluation. (The weighted
scores are in parentheses.)

Table 14.5. Database Evaluation, Weighted Scores

Package/Feature	Weight	YourBASE	MyBASE	HisBASE	HerBASE
Reporting speed	4	4 (16)	2 (8)	3 (12)	6 (24)
Large capacity	2	4 (8)	5 (10)	1 (2)	8 (16)
Easy to maintain	8	10 (80)	2 (16)	4 (32)	7 (56)
Uses mouse	6	0 (0)	3 (18)	9 (54)	0 (0)
TOTAL SCORE		18 (104)	12 (52)	17 (100)	22 (96)

Note that the results from the weighted comparison are somewhat different. Although HerBASE is still highly rated, it has slipped behind HisBASE and YourBASE. HisBASE was boosted by the weighting given to the Uses Mouse feature, and the low priority of Large Capacity dragged HerBASE down a bit. The new winner is YourBASE, chiefly due to its easy maintenance.

Making Your Final Choice

CHECKLIST

Be sure that you can answer the following questions in the affirmative before you write the check for your next software package.

❑ Is it powerful enough to fulfill my requirements?

Consider the speed, file, and record limitations of the system.

❑ Will it suit the system's end users?

❑ Is it easy enough to use? Is the interface intuitive, or at least familiar?

❑ Will the database developer find it suitable?

❑ Will designing the file structure, forms, and reports be easy?

Remember that the amount of money you spend on programming usually exceeds the DBMS software cost, so faster development time can result in significant savings.

❑ Is the application easy to maintain?

❑ Does the software have a future? Is it an industry standard that is sure to enjoy continued support and improvements?

Loyal IBM customers, for example, are often willing to forsake the latest software technology, best performance, and slickest interfaces in exchange for the stability and excellent support of the largest computer company in the world.

❏ Can I afford it?

The system that best meets your two most important criteria is of little use to you if it is $10,000 over your budget.

Considering Special Features

Some features, when needed, can weigh heavily in your buying decision. In addition to standard text, numeric, and date and time fields, some packages can store images as fields. This feature enables a building security database to contain a photo of each employee along with name, employee ID, and other information. Other exotic data types include variable-length text and memo fields.

If your requirement demands a special field type, your choices may be limited. Be sure to check for add-on packages that supplement the standard field types.

Another important consideration when purchasing a DBMS is whether you will need to use your database with different hardware platforms. Although several packages claim to run across many different platforms, moving an application from one machine to another is not necessarily a simple operation. In many cases, large portions of the code must be rewritten to accommodate features that vary from one operating system to another.

Summary

By spelling out your requirements, you can quickly narrow the field of candidate database software to a short list. You then can identify the strongest contenders by ranking their characteristics against a prioritized list of requirements.

Remember that subjective factors can be as important as objective criteria. To create a successful database, you must be comfortable with your software tools.

If you are a first-time database designer, remember that few programmers use their first database package forever. Most people try several packages before settling on a favorite. With the rapid pace of software evolution, nearly everyone will be using a substantially different package in a few years even if it bears the same name as the package they are using today.

Always keep an eye on the future of your database. Beware of relying too much on the proprietary features of your database software. You will have to rewrite functions based on these features if you move the application to a new database package. Even if you stay with your package, its features may change in later releases and jeopardize your applications.

In the final analysis, the goal is to obtain the database software best suited to your needs, not necessarily the best, fastest, or most powerful database on the market. Advanced features that you do not need are a waste of money and might actually clutter up the product, making your work more difficult.

14

Client-Server Architecture

Abolish all private property.

Karl Marx

The most widely touted new technology for relational databases is client-server architecture. Heralded as the successor to networks and mainframes, client-server architecture integrates the best characteristics of personal computers (friendly software and quick response) with the best traits of mainframe computers (high storage capacity and strong security).

Client-server architecture is a combination of hardware and software that enables users to divide computing tasks between the user's workstation (usually a microcomputer) and server computers (micros, minis, or mainframes, depending on the volume of data and the speed required). The user interface runs on the workstation, the database software runs on the server, and a network links the two.

A key benefit of client-server architecture is that it enables several types of applications (such as databases and spreadsheets) to share data. With a client-server system, you can use a graphics program, for example, to create a chart based on numbers stored on the central database.

Client-server architecture promises unprecedented ease of data access at a much lower price than conventional mainframe solutions. The business press is buzzing with stories of companies that have downsized by converting expensive mainframe applications to run on PC networks. Companies of all sizes are retiring their mainframes and converting to less expensive computing power. Some companies, such as the computer manufacturer Compaq, have eliminated mainframes entirely.

Industry analysts are optimistic about the growth of client-server computing. According to Forrester Research of Cambridge, Massachusetts, the U.S. client/server market will grow from $4.9 billion in 1992 to $38 billion in 1995 ("Resizing Client/Server," *The Computing Strategy Report*, December 1991). Many software companies are staking their futures on the success of client-server systems by devoting large amounts of research and development effort to client-server products.

> **NOTE:** This chapter is a bit more technical than the preceding chapters and is meant to be an introduction to a new and exciting database technology rather than a step-by-step guide. All the principles of database design discussed up to this point apply as well to client-server architecture.

Components of Client-Server Architecture

Client-server architecture represents the careful melding of a number of elements (see fig. 15.1). The three main components of client-server architecture are the client, the server, and the network.

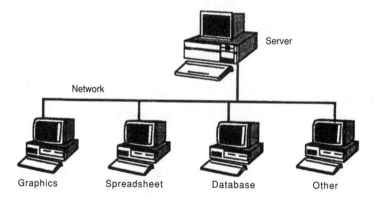

Fig. 15.1. *Client-server architecture.*

The *client* (or *front-end*) workstation is the interface to the user. The client workstation—often a microcomputer—may use any of several operating systems, including DOS, OS/2, UNIX, or Apple Macintosh System 7. Client software can be a database, spreadsheet, word processing program, graphics program, or some other application.

The *server* (or *back-end*) computer stores the data, processes the clients' requests for data, and controls data access and security. The server can be a microcomputer, minicomputer, or mainframe computer, and can run any of several operating systems. Database server software, such as Microsoft SQL Server, Oracle, or DB2, manages the database and processes requests for information from clients.

The *network* provides a communications channel between the clients and the server. The network, which consists of hardware (such as network cards and cables) and software (the network operating system), transmits data among all workstations and servers. Popular network operating systems for client-server include DECnet, Novell, and Microsoft LAN Manager.

Client-server architecture divorces an application's user interface functions (such as menus, forms, and the presentation of reports) from its data storage and retrieval functions. A client-server works differently than does a stand-alone PC application, a mainframe or mini-computer application, or a PC local area network. Table 15.1 lists the main components for each of these database architectures and the role played by each main component. Although these architectures sometimes contain the same hardware components, they are used for quite different purposes.

Table 15.1. Competing Database Architectures

Component	Workstation	Mainframe (Server)	Network
Microcomputer	Stores data, processes queries, handles user interface	N/A	N/A
LAN	Processes queries, handles user interface	N/A	Stores data (file server), transmits files to PC for processing
Mainframe	With emulation software, may be used as a dumb terminal	Stores data, processes queries, handles user interface (dumb terminals)	N/A
Client-Server	Handles user interface, submits SQL queries to database server	Stores data, processes queries received from workstation	Forwards to database server and answers to workstation

15

Division of Labor in Client-Server Architecture

In a typical client-server transaction, the workstation handles the user interface and creates a database query. Suppose that a user searches the records for a person by last name. When the user enters the query, the workstation processes the request and submits a statement such as SELECT FROM CUSTOMERS WHERE LNAME = "Rodriguez" to the database server. The server processes the query and transmits the answer back to the user.

Using a client-server system is quite different from running a database on a local area network (LAN). To run the search described in the preceding paragraph on a LAN, you send the entire Customer table to the workstation, and the workstation central processing unit (CPU) performs the search. If the query searches a large file, this kind of communication and processing can take much longer than under client-server architecture.

If you are searching a 10M file, that entire file (or at least its index file) is transmitted from the disk drive of the file server to the workstation, where the file will be processed. In client-server architecture, on the other hand, the CPU of the database server performs the query, and only the results of the search are transmitted over the network. You, therefore, might receive a 10,000 byte file rather than a 10,000,000 byte file.

The net result is a dramatic reduction in network communications traffic. The processing speed of the workstation (along with the speed of the network to send the files to the workstation) determines database performance on a LAN. Consequently, a slower CPU on a LAN workstation results in dramatically slower performance; in a client-server environment, however, this degradation is minimal.

Structured Query Language

A client-server system needs a common language to make its components communicate with each other. Several relational database manipulation languages are used in client-server applications. You may have used a database language if you have programmed in the dBASE language or Paradox Application Language. Only one language, however, has become the ascendant language.

Structured Query Language (or *SQL*, often pronounced "sequel") is the most popular language for client-server architecture. SQL, which grew out of research conducted by IBM in the late 1970s, is endorsed by the American National Standards Institute and the International

Organization for Standardization. Dozens of vendors use various dialects of SQL in their software. SQL is the language of choice for a number of relational DBMS.

Software written by different vendors can communicate through SQL, using the same commands for entering, retrieving, and manipulating data. The front-end software accepts user input and then generates the appropriate SQL command to process the data. The command is sent through a local area network or other communications channel to the server, which processes the request. The result is sent back to the front end and is displayed on the user's workstation.

Although SQL is the standard, some of its implementations are more standard than others. Some SQL dialects contain syntax or commands that other SQL systems do not understand. More sophisticated front-end packages tailor queries to the dialect of SQL used by the server.

Benefits of Client-Server Architecture

According to its proponents, client-server architecture offers a number of cost and performance benefits. In short, client-server architecture can provide a high level of performance, productivity, and cost effectiveness. These advantages are described as follows:

- *Greater performance than a PC LAN.* Because you may use any size computer as the database server, you are not limited to databases that can fit on PCs. Lower communication traffic and faster processing means improved response time for all users.

- *Better data integrity than a PC LAN.* Database server software, originally written for mainframe and minicomputers, includes much better security features, including password protection, referential integrity, and sophisticated backup and error recovery capabilities.

- *Friendlier software than minicomputers and mainframes.* Users can access data with their favorite PC spreadsheet and graphics programs.

- *Lower cost than minicomputer and mainframe systems.* Performing development on the workstation means reduced expenses for development, because PC CPU is virtually free.

- *Higher productivity for developers.* Advanced programming tools available on workstations can cut dramatically the amount of coding required and produce results more quickly than traditional mainframe methodologies.

- *Easier development than mainframe systems.* Because database designers are insulated from details such as the physical storage of the data, they are free to concentrate on the application itself.

- *Supports more users than a LAN.* The option of large server computers means that a client-server application can grow to accommodate a larger number of users than a LAN database.

- *Reduced network traffic compared to a LAN.* Network communications traffic grows more slowly with each additional user in a client-server environment than on a LAN.

Client-server architecture can make application programmers more productive, because they can develop applications on the PC without contending for limited time on a host computer. Programmers also have access to a large number of development tools for the PC. Client-server architecture thus enables developers to use their PCs to build the application, even if the data ultimately is stored on a minicomputer or mainframe.

Client-server architecture also frees software developers to divide their efforts, specializing in the database engine (server) or the front end (workstation). In the past, some of the best front ends were limited by weak storage and retrieval mechanisms and the fastest engines crippled by unfriendly programmer and user interfaces. In the client-server world, consumers can choose the front and back ends of the database independently.

In client-server systems, you can use multiple front-end software packages to access the same data. These front-end packages do not even have to be databases. Spreadsheets are popular front ends. The spreadsheet cells "point" to records in the corporate database. Each time a spreadsheet is retrieved, it creates a query and the database provides an updated figure. Business graphics programs also make handy front ends, turning pages of boring numbers into slick graphs.

The capability to use multiple front ends means that the database can please more users. One department may prefer Excel on the Macintosh, for example, but another may use an Oracle application on UNIX workstations. With client-server architecture, the two departments can keep their favorite hardware and software while sharing a common database.

Database server software offers a higher level of security than a PC DBMS. Security features include transaction logs that can help users recover data after the system crashes, two-phase commit (so that you can "roll back" or undo changes to the database in the event of a crash), and options to enforce sophisticated rules that control access to various portions of the database. Many database servers enable you to create access control lists containing names of users and assign each list with specific privileges. This kind of security is not usually available in PC DBMS.

Upgrading a database server in a client-server system improves performance much more than upgrading a file server on a LAN. Moreover, nearly any class of computer—from PC to mainframe—can act as a database server. As your needs grow, you may upgrade the server to provide additional storage or processing speed without modifying the applications that use the data.

Costs of Client-Server Architecture

The numerous benefits of client-server architecture are not without cost. The following list includes some of the drawbacks of client-server architecture:

- *More expensive than PC LAN.* Server software usually costs more than LAN software, running several thousand rather than several hundred dollars.

- *More complex to develop than PC or LAN systems.* Developers must deal with several layers of software, from the workstation to the communications protocols to the database server. More skill and training are needed for client-server development than for PC or mainframe applications.

- *More expensive to maintain than a LAN.* Again, the greater complexity of client-server means that more things can go wrong.

- *More difficult to install than a LAN.* Especially at this early stage of client-server evolution, not all hardware and software pieces work together as advertised. You must spend extra time testing and configuring the system.

- *Possibly worse performance than a mainframe system.* Compared to a mainframe application with dumb terminals, response time may not be faster with client-server architecture, depending on the speed of the workstation and network.

- *Sometimes worse performance than a stand-alone or a LAN.* For small databases that run quickly on a PC or PC LAN, the extra layers of software in client-server actually may make response time worse. An application must be rather large to justify client-server architecture.

Summary

Client-server architecture is the most exciting development in database technology. Combining the friendliness of the PC with the brute force of the mainframe or minicomputer, client-server architecture promises the best of both worlds. This chapter offers an overview of the benefits and potential pitfalls of client-server architecture.

For demanding applications, client-server architecture is an attractive alternative to LAN, minicomputer, or mainframe solutions. New advances in hardware, especially parallel processing, will make client-server architecture even more tempting.

A growing number of businesses have pioneered the use of client-server architecture to downsize from mainframes to networks, and to speed development of new applications. Client-server is still in its early stages, however—commercially if not technically—and is not yet widely adopted.

If you are responsible for a large database effort, you should become familiar with client-server architecture and find out what it can offer. Over the coming decade, client-server architecture is likely to become as common as the local area network.

Glossary

For additional help on computer terminology, consult *Que's Computer User's Dictionary*, by Bryan Pfaffenberger.

1NF. See *first normal form (1NF)*.

2NF. See *second normal form (2NF)*.

3NF. See *third normal form (3NF)*.

ad-hoc reporting. A facility that enables users to create new reports as needed, often through use of query by example. See also *query by example*.

American National Standards Institute (ANSI). An organization devoted to enhancing the productivity of American industrial enterprises through the development of voluntary standards. ANSI committees have developed standard versions of several computer languages.

American Standard Code for Information Interchange (ASCII). The code used to store and communicate text. ASCII files consist of text that a large number of programs can view and edit; ASCII files, unlike compiled programs or graphics, do not include binary characters.

AND. The relational operator indicating that both of two conditions must be met to satisfy search criteria. The AND operator often is called *exclusive* because it narrows the scope of a search. See also *relational operator*.

ANSI. See *American National Standards Institute (ANSI)*.

application. A computer program consisting of elements, such as forms, reports, procedures, menus, and imports, that address a particular business problem or need. Some database packages refer to applications as *databases* or *projects*.

application generator. Software that generates database programs based on operator input (usually through a series of menus), rather than based on writing a program line-by-line.

archive. A file or table used to store inactive records. Archives can be stored on-line or off-line.

ASCII. See *American Standard Code for Information Interchange (ASCII)*.

attribute. A characteristic of a database entity. Attributes are represented by fields in database tables. See also *field* and *table*.

audit trail. A record of transactions, used to re-create a series of database events. Some database software automatically record a transaction log for this purpose.

backups. Extra copies of files, created in case of system failure.

baud rate. The rate that data is transmitted; roughly synonymous with *bits per second (bps)*.

BCNF. See *Boyce/Codd Normal Form (BCNF)*.

bits per second (bps). A unit of measurement used for the speed of data transmission.

Boyce/Codd Normal Form (BCNF). A stricter version of third normal form in relational database theory. See also *third normal form (3NF)*.

bps. See *bits per second (bps)*.

business rules. The policies of a business as they relate to handling data. A business rule might define a customer, for example, as a person who has made a purchase in the last 12 months.

calculated fields. Fields that have values determined by the system rather than entered by a user. Sales tax, for example, might be calculated as a percentage of total cost.

CASE. See *computer-assisted systems engineering (CASE)*.

choice field. A field that restricts data entry to a predesignated list of options.

column. In a database table, a single field (or attribute) is shown as a vertical column. See also *field* and *attribute*.

comparison operators. The ways to express selection criteria in terms of how records relate to one another or to a constant. The comparison operators usually include: = (equal), > (greater than), < (less than), <= (less than or equal to), and >= (greater than or equal to). Some database software includes other comparison operators.

computer-assisted systems engineering (CASE). Software used for designing computer systems.

conditional. A program or subroutine executed only if a certain condition is true. Usually, programs use a structure with words such as IF, THEN, and ELSE to show the parts of the condition.

data dictionary. A list of all database tables and fields. An active data dictionary automatically updates all occurrences of a field when the field is changed; a passive data dictionary merely stores the original information. Passive data dictionaries can be on paper or automated.

data-entry form. A logical grouping of fields displayed on-screen, often based on a paper business form. Data entered in forms is stored in tables.

database. A computerized collection of information.

database administrator (DBA). The person in charge of maintaining a database.

database design. The practice of constructing a database.

database management system (DBMS). Software (and sometimes hardware) specially designed to store and retrieve information. A DBMS enables users (or other programs) to enter, edit, and retrieve information.

data flow diagram. An illustration that shows how information moves in an organization or process. Special symbols represent different types of data flow.

data independence. A goal of database management systems to insulate users and applications from details of the data storage structures.

data integrity. The completeness and consistency of a database. Key features for data integrity include uniqueness checks and referential integrity. See also *referential integrity*.

data interchange format (DIF). A format that uses ASCII text files for exchanging data between software packages. The DIF format commonly is supported by spreadsheets and databases.

data validation. Testing data against a range of acceptable values to ensure integrity.

DBA. See *database administrator (DBA)*.

DBMS. See *database management system (DBMS)*.

default. A standard value to be entered in a field. Typically, the user can override the default value as necessary. This term also refers to standard settings used for printer control, page control, and other functions.

delimiter. A character used to mark the end of a data field or record; delimiters are used for variable-length ASCII exports from databases.

derivation formula. A lookup or calculation used to fill in the value of a field.

derived field. A field with a calculated value based on other fields. The city and state fields, for instance, might be derived based on the ZIP code field.

development cycle. The process by which applications are developed. Main phases of the development cycle include analysis, implementation, testing, and documentation.

DIF. See *data interchange format (DIF)*.

encrypt. To encode sensitive data for security reasons.

entity. Something tracked in a database. Entities can be concrete (inventory, people, places) or abstract (accounts, transactions, assignments). Each entity is represented by a database table.

entity-relationship (E-R) model. A theoretical framework for representing data requirements, often using symbols to represent the relationships among data elements.

export. Output of data from a program in a format suitable for use by another program. Typical export formats include fixed- and variable-length ASCII files.

extract. To select a set of items from a larger group, such as in choosing a set of records from a database according to particular selection criteria.

field. The smallest meaningful unit of a database. See also *column* and *attribute*.

file. Generally, a computer file is a stream of information. Many file types exist, including files that store programs (binary files), and data files suitable for various programs. Files are stored on peripheral devices, such as a disk or tape drive. Some DBMS refer to tables as files.

first normal form (1NF). In relational database theory, a state achieved when a relation (represented by a table) contains no repeating fields. See *normalization, second normal form (2NF),* and *third normal form (3NF).*

flat-file database. A database with limited support for multiple-file operations. In a flat-file database, as opposed to a relational database, information is stored in one or more single files, accessed individually. Flat-file databases are typically easier to use and less expensive than relational databases. See also *relational database.*

foreign key. In a relational database table, a field that is the primary key field for another table. The customer number in an invoices table, for instance, is a foreign key. See also *key field* and *primary key.*

form. See *data-entry form.*

graphical user interface (GUI). A design in which a computer interacts with a user by means of graphical menus and symbols rather than a command language. Microsoft Windows, the Apple Macintosh, and GeoWorks are examples of graphical user interfaces.

GUI. See *graphical user interface (GUI).*

horizontal application. A database application designed for use across industries. A word processing program is an example of a horizontal application. See also *vertical application.*

horizontal menu. Also referred to as a Lotus-style menu; this type of menu appears across the top of the screen and often displays submenu choices when you select a menu option; menu options typically are chosen by entering the first letter of the choice or by using the arrow keys.

icon. A graphical symbol used in graphical user interfaces. Generally, menu options are selected by positioning the mouse pointer on the icon that represents the desired option, and clicking. See also *graphical user interface (GUI).*

import. To bring foreign data into a database.

index. A file that maintains the logical order of records in a table; an index facilitates quick information retrieval.

interface. The way that users communicate with a computer system. In a database, the interface consists of elements such as menus, forms, tables, reports, and queries. See also *graphical user interface (GUI)*.

intersection. In set theory, the area where two sets overlap. An intersection is produced by using the AND query operator.

join table. The result of a query that combines two or more tables. Several types of joins exist depending on the rules for inclusion of records in the query.

key fields. Fields in a table which identify a record. See also *primary key* and *foreign key*.

LAN. See *local area network (LAN)*.

link. A key field that relates multiple tables; for example, a customer number may be the link between a customer table and an invoices table. See also *key fields*.

logical data model. The structure of the data as seen by users, independent of hardware considerations. See also *physical data model*.

local area network (LAN). Hardware and software that enable computer workstations to share programs and data.

Lotus-style menu. See *horizontal menu*.

macro. A single command that executes a series of different commands; extensively used in databases such as Paradox.

mainframe. A multiuser computer designed to meet the needs of a large organization; a mainframe has a greater capacity than that of a minicomputer or microcomputer. The mainframe is the basis for supercomputers. See also *microcomputer* and *minicomputer*.

management information system (MIS). An automated means of providing information for decision making to managers at various levels in an organization. MIS also refers to the academic discipline relating to these systems.

many-to-many relationship. A relationship between two tables in which each record in table A is related to multiple records in table B, and vice versa. See also *one-to-many relationship* and *one-to-one relationship*.

match field. A field defined as the basis for a relationship between two tables.

menu. A list of options displayed on-screen in a computer program, from which the user chooses; choices can include subsequent menus, data-entry forms, reports, or other procedures.

metadata. Data that describes other data, such as tables that contain lists of database entities and attributes.

microcomputer. A computer with a central processing unit based on a microprocessor chip. More commonly referred to as a personal computer (PC). See also *mainframe* and *minicomputer*.

minicomputer. A multiple-user computer, sometimes based on multiple processors, that is larger than a microcomputer and smaller than a mainframe. Traditionally, minicomputers used 32-bit processors, and microcomputers used 8- and 16-bit processors. With increasingly powerful PCs, however, the distinction between micro-, mini- and mainframe computers has become blurred. See also *mainframe* and *microcomputer*.

MIS. See *management information system (MIS)*.

normalization. The process of organizing data into a structure of one or more tables. Normalization is necessary to achieve the optimum structure for a relational database. See also *first normal form (1NF)*, *second normal form (2NF)*, and *third normal form (3NF)*.

one-to-many relationship. A relationship between two tables in which table A can have multiple related records in table B, but each record in table B is related to only one record in table A. See also *many-to-many relationship* and *one-to-one relationship*.

one-to-one relationship. A relationship between two tables in which table A can have one and only one related record in table B, and each record in table B is related to one and only one record in table A. See also *many-to-many relationship* and *one-to-many relationship*.

operator. A symbol or word that defines an operation to be performed on a value or values; operators can define arithmetic functions, relational functions, and other commands. See also *relational operator*.

OR. The relational operator indicating that either of two conditions must be met to satisfy the search criteria. The OR operator is often called inclusive because it broadens the scope of a search. See also *relational operator* and *union*.

output. Data that has been processed and then made available to the user. Output can be directed to a printer, the screen, or a disk file.

overnormalization. The process of breaking the structure of a relational database into many small tables that should be combined to produce optimum performance. See also *normalization*.

password. A code used to control access to various parts of a computer program. Many DBMS enable the developer to define password protection for sensitive data.

PC. See *microcomputer*.

physical data model. The structure of the data as stored on hardware such as disk drives, as compared with a logical data model. Modern database management software insulates the user and developer from many details of the physical storage. See also *logical data model*.

primary key. In a relational database table, the field or combination of fields that uniquely identifies a record, such as the Social Security number in a personnel table. The primary key is used to prevent duplicate records from being entered and to search for records. In a relational database, you can designate the primary field when you create a table. See also *key field* and *foreign key*.

project table. A temporary table created by a query; contains a subset of the columns (fields) from the source table.

prototype. A working model of the finished application. Prototypes can be simple but should realistically demonstrate all database functions.

pseudocode. An English-language simplification of actual computer instructions. Instead of using symbols to describe the programming logic steps, as do flow charts, pseudocode uses words to express the actions to be performed by a program.

pull-down menu. A list of choices that expands from a menu at the top of the screen; Windows applications rely extensively on pull-down menus.

query. An action to retrieve information from a database. Queries can be used also to add, modify, or delete records.

query by example. A query technique whereby users can retrieve information from a table by giving an example of the answers they want to find. Query by example is an alternative to using a query language. See also *query language*.

query language. An English-like language that enables users to retrieve or manipulate information in a database.

range validation. The process of setting upper and lower limits for the value that can be entered in a field.

record. A collection of related data items; a group of records is called a table. Records are known also as rows or tuples. See also *row*, *table*, and *tuple*.

referential integrity. A guarantee of internal consistency in data even when the information about one entity is stored in two or more tables or forms.

relational database. A database in which the information is stored in tables or forms. The information in different tables can be related though links established by a common column or field. See also *flat-file database*.

relational operator. An operator that compares the values of two data items; < (less than) and > (greater than) are examples of relational operators. See also *operator*.

relationship. The link between two files in a database, based on specific criteria. Defined relationships are two-directional and are based on an exact match of values in linking fields in the two files, as specified on the relationship form. Ad-hoc relationships are defined during the transaction that uses them and also can be based on other criteria.

report. Printed information from tables. Reports also can be viewed on-screen before printing or sent to a DOS file.

required field. A field that must be filled with a value in order for a record to be saved.

restore. To return to an original (initial) value or condition. In the context of a database, information is often restored from disks or tapes.

row. In a database table, all the information pertaining to a particular record, arranged horizontally across the display. See also *record* and *table*.

schema. A visual representation of the logical structure of a database. Special symbols often are used to show relationships among database tables.

search criteria. Conditions that records must meet to be retrieved in a query.

second normal form (2NF). A relational database table that meets the criteria of first normal form and whose attributes (fields) all describe the entity tracked. See also *first normal form (1NF), normalization,* and *third normal form (3NF)*.

sequenced fields. Numeric fields with numbers that increase by one for each new record written.

sequential. A search method that reads a file from start to finish, as opposed to indexing and other performance-boosting techniques.

sort. A process used to arrange records in a particular order, such as alphabetical, numerical, or chronological.

Soundex. A feature available in some DBMS that searches for words that "sound like" the target entry. Soundex searches are useful for finding names of persons because many spelling variations may exist for the same name.

spreadsheet. A popular type of financial modeling package based on the paper ledger. Lotus 1-2-3, Excel, and Quattro Pro are examples of spreadsheets.

SQL. See *Structured Query Language (SQL)*.

string functions. Programming commands that manipulate character strings by retrieving substrings, changing capitalization, and so on.

Structured Query Language (SQL). A relational database language widely adopted as a standard and available in a large number of commercial databases. A version of SQL has been adopted by the ANSI. See also *relational database* and *American National Standards Institute (ANSI)*.

system documentation. A manual for the database administrator that includes detailed listings of all table, form, and report definitions. See also *database administrator (DBA)*.

table. The building block of databases. Tables consist of rows (records) and fields (columns). Relational database tables have special properties, including safeguards against duplicate entries. See also *column, field, record, and row*.

third normal form (3NF). In reference to a relational database, a relation (represented by a table) consisting of a primary key value that identifies an entity, and zero or more mutually independent attributes describing that entity. A table must also meet the requirements of first and second normal form to qualify as third normal form. Normalization has third normal form as its minimum goal. See also *first normal form (1NF)*, *normalization*, and *second normal form (2NF)*.

tuple. A row or record in a database table. See also *record, row, and table*.

union. In set theory, the combination of two sets. Union is the result of using the OR operator. See also *OR*.

unique field. See *primary key*.

uniqueness constraint. A table rule that prevents two records from being saved if they have the same value in the primary key. See also *primary key*.

user documentation. Manuals that explain a computer application to people who use it. User documentation accompanies most commercial software.

user interface. See *interface*.

utilities menu. A menu included in many database applications. A utilities menu includes such functions as File Copy, Backup, Restore, and other administrative functions.

validation. Data tests to determine whether an entry adheres to a designated criterion, such as range limits, or to a list of acceptable values.

vertical application. A database application designed for a particular business or industry. A real estate sales application is an example of a vertical application. See also *horizontal application*.

virtual field. A field in which a value is not saved but is derived anew each time the record is accessed.

word processing program. Computer software for creating text files and other types of documents.

Bibliography

Here are sources for additional information on database design and related subjects. I have not attempted to put together an exhaustive bibliography but rather a select group of books and periodicals I have found useful in my work. Many of these books are college textbooks and rather tough reading for all but the dedicated database student. Textbooks are the best places to turn for exhaustive treatment of database theory, at which I have only hinted in this book.

This bibliography is divided into general database books, other software engineering books, software-specific books, and periodicals.

General Database

Brathwaite, Kenneth S. *Systems Design in a Database Environment.* New York: Intertext Publications/Multiscience Press, Inc., 1989.

A technical work focusing on overall database concepts. The approach is analytical and logical, but exhaustively theoretical.

Codd, E. F. *The Relational Model for Database Management: Version 2.* Reading, Massachusetts: Addison-Wesley Publishing Company, 1990.

Date, C. J. *Database A Primer.* Reading, Massachusetts: Addison-Wesley Publishing Company, 1983, 1990.

The Codd and Date books, written by the fathers of relational database theory, are classics. Like all classics, however, these are books to which everyone refers but few people read. The reason is their difficult language combined with heavy doses of mathematics. The writing is clear, but requires quite an investment of time to understand. The reader must understand the meaning of words such as tuple, scalar, canonical, domain, recursive, and orthogonality in the context of relational database theory. These books are unapproachable for the business reader. Date's *Primer* is the simplest, but may be more of a textbook than general readers desire. Most examples use SQL.

Fidel, Raya. *Database Design for Information Retrieval.* New York: John Wiley & Sons, 1987.

Focus is on the design stage of development. Written in a relatively relaxed style. Emphasizes the entity-relationship model heavily. Unfortunately, the author does not give many practical examples.

Gardarin, Georges; Patrick Valduriez. *Relational Databases and Knowledge Bases.* Reading, Massachusetts: Addison-Wesley Publishing Company, 1989.

A book for the programmer. Examines theory and examples on an advanced level and with a jargon-rich vocabulary. dBASE oriented.

Gillenson, Mark L. *Database, Step-by-Step.* New York: John Wiley & Sons, 1990.

Textbook-style introduction to databases covers network, hierarchical, and relational models. Includes history of computer hardware and software. Most examples from IBM mainframe software, with some references to dBASE. Contains good illustrations.

Grant, John. *Logical Introduction to Databases.* Washington, DC: Harcourt Brace Jovanovich, Publishers, 1987.

Textbook covering hierarchical, network, and relational models. Includes discussion of relational algebra, relational calculus, E-R modeling, and other advanced topics. Mainframe oriented, geared toward MIS or computer science students. Some references to Ingres, Nomad, dBASE III Plus, but not extensive practical examples. Includes chapter bibliographies and exercises.

Hogan, Rex. *A Practical Guide to Database Design.* Englewood Cliffs, New Jersey: Prentice Hall Inc., 1990.

Textbook covering hierarchical, network, and relational models. Mainframe oriented, geared toward MIS or computer science students. Some references to DB2, but not DBMS-specific.

Jackson, Glen A. *Relational Database Design with Microcomputer Applications.* Englewood Cliffs, New Jersey: Prentice Hall Inc., 1988.

Textbook covering hierarchical, network, and relational models. Mainframe oriented, geared toward MIS or computer science students. Uses graphical notation and confusing abbreviations for data modeling. Employs dBASE III and R:BASE 5000 for student-oriented, trivial examples. Includes chapter exercises.

Loomis, Mary E. S. *The Database Book*. New York: Macmillan Publishing, 1987.

Textbook covering hierarchical, network, and relational models. Mainframe oriented, geared toward MIS or computer science students. Not DBMS-specific; no program examples are furnished.

Ozkarahan, Esen. *Database Management—Concepts, Design, and Practice*. Englewood Cliffs, New Jersey: Prentice Hall Inc., 1990.

Textbook covering hierarchical, network, and relational models. Mainframe oriented, geared toward MIS or computer science students. Some references to SQL and ANSI/SPARC, but not DBMS-specific. Covers advanced topics such as knowledge bases, multimedia, and object-oriented databases. Mind-numbingly boring, with obscure acronyms.

Pascal, Fabian. *SQL and Relational Basics*. Redwood City, California: M&T Publishing, Inc., 1990.

Good discussions of relational database concepts. Uses SQL for examples, dismissive of nonrelational PC DBMS such as dBASE and its offshoots. Clear in its exposition of theory, the book contains some preaching of relational gospel and attacks on heretics. Good for the serious student of relational database design but probably not direct enough for the business reader.

Walters, Richard F. *Database Principles for Personal Computers*. Englewood Cliffs, New Jersey: Prentice Hall Inc., 1987.

Textbook covering hierarchical, network, and relational models. Rather long section on computer hardware, operating systems, and other background information. Geared toward MIS, computer science, or business students. Uses DataEase and dBASE III Plus for examples. Includes case study of student enrollment database, chapter bibliographies.

Software Engineering

Beyond the literature that specifically addresses database issues, a wealth of knowledge is available on general computer science topics that will assist the database designer. I have found the books on requirements analysis and interface design to be particularly helpful.

Boehm, Barry W. *Software Engineering Economics.* Englewood Cliffs, New Jersey: Prentice Hall Inc., 1981.

Hardcore graduate-level college textbook. Holds up well despite its age, but not appealing to general readers. Not database-specific.

Brockman, R. John. *Writing Better User Documentation/From Paper to Hypertext.* New York: John Wiley & Sons, Inc., 1990.

Not database-oriented, but a good guide to documentation.

Cutts, Geoff. *Structured Systems Analysis and Design Methodology.* Oxford: Blackwell Scientific Publications, 1991.

Excellent guide to systems analysis. Clear examples and much common sense. Not database-oriented per se, but quite useful for database designers. Geared for college course on systems analysis and design. Uses British government's SSADM Version 4 database software in examples.

Gause, Donald C.; Gerald M. Weinberg. *Exploring Requirements: Quality Before Design.* New York: Dorset House Publishing Company, 1989.

A helpful guide for the early stage in the development process. Style is conversational, and the examples are entertaining. The book utilizes practical experience well.

Powell, James E. *Designing User Interfaces.* San Marcos, California: Microtrend Books, 1990.

Despite its broad title, this book is geared toward database applications, using FoxPro for all examples. Its cute tone can be annoying at times, and the depth of coverage varies widely, but it contains a wealth of practical pointers for applications design, particularly for data-entry screens and reports.

Yourdon, Edward. *Managing the Structured Techniques/Strategies for Software Development in the 1990's*, 3rd Edition. Englewood Cliffs, New Jersey: Yourdon Press—A Prentice Hall Company, 1986.

Textbook covering structured software design techniques. Not database-specific. Mainframe oriented, geared toward MIS or computer science students. Lots of COBOL references.

Software-Specific Books

If you are not happy with the user documentation that comes with your software, you have many other options. Software reference books present the information in user documentation in a clear, understandable way and add extra discussion of difficult concepts and program features. The following Que books are aimed at users of particular database programs.

Bruce, Walter. *Using DataEase.* Carmel, Indiana: Que Corporation, 1991.

Bruce, Walter R. *Using Paradox 3.5.* Carmel, Indiana: Que Corporation, 1991.

Chou, George T. *dBASE III Plus Handbook,* 2nd Edition. Carmel, Indiana: Que Corporation, 1991.

Crooks, Ted. *Using Oracle.* Carmel, Indiana: Que Corporation, 1991.

Dasef, Marva. *Using R:BASE.* Carmel, Indiana: Que Corporation, 1991.

Ewing, David; Bill Langenes. *Using Q&A.* Carmel, Indiana: Que Corporation, 1991.

Que Development Group. *dBASE IV PC Tutor.* Carmel, Indiana: Que Corporation, 1991.

Que Development Group. *dBASE IV Quick Reference.* Carmel, Indiana: Que Corporation, 1991.

Que Development Group. *Q&A Database Techniques.* Carmel, Indiana: Que Corporation, 1991.

Que Development Group. *Q&A Quick Reference.* Carmel, Indiana: Que Corporation, 1991.

Que Development Group. *Q&A Que Cards.* Carmel, Indiana: Que Corporation, 1991.

Que Development Group. *Q&A Quick Start.* Carmel, Indiana: Que Corporation, 1991.

Que Development Group. *Using dBASE IV.* Carmel, Indiana: Que Corporation, 1991.

Shepherd, Steve. *Paradox Programmer's Reference.* Carmel, Indiana: Que Corporation, 1991.

Slater, Lisa C. ; Steven E. Arnott. *Using FoxPro 2.* Carmel, Indiana: Que Corporation, 1992.

Tiley, Ed. *Clipper Programmer's Reference.* Carmel, Indiana: Que Corporation, 1991.

Tiley, W. Edward. *dBASE IV Programming Techniques.* Carmel, Indiana: Que Corporation, 1991.

Tiley, W. Edward. *Using Clipper,* 2nd Edition. Carmel, Indiana: Que Corporation, 1991.

Slater, Lisa C.; Steven E. Arnott. *Using FoxPro 2*. Carmel, Indiana: Que Corporation, 1992.

Periodicals

The computer industry changes so quickly that many books are obsolete by the time they are produced. For the most up-to-date information on database software and techniques, you must turn to magazines and journals.

Database Journals

A number of magazines cater to the database developer.

Data Based Advisor
Data Based Solutions, Inc.
4010 Morena Blvd.
Suite 200
San Diego, CA 92117
(619) 483-6400

> Mostly oriented toward PC database management systems, with particular attention to Xbase languages. Columns for popular packages, and code listings for innovative programming techniques.

Database Programming and Design
Miller Freeman Publications
500 Howard Street
San Francisco, CA 94105
(415) 905-2200
(800) 289-0169

> Focus on mainframe database software and large applications. Good coverage of relational design theory, accompanied by sometimes obscure articles on particular DBMS.

DBMS
M&T Publishing
P.O. Box 57511
Boulder, CO 80322-7511
(800) 456-1859
(303) 447-9330

Serious magazine for corporate database application developers. Includes columns for certain products such as Oracle, Paradox, and Clipper, feature articles on design issues, interviews and product reviews.

Product-Specific Journals

Each popular database software product inspires one or more newsletters or journals devoted to hints for that package. You also can ask your software vendor for a listing of user groups. User group listings are published periodically in several computer magazines, including *Data Based Advisor*. Large user groups often produce inexpensive newsletters, which contain inside information on your favorite product, information on technical support bulletin boards, and extensive code listings.

Pinnacle Press offers several monthly journals geared toward specific database products, including the following:

Journal	Product
ExpertEase	DataEase
.dbf	dBASE
foxtalk	FoxBase and FoxPro
Reference (Clipper)	Clipper
The Quick Answer	Q&A
R:VIEW	R:BASE
SMART Times	SMART

For additional information, contact the following organizations:

Pinnacle Press
P.O. Box 1088
Kent, WA 98035-1088
(206) 251-1900

Paradox Developer's Journal
The Cobb Group
9420 Bunsen Parkway
Suite 300
Louisville, KY 40220
(502) 491-1900
(800) 223-8720

Paradox Informant
8525 Elk Grove Blvd. #126
Elk Grove, CA 95624-1777

Computer Magazines

Byte
McGraw-Hill, Inc.
One Phoenix Mill Lane
Peterborough, NH 03458
(603) 924-9281

PC Computing
Ziff-Davis Publishing Company
P.O. Box 58229
Boulder, CO 80321-8229
(800) 365-2770

PC Magazine
Ziff-Davis Publishing Company
P.O. Box 54093
Boulder, CO 80322-4093
(212) 503-3500

PC Novice
Peed Corporation
120 West Harvest Drive
Lincoln, NE 68521
(800) 848-1478

PC Today
Peed Corporation
120 West Harvest Drive
Lincoln, NE 68521
(800) 424-7900

PC Week
InfoWorld
P.O. Box 1172
Skokie, IL 60076
(708) 647-7925
(800) 457-7866

INDEX

2535

QA
76.9
.D26
T69
1992

QA
76.9
·D26
T69
1992

24.15